Intellectual Property Rights in Science, Technology, and Economic Performance

Intellectual Property Rights in Science, Technology, and Economic Performance

International Comparisons

EDITED BY

Francis W. Rushing and
Carole Ganz Brown

Routledge
Taylor & Francis Group
LONDON AND NEW YORK

First published 1990 by Westview Press

Published 2018 by Routledge
52 Vanderbilt Avenue, New York, NY 10017
2 Park Square, Milton Park, Abingdon, Oxon OX14 4RN

Routledge is an imprint of the Taylor & Francis Group, an informa business

Library of Congress Cataloging-in-Publication Data
Intellectual property rights in science, technology, and economic performance : international comparisons / edited by Francis W. Rushing and Carole Ganz Brown.
p. cm. -- (WVSS in science, technology, and public policy)
Includes bibliographical references.
ISBN 0-8133-7916-4
1. Intellectual property. 2. Patent laws and legislation.
3. Inventions. I. Rushing, Francis W. II. Brown, Carole Ganz.
III. Series: Westview special studies in science, technology, and public policy.
K1401.I57 1990
346.04'8--dc20
[342.648] 89-49119
CIP

ISBN 13: 978-0-367-01464-3 (hbk)

ISBN 13: 978-0-367-16451-5 (pbk)

Contents

PART III
INTERNATIONAL COMPARISONS: DEVELOPING COUNTRIES

PART IV
INTERNATIONAL COMPARISONS: DEVELOPED COUNTRIES

Foreword by Adolph Posnick

For many decades, international business and government have worked mainly on policies related to trade and investment in physical goods. Only recently have services entered the picture. The GATT has reflected these traditional concerns.

The times have changed in a fundamental way. Countries with development ambitions now recognize that know-how and technology are the most essential ingredients to growth. The speed of technological change has forced virtually all businesses to pay more attention to research and development and to protecting their rights in the fruits of their labors. This recognition is now reflected in government policies and in the Uruguay Round negotiations of the GATT.

Just as trade and investment have prospered most in areas where property rights are carefully honored, technological development will favor those societies that scrupulously safeguard economic rewards to innovators.

This book, <u>Intellectual Property Rights in Science, Technology, and Economic Performance: International Comparisons</u>, thus comes out at a critical juncture in international relations. It discusses the economic, political, legal, and social concerns of the world's governments on intellectual property rights. This volume analyzes the systems of both developed and developing economies and draws a clear picture of the status of intellectual property regimes around the world. The impact of intellectual property rights on innovation and technological change is evaluated, and recommendations are presented for a set of standards to orient productive intellectual property rights systems in the GATT, WIPO, and individual countries.

It is an honor for the Brazil-U.S. Council and a personal pleasure to be associated with such a useful contribution to this important and critical subject for international business.

Adolph Posnick
Chairman, U.S. Section,
Brazil-U.S. Business Council;
President and CEO,
Ferro Corporation

Foreword by Robert B. Hardy

Intellectual property protection is required to encourage the emergence of important new technologies, stronger protection to continue productive investment in increasingly expensive research and development, and worldwide protection to enhance global distribution of the products of intellectual efforts. Today, the United States and other industrial countries are no longer the only players in developing these policies to advance the world economy through science and technology.

This volume reflects the many unresolved issues surrounding intellectual property protection and the advancement of research encountered by U.S. government, industrial, and academic communities. Similar questions are being faced by counterpart institutions in both industrial and newly developing nations around the world.

Intellectual property policies can no longer be viewed solely as national issues but must be seen as international concerns. Increasing attention is paid to the intellectual property clauses of U.S. international agreements concerning cooperation in science and technology. The U.S. Omnibus Trade and Competitiveness Act of 1988 amends the Foreign Relations Act, adding that cooperative science and technology agreements should enhance the protection of U.S. intellectual property rights abroad.

This project brought together distinguished individuals in research, government, and the business community to examine these and other relationships between science, technology, and intellectual property protection worldwide and to lend insight to national and international policies in protecting the products of research and development.

This book, as the end product of the project, should enhance understanding of the economic and legal foundations for improved protection and more equitable exchange of knowledge among countries. Only with improved understanding can constructive dialogue follow among countries about the policies guiding international trade and the transfer of science and technology.

Robert B. Hardy
Deputy Director,
Division of International
Programs, National Science
Foundation

Acknowledgments

This volume on intellectual property rights is the culmination of a project sponsored by the International Division of the National Science Foundation and the U.S. Section, Brazil-U.S. Business Council of the Chamber of Commerce of the United States. The editors would like to express their gratitude to these organizations, while freeing the sponsors from any responsibility for the research, analysis and findings presented in this book. We especially thank Keith Miceli, Executive Director, U.S. Section, Brazil-U.S. Business Council for his patience, advice, and thoughtful recommendations throughout the project.

The authors of the chapters in this volume benefited from the presentations and discussion at the project symposium held in Washington, D.C., in May 1989. The symposium agenda is in Appendix A and the participants are listed in Appendix B. The Science and Technology Policy Program, SRI International, provided both logistic and professional support for the symposium which we gratefully acknowledge. We would like to express special appreciation to Tony Motley, President, L.A. Motley & Company; John Boright, National Science Foundation and U.S. Department of State; Emery Simon, Office of the U.S. Trade Representative; Richard Levin, Yale University; Kevin O'Connor, Office of Technology Assessment; and R. Michael Gadbaw, of Dewey, Ballentine, Bushby, Palmer and Wood, all of whom influenced the final drafts of the papers published. Appreciation also goes to Henry Hertzfeld, Legal and Economic Consultant, who served as Rapporteur for the symposium.

The production of Intellectual Property Rights in Science, Technology, and Economic Performance: International Comparisons would not have been possible without the commitment of Elizabeth Deal Rushing, a Georgetown University graduate in Government and International Relations who was editorial consultant to the project. She diligently and professionally prepared the manuscript for publication by attending to a myriad of details and problems. She has done an outstanding job.

Finally, an edited volume relies upon the expertise of the contributing authors. We have been fortunate to have been associated with such an exemplary group of scholars.

Francis W. Rushing
Carole Ganz Brown

PART ONE

Introduction

1

Intellectual Property Rights in the 1990s

Problems and Solutions

Carole Ganz Brown and
Francis W. Rushing

THE PROBLEMS

The 1474 Venetian statute considered to be the prototype for modern patent systems says in its preamble:

> We have among us men of great genius, apt to invent and discover ingenious devices.... Now, if such provision were made for the works and devices discovered by such persons, so that others who may see them could not build them and take the inventor's honor away, more men would then apply their genius, would discover, and would build devices of great utility to our commonwealth.1/

Since then few institutions have stirred such heated debate over so many centuries as the protection of intellectual property.

This volume is a direct consequence of such debate. From the editors' perspective, the time for a new look at the conceptual foundations of intellectual property systems seems appropriate. Until recently, discussion was remarkedly devoid of hard evidence, as distinguished from advocacy. But during the last few years, impartial scholarly work has been accomplished on the effects of differing intellectual property policies on the nature, costs, and risks of research and development (R&D). Our task in this volume is to use these insights to advance national and international policymaking in intellectual property protection, science, technology, and economic performance.

Frequently, at the center of such debate are proposals to waive inventors' exclusive rights in favor of a public interest in wider availability. Even so, no one doubts that the protection of intellectual property does have an impact. There are almost surely innovations that would not occur or that would be delayed in the absence of protection. Protection has also been used, and will presumably continue to be used, to exclude competitors. Sometimes such exclusion is an essential part of the incentive to innovate. But under other circumstances, protection may lead to rewards beyond what is required to call forth the necessary innovative effort. In addition, monopoly power may slow the dissemination of new ideas, processes, and innovations; the cross-fertilization of ideas; and the broadening of basic knowledge to build other technological advances.

The essential problem is to strike a balance: enough protection to sustain incentives to the innovator, but not too much protection to allow for the maximization of the social good.

Given this conceptual framework, the chapters that follow review the evidence on experiences in the United States, other industrial countries, and the developing world. They also consider the kinds of innovative activities national governments seek to stimulate by conferring rights to intellectual property and the essential logic of the intellectual property-innovation nexus.

Some nations completely exclude certain products and processes from patent protection such as pharmaceuticals and food-related inventions. These categories are most commonly singled out for special treatment ostensibly because they are considered especially important to public health and welfare. The rationale for such exceptions is somewhat paradoxical. If patents encourage innovation, one might be particularly concerned about maintaining strong incentives for medicinal and nutritional invention.

One extenuating consideration is that in developing nations, many more patents are held by foreigners than by domestic citizens, and the control of health-related technologies by foreign interests is viewed with concern. Whatever the rationale, this volume considers these international differences in patent policy from the perspective of their possible effects on innovation. Overall, developing countries are drawing a balance between the "free" use of ideas and incentives to the inventor; however, they tend to draw this balance much further in favor of "free" use of ideas than do their industrialized counterparts.

Today, the United States and other industrial country policymakers are engaging in significant efforts to seek stronger intellectual property protection worldwide and diminish international infringement of their products and innovative activity. The U.S. government has taken a trade-oriented approach to international protection issues -- an approach that consists of multilateral and bilateral negotiations and unilateral trade measures. This strategy is being implemented in a dynamic world economy in which the forces propelling development are new: the importance of industrial country markets to economic development, the technical revolutions in microelectronics and biotechnology demanding new kinds of protection, and the restructuring of the economies of most countries. This volume summarizes the most important of these changes and considers the policy implications for strengthened protection in developing countries.

At the international level, an effective intellectual property rights regime must also achieve a balance between policies that promote worldwide diffusion of new science and technology and the proprietary interests of researchers, companies, and nations. At the national level, ongoing political and policy processes consider the relevant dimensions of the problem and some balance is likely to emerge. At the global level, however, there do not appear to be international institutions with the capability to balance these diverse interests. This makes it difficult to accomplish the kind of international agreement that would extend intellectual property rights systems worldwide. Thus, to begin to do this effectively, nations seek to:

1. strengthen the economic and legal foundations of intellectual property protection;
2. better understand the emerging technologies demanding new forms of protection unfettered by historical differences among nations;

3. better relate protection to national industrial and economic development policies;
4. improve understanding of the attitudes of academic and business organizations to strengthened protection; and
5. suggest innovative approaches to achieving constructive consensus among nations on balancing national interests with advancing the flows of science and technology across national borders.

THE EVIDENCE

In the chapter which follows, Edwin Mansfield examines the relationships among intellectual property, technology, and economic growth. He emphasizes that the schism between industrial and developing countries in their perception of intellectual property is very real. Developing countries think of intellectual property -- the results of science and technology -- as a public good. On the other hand, industrial countries view intellectual property primarily as a means of maintaining a competitive edge in the marketplace as well as of providing monetary returns to the individual investor.

Mansfield goes on to say that industrial countries should assist developing ones in technological advancement. But weak intellectual property protection would not be the mechanism to achieve this objective. Mansfield also believes that reducing rewards for invention in an already weak incentive system does not make sense.

Richard Levin complements Mansfield's conclusions by making several important distinctions:

1. One must look at individual industries to determine what constitutes adequate protection.
2. In all cases, one cannot simply look at the number of patents, but must also take into consideration the value of those patents.
3. The evidence is weak that stronger protection alone increases investment in R&D. Importantly, however, other factors should be taken into consideration such as the diffusion that results from patent protection, and the freer

mobility of researchers. Rapid information flow is conducive to rapid technological advance (the licensing of the transistor by AT&T Laboratories being the most powerful example).

From this, several conclusions follow:

1. More technical advance from stronger appropriability is not a given because other policies and conditions must be present.
2. Since industries differ widely in the conditions necessary to appropriate returns from their technology, industrial country efforts to strengthen intellectual property protection should be targeted to specific industries.
3. Pharmaceuticals and fine chemicals are areas in which protection is needed, and thus the United States should focus its efforts on strengthening protection for these industries in other countries.2/

In Chapter 3, Richard P. Rozek develops criteria to prioritize the industries and countries which the United States and other industrial nations believe have a need to enhance their intellectual property protection system. These criteria include:

1. the extent of damages to intellectual property owners by unauthorized use of their property in other countries;
2. the level and effectiveness of protection in certain nations;
3. the prospects for change to strengthen protection.

Overall, today's climate is one in which a significantly improved basis for more constructive dialogue among the United States, its industrial partners, and the developing countries can be achieved.

Anne Wells Branscomb considers new property rights for computer technologies in Chapter 4. The traditional intellectual property system is breaking down in the wake of these new information and communication technologies. Further, intellectual property rights should not be limited to discussion of patents, as the use of copyrights in protecting software, the "crown jewels" of the information economy, demonstrates. The line between forms of protection has begun to erode, and in dealing with new technologies, current protection requirements cannot be easily met and should move toward a less costly and more flexible system. Technologists must be partners in advancing these new laws.

Software is joined by other new technologies and applications in deviating from past patterns of protection. For instance, biotechnology is a new challenge to the question of whether to protect advances and what form the protection should take. Kevin O'Connor addresses these issues.3/

The authors of the ten chapters that follow focus on national and individual firm intellectual property protection policies in the developing countries of Brazil, India, Korea, Taiwan, Singapore, and Thailand, and the industrial countries of the United States, Japan, and Western Europe.

Claudio R. Frischtak enumerates "gaps" in intellectual property protection in Brazil:

1. Legislative gaps result from the fact that some products (such as pharmaceuticals) as well as processes are not patentable.
2. Trade secret law is nonexistent in Brazil.
3. The patent office is small and understaffed, leading to administrative gaps.
4. To litigate intellectual property matters in Brazilian counts is not easy, resulting in judicial gaps.

According to Frischtak, it is in Brazil's own interest to strengthen the many factors that drive technological change and advancement. The nature of these factors depends very much on the size and nature of the firm. Those areas in which the strengthening of protection would have a major impact must be chosen carefully. One should take into consideration that Brazil still spends a relatively small proportion of its GNP on R&D of which the government finances 80 percent and the private sector finances only 20 percent.

Frischtak goes on to say that weak protection cuts off creation of new technology and lowers the innovation rate. Strategies to strengthen protection in Brazil should focus on areas that would benefit from strengthened protection; these are areas in which Brazil exhibits growing national capabilities, such as software. Strengthened protection for such areas as pharmaceuticals, on the other hand, will only emerge in five to ten years.

The chapters of Flavio Grynszpan and Robert M. Sherwood are directed towards understanding the "business culture" of Brazil and the influence of this culture on protection. Grynszpan analyzes the disparities among various sectors of the Brazilian economy in their tendencies to oppose or advocate intellectual property protection. State supported firms show little support for intellectual property protection while firms in the advanced or emerging technologies demonstrate support. Awareness of the need for and benefits from intellectual property protection is a prerequisite for building a constituency for protection in Brazil.

Overall, Brazilian science and technology-related activities lack confidence in the system of protection, and this does not make for an atmosphere of innovation. Sherwood cites many examples of this atmosphere:

1. Lack of trade secret protection inhibits mobility of researchers in Brazil, a country that traditionally has more mobility than Western Europe and the United States.
2. Lack of protection leads to diminished investments in R&D in both large and small companies, and a reluctance of highly-trained scientists and engineers to work for industry.
3. The paucity of small businesses in Brazil may be related to the lack of protection as well as the lack of venture capital.
4. Within R&D organizations, researchers are reluctant to communicate with one another for fear of disclosure of trade secrets.
5. Academics appear to favor protection because they do not wish to exclude the possibility of commercialization of their research.

International transfers of technology are also adversely affected by lack of protection. The Brazilian military has problems in getting up-to-date foreign suppliers of technology. Foreign sources in general seem unwilling to provide technology without protection, and the problem of Brazilian researchers leaving firms with foreign technology appears particularly threatening to foreign suppliers.

In Chapter 8, Falguni Sen examines the relationship between protection and the management of R&D in India. He assesses the Indian government to be extremely opposed to strengthening protection. One reason may be that the government funds approximately 90 percent of R&D, and there is no business community to counterbalance the government. Indian R&D funding is similar to Brazil in this respect.

The change in Indian government policy toward weak protection came in the early 1970s. Importantly, those industries in which protection plays a strong role, such as pharmaceuticals, are denied protection. Further, the Indian government gives itself broad rights to use patents. These policies, the Indian government holds, break up foreign monopolies, and encourage the development of indigenous technology. In contrast to these areas, software is protected in India by copyright provisions. While one cannot prove a causal link, the general conclusion is that protection of software played a role in the accomplishment by India of international partnerships in software development.

Gunda Schumann focuses on the critical question faced by developing countries: Are the overall technological and economic advances gained from strong protection sufficient to offset the short-term gains from weak protection? Strong protection is beneficial when used in conjunction with a package of other development policies such as human resources improvements, investments in R&D, export-oriented strategies, and willingness to allow international competition for domestic products. Further, countries adopting these policies realize the positive role of direct foreign investment in development and the importance of diversified economies.

In countries such as Korea, attitudinal changes towards strong protection probably occur in association with their own indigenous technological development. Another factor is that in Korea 80 percent of the R&D is private as compared with the large amounts of public funding of R&D in countries such as Brazil and India. Overall, intellectual property systems cannot be taken independently of the other development policies followed by a country, and the strength of the private sector.

In Chapter 10, Ashoka Mody reemphasizes a point made by Edwin Mansfield -- the standoff between developing and industrial countries with respect to protection is quite dramatic. Intellectual property protection is likely to become an even more important issue in the future because increasing amounts of R&D are needed to produce new products. In addition, nonlegal means of appropriating the returns from intellectual property are becoming weaker, thereby putting pressures on the need to strengthen the legal environment for protection. Finally, the rate at which technology is being bought or exchanged has increased. These factors will lead over the next decade to higher prices and/or less access to technology by developing countries.

Mody observes that for the United States, protection has been strengthened, and minimum standards are being demanded of other countries by U.S. companies. The pendulum has swung very much in favor of increased protection for the United States, and there is speculation about how far the country will go in that direction.

Atul Wad conceptualizes intellectual property as a technology asset of the U.S. firm. The returns on these technology assets are broader in scope than just monetary rewards. Patents, for example, raise the visibility of the firm and attract both capital and highly skilled laborers. Thus, patent infringement cannot be looked at narrowly as inadequate return on research investment.

Wad emphasizes that the rising costs of R&D are contributing to the importance of intellectual property issues in today's world. Other reasons for this new focus on protection are: the internationalization of production with its consequent increased potential of leakage of technology, rapid diffusion of products, and the growing worldwide marketplace for technology. In the end, the impetus for strengthened protection would come from the power and clout of small and medium businesses seeking to influence government actions.

R. Michael Gadbaw points out the interface between U.S. domestic technology policies and the dynamics of international protection.4/ Protection of semiconductor chips is an example. Because the United States faced strong foreign challenge to its technological leadership, its profits began to fall. Part of the explanation is the effective adoption and use of U.S. technologies without proper renumeration. U.S. industry saw erosion around the world in protection, and consensus grew that this protection was essential to U.S. competitiveness. A U.S. government objective became the adoption of minimum standards of protection throughout the world.

According to Gadbaw, in this government support for domestic industry, the United States becomes more like other countries. For other nations, trade and economic policies have commonly been used to foster national growth and competitiveness. Further, strengthening protection is seen as a far better alternative to trade protectionism and the lack of competition it entails.

Currently countries differ widely in traditions and approaches to intellectual property. Gadbaw points out that the news is not all bad. Software, in the course of a decade, has become widely recognized as appropriate for protection. Korea, Brazil, Singapore, and Taiwan have increased protection overall. The joining of India to the Paris Convention for Patent and Trademark Laws is a major political step in the right direction.

Looking toward the future, the United States should follow several strategies:

1. Seek to improve minimum standards for protection.
2. Pursue improved methods of enforcement.
3. Encourage more beneficial linkages between protection and trade.

It is a given that countries more likely to strengthen protection in response to U.S. pressures are those more heavily dependent on trade with the United States.

In Chapters 12 and 13, Michael Borrus and Dennis S. Karjala consider the relationships between intellectual property rights and Japan's economic performance. Borrus foresees that Japan will move towards stronger protection of intellectual property. The major reason is that Japan will shift to protect its own innovations against newly industrializing countries that now claim the same right to reverse engineer and copy that Japan once incorporated as part of its own industrial policy. These pressures, however, provide little guarantee that protection in Japan will equal that of other industrial countries. Given its traditions, practices, and institutions, Japan is likely to draw the line between innovation and imitation in unique ways. Even as the innovator is better protected, Borrus concludes, the economic usefulness of the imitator is not likely to be entirely sacrificed in Japanese growth strategies.

On the other hand, Karjala believes that arguments assessing Japan to be more lenient in protection than the United States are superficial. As one example, employer/employee contracts in Japan serve to replace trade secret protection, and Japan is also considering a trade secret law. Less researcher mobility also makes trade secret protection less of a problem for Japan than for the United States. Further, Karjala's opinion is that Japan's patent laws do not systematically discriminate against foreigners. With respect to copyright protection of technology, Japan is as much a novice as the United States. He sees the Japanese statute regarding protection of software under copyright law as a more reasonable balance between diffusion of innovation and incentives to innovate than the U.S. counterpart. Concluding his comparisons between the United States and Japan, Karjala observes no systematic patterns that demonstrate that Japanese courts are more or less protective than their U.S. counterparts.

Wolf Brueckmann focuses on the future objectives and modes of intellectual property protection for the European Community. New protection for emerging technologies was one theme. For example, the problem of legitimizing downloading of databases is one anticipated problem, and new sui generis protection of databases is another. A second theme is the emerging European consensus on the appropriateness of GATT -- the General Agreement on Tariffs and Trade signed in 1947 -- versus bilateral actions to strengthen protection.

The overall objective of policy is to reduce foreign misappropriation of European technology, and ensure a fair return on R&D investments. The European position is parallel to that of the United

States: to incorporate principles of protection, dispute settlement procedures, and enforce sanctions into GATT. No appealing alternatives are currently available. WIPO -- the World Intellectual Property Organization organized in 1963 to administer major intellectual property conventions -- is an inadequate forum for dispute resolution and enforcement of property rights.

In Chapter 15, the concluding chapter of this volume, Alden F. Abbott sketches a framework for protection to advance innovation. The microeconomics of firm behavior regarding R&D investment is crucial. To the extent that R&D investments are considered sunk costs, appropriate returns from these investments are increasingly important to firms in the knowledge industry. The rights associated with intellectual property should not be considered iron-clad monopoly rights. Patents, for example, are of limited scope and duration. Patents encourage licensing to diffuse technologies. Firms may also turn outside the legal system of protection, using other means to protect their property such as scrambling techniques, leasing penalties, and bundling strategies.

Abbott agrees strongly with Brueckmann in noting that WIPO lacks enforcement mechanisms and that the primary multilateral approach should be to incorporate principles of protection into GATT. Finally Abbott discusses the means of strengthening intellectual property protection in the United States by lowering antitrust and patent disincentives, strengthening process patent protection, passing a federal trade secret law, removing disincentives to joint R&D, and encouraging foreign countries to increase their intellectual property protection.

THE SOLUTIONS

The editors intended this volume to be prescriptive as well as descriptive. The chapters effectively characterize the current status of intellectual property systems throughout the world and the critical differences among them. The prescriptions are based on a fundamental premise: intellectual property protection provides greater benefits than costs in the advancement of science, technology, and economic performance. However, the benefits to intellectual property protection often accrue in the future thereby making the near-term costs seem large. The protection benefits both the private and the public sectors and it is the allocation of the return which is determined by public policy. But taken together, the components of the prescriptions offer new opportunities to secure international agreement on protection beneficial to global economic advancement.

First, intellectual property systems cannot be taken independently of the developmental and competitiveness policies followed by a country and the strength of their private sectors. Therefore, trade-oriented approaches to enhance protection should target specific countries and industries to achieve their goals.

Second, the distinction between science and technology is becoming blurred. Scientific discovery is more rapidly converted to technological advancement. Care, however, should still be taken that efforts to enhance the protection of technology worldwide do not diminish flows of scientific knowledge across national boundaries.

Third, trade strategies must be undertaken in conjunction with development assistance and educational/awareness efforts on the effects of protection on economic performance. The strategies must recognize the linkages between intellectual property protection and technology, investment, and trade flows. Current realities reflect the interdependencies of policies of nations.

Fourth, these educational efforts must emphasize that the benefits to organizations from protection are more broad-based than economic returns from their research and development efforts. The value, as well as the number of patents, and their conceptualization as technological assets to private sector institutions should be emphasized.

Fifth, governments alone cannot evolve an international regime for protection in a vacuum. The needs and advice of business and academic communities in all countries must play a strong role. Domestic constituencies for intellectual property protection emerge as domestic technology capabilities increase, the stage of development is enhanced, and private sector funding of R&D grows.

Sixth, increased protection is not to be expected tomorrow, and the movement will be evolutionary rather than revolutionary. Strategies to advance protection should take long-range approaches, say, a five to ten year time frame. Advocate nations should support a scheduled phasing in of genuine intellectual property protection -- enforcement as well as legislation.

Seventh, the new technologies provide opportunities for countries to join in the development of new forms of protection, unfettered by past differences. These advances should be emphasized in evolving international agreement.

Eighth, the recent entry of new players such as Eastern Europe and the USSR into the mainstream of the global economy, and the movement of such countries as Thailand and Malaysia towards the technological status of Brazil and Korea require more room at the negotiation table for discussion of enhanced protection. This expansion requires recognition of the advantages of multilateralism in the long-term solution to intellectual property rights issues.

Finally, as the writing of this volume demonstrates, impartial scholarly work has been accomplished on the effects of differing intellectual property regimes. Sustained progress towards improved economic performance from enhanced property rights in science and technology will only be achieved through hard evidence and informed discussions.

NOTES

1. F.M. Scherer, The Economic Effects of Compulsory Patent Licensing, New York University Monograph 1977-2 (New York: New York University, 1977), p. 4.

2. Comments by Levin at the symposium, "Intellectual Property Rights in Science, Technology, and Economic Performance: International Comparisons," Washington D.C., May 8-9, 1989. For an elaboration of Levin's views, see Richard C. Levin et al., "Appropriating the Returns from Industrial Research and Development," in Brookings Papers on Economic Activity: Special Issue on Microeconomics, eds. Martin N. Baily and Clifford Winston

(Washington DC: The Brookings Institution, 1987). The authors describe the results of their major project to assess the effectiveness of patents as a method of appropriating returns and to compare their effectiveness with other methods such as keeping technology secret.

3. Comments by Kevin O'Connor at the symposium. See also, New Developments in Biotechnology: Patenting Life -- Special Report, OTA-BA-370 (Washington D.C.: Office of Technology Assessment, 1988). Kevin O'Connor was Study Director and Legal Analyst for this project which reviews the protection issues surrounding inventions that are themselves alive.

4. Comments by R. Michael Gadbaw at the symposium. For an elaboration of Gadbaw's views, see R. Michael Gadbaw and Rosemary E. Gwynn, "Intellectual Property Rights in the New GATT Round," in Intellectual Property Rights: Global Consensus, Global Conflict?, eds. R. Michael Gadbaw and Timothy J. Richards (Boulder, Colo.: Westview Press, 1988).

PART TWO

Issues in Intellectual Property Rights

2

Intellectual Property, Technology and Economic Growth

Edwin Mansfield

INTRODUCTION

The past thirty years have seen a remarkable growth in the attention devoted by economists and others to technological change, due in large part to studies indicating that economic growth has resulted in substantial measure from changes in technology. There also has been a notable revival of interest in the patent system and in the general topic of intellectual property rights.

In this article, I analyze and summarize aspects of both of these subjects, including the importance of the social rate of return on investments in new technology; I conclude with a discussion of some policy issues regarding intellectual property rights.

MEASURING ECONOMIC GROWTH

It is generally accepted that economic growth is an important goal in our society. This does not imply that economic growth is, in some simple sense, what public policy should attempt to maximize. Clearly, the desirability of a particular growth rate depends on the way it is achieved, how the extra output is distributed, how growth is measured, and many other things. Nor does my focus here on the economic effects of research and technological change imply that only these effects are important or relevant. On the contrary, increased knowledge is of great importance beyond its strictly economic benefits.

What is the relationship between technological change and economic growth? The pioneering studies in this area -- by Robert Solow, Moses Abramowitz, and Solomon Fabricant -- occurred in the mid-1950s. Solow's paper, part of the work for which he recently received the Nobel Prize, was most influential. Assuming that there were constant returns to scale, that capital and labor were paid their marginal products, and that technological change was neutral, Solow attempted to estimate the rate of technological change for the American nonfarm economy during 1909-1949. His findings suggested that, for the period as a whole, the average rate of technological change -- the increase in the amount of output that could be derived from a fixed amount of inputs -- was about 1.5 percent per year. On the basis of these findings, Solow concluded that about 90 percent of the increase in output per capita during this period was attributable to technological change.

The basic methodology used in the early studies in essence was the following: Economists, who view the total output of the economy as being due to various inputs of productive services into the productive process, began by specifying these inputs as labor and capital and by attempting to estimate their contribution to the measured growth of output. Whatever portion of the measured growth of output could not be explained by these inputs was attributed to technological change. The crudeness of this procedure is obvious. The resulting measure of the effect of technological change does not isolate the effects of technological change alone. In addition, it contains the effects of whatever inputs are excluded, which, depending on the study, may be economies of scale, improved allocation of resources, changes in product mix, increases in education, or improved health and nutrition of workers.

To eliminate some of these deficiencies, a number of additional studies were carried out in the early 1960s, the most comprehensive and influential of which was by Edward Denison. Denison attempted to include many inputs -- particularly changes in labor quality associated with increases in schooling -- that were omitted in earlier studies. Since his study was relatively comprehensive, it resulted in a relatively low residual increase in output unexplained by inputs included in his study. Specifically, Denison concluded that the "advance of knowledge" -- his term for the residual -- was responsible for about forty percent of the total increase in national income per person employed during 1929-1957. In subsequent studies, Denison estimated that the advance of knowledge was responsible for 1.4 percentage points of the annual growth rate of national income per person employed during 1948-1969, and for 1.6 percentage points of its growth rate during 1969-1973.

While Denison's studies removed some of the deficiencies, others remain. For one, the measured rates of growth of output on which these estimates are based fail to give proper weight to improvements in the quality of goods and services produced. In general, only those changes in technology that reduce the costs of existing end products have an effect on measured economic growth. Unfortunately, the measured growth of national income fails to register or indicate the effects on consumer welfare of the increased spectrum of choice arising from the introduction of new products.

Nonetheless, based on available evidence, technological change seems to have been a very important factor, perhaps the most important factor, underlying long-term economic growth in the United States and elsewhere.

RETURNS ON INVESTMENT

The social rate of return from an investment in new technology is the interest rate realized by society as a whole from that investment -- the payoff to society. A high social rate of return indicates that society's resources are being used effectively and that more should be devoted to such investments, if the rate of return remains high.

The first attempt to measure the social rate of return from investments in industrial innovations was a study conducted by myself and others, the results of which were published in 1977. The innovations that were included in the study occurred in a variety of industries, including primary metals, machine tools, industrial controls, construction, drilling, paper, thread, heating equipment, electronics, chemicals, and household cleaners. They occurred in firms of quite different sizes, and most of them were of average or routine importance, not major breakthroughs. The results (shown in Table 2.1) indicated that the median social rate of return from the investment in these innovations was 56 percent, a very high figure. This high rate of return was borne out in two studies commissioned by the National Science Foundation. Based on separate samples of twenty innovations each, the studies found the median social rate of return to be 70 percent and 99 percent, respectively.

TABLE 2.1
Social and Private Rates of Return from Investment in Innovation

	Rate of Return (percent)	
Innovation	Social	Private
Primary Metals Innovation	17	18
Machine Tool	83	35
Component for Control System	29	7
Construction Material	96	9
Drilling Material	54	16
Drafting Innovation	92	47
Paper Innovation	82	42
Thread Innovation	307	27
Door Control Innovation	27	37
New Electronic Device	neg.	neg.
Chemical Product	71	9
Chemical Process	32	25
Chemical Process	13	4
Major Chemical Process	56	31
Household Cleaning Device	209	214
Stain Remover	116	4
Dishwashing Liquid	45	46
MEDIAN	56	25

Source: Edwin Mansfield and others, "Social and Private Rates of Return from Industrial Innovations," Quarterly Journal of Economics, May 1977. Copyright © 1977 by John Wiley & Sons, Inc.; reprinted by permission.

The foregoing results pertain to the <u>average</u> rate of return. In earlier investigations based on econometric estimation of production functions, J. Minasian and I, in separate studies, estimated the marginal rate of return from research and development (R&D) in the chemical and petroleum industries. My results indicated that the marginal rate of return was 40 percent or better in the petroleum industry and about 30 percent in the chemical industry if technical change was capital-embodied (but much less if it was disembodied). Minasian's results indicated about a 50 percent marginal rate of return on R&D investment in the chemical industry.

In a much more recent study of this sort based on approximately 1,000 of the largest U.S. manufacturing firms, Zvi Griliches concluded that the "average (at the geometric mean of the sample) gross rate of return to R&D investment rises... from...0.51 in 1967 to 0.62 in 1972.... The estimated rate of return is quite high, and there does not appear to be any dramatic fall in it over time."

Although the social returns from innovative activities are very high, this does not mean that the private returns -- the returns to the innovating firm -- are high. In my 1977 study cited above, whereas the median social rate of return was 56 percent, the median private rate of return was only 25 percent. Similarly, one of the nation's largest firms made a careful inventory of the technological innovations arising from its R&D and related activities for the years 1960 to 1972, as well as detailed estimates of the effect of each of these innovations on its profit stream. The average private rate of return from this firm's total investment in innovative activities was about 19 percent, which was much less than the social rate of return.

One of the major reasons why the private rate of return from innovative activity is so much lower than the social rate of return is that the innovator frequently finds it difficult to appropriate the returns from the innovation. Many of these benefits accrue to imitators, who frequently obtain information quickly concerning the detailed nature and operation of new products and processes. According to a study of 100 American firms, this information is in the hands of at least some of their rivals within about a year, on the average, after a new product is developed. Indeed, for over one-third of the firms, it is diffused within six months.

There are many channels by which information on innovation is spread -- the movement of personnel from one firm to another, informal communications networks among engineers and scientists working at various firms, and professional meetings at which information is exchanged. In other industries, input suppliers and customers are important channels (since they pass on a great deal of relevant information), patent applications are scrutinized very carefully, and reverse engineering is carried out. In still other industries, the diffusion process is accelerated by the fact that firms do not go to great lengths to keep such information secret, partly because they believe that it would be futile. Overall, although the diffusion process varies considerably from industry to industry and from case to case, there seems to be little difference among industries in the _rate_ of diffusion of such information. In practically all industries included in this study, the median time lag for products was between six and twelve months and that for processes (other than chemicals and drugs, where processes frequently can be kept secret for a number of years) was six to eighteen months.

Although information on innovative products and processes leaks out relatively quickly, this does not mean that imitation will occur equally fast. It often takes considerable time to invent around patents (if they exist), to develop prototypes, to alter or build plant and equipment, and to engage in the manufacturing and marketing start-up activities required to introduce an imitative product or process. Nonetheless, the basic information concerning the nature and operation of the innovation is of great importance to the innovator's rivals. And because information of this sort is likely to find its way into the hands of rivals within a year or two, this has obvious and important implications concerning the incentives for innovation in the United States.

Given the very high social rates of return from innovative activity and the much lower private rates of return from such activity, some economists have been concerned that there may be some underinvestment in such activities. Because it is often difficult for firms to appropriate the benefits that society receives from new technology, there may be a tendency for too few resources to be devoted to the development of new technology. It is generally agreed that the extent to which these benefits are appropriable is related to the extent of competition faced by the potential innovator and to the kind of research or development activity in question. In particular, the more competition there is and the more basic the information, the less appropriable it is likely to be.

THE PATENT SYSTEM

One of the principal instruments of public policy aimed at protecting intellectual property rights in the United States is the patent system. Patent laws grant the inventor exclusive control over the use of his or her invention for seventeen years in exchange for making the invention public knowledge.

Since the U.S. Congress passed the original patent act in 1790, the arguments used to justify the existence of the patent laws have not changed very much. First, these laws are regarded as an important incentive to induce the inventor, particularly the individual inventor, to put in the work required to produce an invention. Second, patents are regarded as a necessary incentive to induce firms to make the investment in pilot plants and other items required to bring the invention to commercial use. Third, because of the patent laws, inventions are disclosed earlier than would otherwise be the case, thus facilitating other inventions.

New technological knowledge differs from other goods in an important way: It cannot be used up. A person or firm can use an idea repeatedly without wearing it out, and the same idea can serve many users at the same time. This property of knowledge creates an important problem for any firm that would like to make a business of producing knowledge. For an investment in research and development to be worth considering, a firm must be able to sell its results, directly or indirectly, for a price. But who would be willing to pay for a commodity that, once produced, becomes available to all in unlimited quantity? Why not let someone else pay for it, since then it would be available for nothing?

The patent laws are a way of handling this problem. They make it possible for firms to produce new knowledge and to sell or use it profitably. However, the patent system has the disadvantage that new knowledge is not used as widely as it should be, from the viewpoint of static efficiency. This is because the patent holder, who attempts to make a profit, will set a price sufficiently high so that some people who could make productive use of the patented item will be discouraged from doing so. From the point of view of society, all people who can use the idea should be permitted to do so at a very low cost, since the marginal cost of their doing so is often practically zero. But this, of course, would provide no incentive for invention.

Without question, the patent system enables innovators to appropriate a larger portion of the social benefits from their innovations than would be the case without it, but this does not mean that patents are very effective in this regard. Within four years of their introduction, 60 percent of the patented successful innovations included in one study were imitated. Nonetheless, patent protection generally increases imitation costs. In the same study, the median estimated increase in imitation costs was 11 percent. In the ethical drug industry, patents had a bigger impact on imitation costs than in the other industries; the median increase in imitation costs was about 30 percent in ethical drugs in contrast to about 10 percent in chemicals and about 7 percent in electronics and machinery.

Clearly, patents are much more important in some industries than in others. Based on a random sample of 100 firms from twelve industries (excluding very small firms) in the United States, patent protection was judged to be essential for the development or introduction of 30 percent or more of the inventions in only two industries -- pharmaceuticals and chemicals. In another three industries (petroleum, machinery, and fabricated metal products), patent protection was estimated to be essential for the development and introduction of about 10 to 20 percent of their inventions. In the remaining seven industries (electrical equipment, office equipment, motor vehicles, instruments, primary metals, rubber, and textiles), patent protection was estimated to be of much more limited importance in this regard. Indeed, in office equipment, motor vehicles, rubber, and textiles, the firms were unanimous in reporting that patent protection was not essential for the development or introduction of any of their inventions during 1981-1983 (as shown in Table 2.2).

TABLE 2.2
Percent of Inventions that would not have been Developed or Commercially Introduced without Patent Protection, 1981-1983a/

Industry	% that would not be introduced	% that would not be developed
Pharmaceuticals	65	60
Chemicals	30	38
Petroleum	18	25
Machinery	15	17
Fabricated Metals	12	12
Primary Metals	8	1
Electrical Equipment	4	11
Instruments	1	1
Office Equipment	0	0
Motor Vehicles	0	0
Rubber	0	0
Textiles	0	0

a/ Based on a random sample of 100 U.S. firms. Some inventions that were developed in this time period were not introduced then, and some inventions that were introduced then were not developed then. Thus the left-hand column of the table may refer to different inventions than the right-hand column.
Source: Reprinted by permission from Edwin Mansfield, "Patents and Innovation: An Empirical Study," Management Science, Vol. 32, No. 2, February 1986. Copyright © 1986, The Institute of Management Sciences.

Estimates were also obtained from each firm in the sample concerning the percentage of its patentable inventions in 1981-1983 that were patented. If we divide the sample into two parts, one consisting of firms in the five industries where patents seem more important and the other consisting of firms in the seven industries that report that patents are less important, the results indicate that over 80 percent of the patentable inventions in the former group of firms were patented and that over 60 percent of those in the latter group were patented. Thus, even though firms in the latter seven industries seldom regard patent protection as necessary to the development or commercial introduction of an invention, this does not mean that they do not take out patents. On the contrary, in each of these industries at least half of the patentable inventions were patented. The reason seems to be that the prospective benefits of patent protection, including (besides royalties) whatever delay is caused prospective imitators and the use of patents as bargaining chips, are judged to exceed costs.

The percentage of inventions that is patented can vary over time. According to one influential hypothesis, this percentage has tended to decline over the past decade or two as firms have become disillusioned with the patent system and as they have devised ways of protecting their technology that are more cost-effective than patents. Proponents of this hypothesis often argue that this decline in the propensity to patent is at least partly responsible for the well-known drop from the late 1960s and early 1970s to the early 1980s in the annual number of patents granted to U.S. inventors, as well as for the decline in the patent rate in many other major countries at that time.

To help shed some light on this score, information was obtained from a sample of 100 firms concerning the percentage of their inventions in 1965-1969 and 1980-1982 that were patented. The results provide no evidence supporting the hypothesized decline in the propensity to patent in the United States. One-half of the firms in the sample reported that there was essentially no difference between 1965-1969 and 1980-1982 in the percentage of inventions that were patented. Of the remaining half of the firms in the sample, more reported an increase than a decrease from 1964-1969 to 1980-1982 in the percentage patented. Even in the electrical equipment industry, which is often cited as a case where the propensity to patent has declined, more firms reported an increase than a decrease.

If there has been no decline in the propensity to patent, the decrease in the annual number of patents granted to U.S. inventors during the 1970s must have reflected a real decrease in the number of inventions. From many points of view, this is not good news. But the extent to which such a decrease in the number of inventions resulted in a decrease in the rate of technological change depended, of course, on whether the average economic importance of an invention changed during this period.

CURRENT ISSUES

There are important and well-known differences between the industrialized countries and the developing countries in their attitudes toward intellectual property rights. The latter countries tend to feel that intellectual property rights give inventors and innovators an undesirable monopoly on advanced technology that can be used to extract unjustifiably high prices, as well as unwarranted restrictions on the application of the technology. In their view, the enforcement of intellectual property rights would do little to aid their own development; indeed, it would tend to hinder their development and to prolong the period during which their per capita income falls considerably short of that in the industrialized countries.

A view sometimes expressed in developing countries is that knowledge should be made available at minimal cost to everyone since it is a common property of all. Also, it is argued that because the development of the relatively impoverished countries of the world is a goal that benefits everyone, the technology needed by these countries should be given to them at a low cost. For these and other reasons, many developing countries have relatively weak laws to protect intellectual property and less than diligent enforcement of the laws that exist. Also, they have adopted policies with regard to direct foreign investment and licensing designed to improve the terms on which they can obtain advanced technology.

Obviously, the industrialized countries tend to disagree with the foregoing arguments. In their view, intellectual property rights must be respected to provide a fair return to the private investors who take the substantial risks involved in developing and commercializing a new technology. Unless such returns are forthcoming, the incentives for inventive and innovative activity will be impaired, to the detriment of all nations, rich or poor. Moreover, the industrialized countries sometimes argue that the establishment of stronger intellectual property rights would help to promote indigenous technological and innovative activities in the developing countries, although it is recognized that this is only one of many factors involved.

Superimposed on these differences of philosophy between industrialized and developing countries is a bewildering array of exceedingly complex issues that have arisen due to the development and diffusion of new information and communications technologies. There are basic questions concerning data ownership and control and concerning ways to monitor computer activity. Governments find it hard to control the information crossing their borders, and firms have difficulties in protecting their data bases. A variety of new technologies have come into being that fit awkwardly, if at all, into traditional concepts of intellectual property.

Consider, for example, the case of computer software. In the United States, the Federal Republic of Germany, and Britain, there has been a tendency to use copyright law to protect software. But other countries, such as Japan, have opposed copyright protection. Proponents of copyright protection say that software is like writing, except that it is in a new form resulting from technological advance. Opponents argue, among other things, that at least some software is not like writing because it is addressed to machines, not people. Even if all nations agreed that copyright protection should be granted, it is not clear whether imitators could not still duplicate the essential features of a program, if they changed it in minor ways.

A myriad of problems has also arisen with regard to the protection of semiconductor chips. Patents are regarded by many observers as inappropriate because the fundamental technology for making chips is well-known. The U.S. Congress has rejected the argument that copyright protection should be granted in this area. Instead, the Semiconductor Chip Act of 1984 gives creators of mask works exclusive rights concerning the sale, distribution, import, and reproduction of a mask work for ten years if it is original and registered within two years of its creation.

Coupled with these vexing problems associated with new technologies are very significant losses by American manufacturers and others due to outright piracy and counterfeiting. The U.S. International Trade Commission and the U.S. Department of Commerce have estimated that American business has lost over $10,000 million per year in worldwide sales on this account. Among the industrial sectors where counterfeiting is particularly serious are wearing apparel and footwear, transportation equipment parts and accessories, computer hardware, chemicals, records and tapes, sporting goods, toys, video games, and machinery and electrical products.

Given the importance of the trade deficit and the competitiveness issue in the United States at present, it is not hard to understand why American officials are concerned about these issues. For example, the Trade and Tariff Act of 1984 covers intellectual-property-related trade practices, and beneficiaries of the Generalized System of Preferences have been informed that their protection of American intellectual property rights will be scrutinized in deciding benefits under this program, and a discussion of intellectual property rights was put on the agenda of the General Agreement on Tariffs and Trade (GATT) talks. However, it seems fair to say that, from an American point of view, progress has been limited.

PROTECTING INTELLECTUAL PROPERTY

Based on the foregoing discussion, it is clear that intellectual property rights are of fundamental importance. Unless these rights are protected, the incentives for industrial innovation, already relatively weak in industries where patents are ineffective and entry is easy, will wither to the point where the investment in new and improved products and processes is far below the socially optimal level. Given the central importance of industrial innovation for economic growth, such an eventuality would do considerable harm both to the United States and to other countries.

Particularly in the developing countries, there is widespread resistance to a strengthening of intellectual property rights. While there are good reasons why the industrialized countries should help the developing countries and be sympathetic to their problems, there also are important reasons for the protection of intellectual property rights. To a far greater extent than most people realize, economic growth depends on a relatively small cadre of talented people, supported by organizations capable of amassing and managing the necessary complementary resources, who are able to extend the limits of human understanding. In many industries in both the United States and abroad, there is reason to believe that too little currently is being spent on such work. Unless there is a reasonable amount of respect for intellectual property rights, the prospect is for even less being spent.

NOTE: This chapter was previously printed in Intellectual Property Rights and Capital Formation in the Next Decade, edited by C. Walker and M. Bloomfield, (Washington D.C.: University Press of America, 1988). Reprinted by permission.

3

Protection of Intellectual Property Rights

Research and Development Decisions and Economic Growth

Richard P. Rozek

INTRODUCTION

The United States Constitution gives Congress the power to promote scientific and literary activities by granting innovators exclusive rights to their discoveries and writings. From the first U.S. patent law in 1790, the current system of laws regarding patents, trademarks (including trade dress and industrial designs), copyrights, and trade secrets has evolved.1/ Collectively, these laws constitute the intellectual property protection mechanism of the U.S. However, this sophisticated system of legal rights does not provide innovators perfect appropriability (monopoly) for the use of their innovative output. Congress has attempted to improve the system during nearly all of its sessions. During the 99th Congress, for example, patents, trademarks, and copyrights were involved in approximately 200, 100, and 90 bills respectively. Nevertheless, the mechanism for protecting intellectual property in the U.S. is one of the most effective in the world.

For centuries, societies have recognized the importance of providing an incentive to encourage innovative activity by allowing innovators to earn a return from their ideas. A grant of monopoly to encourage artistic activities was made by Sybaris around 500 B.C. Antonius Marini received the first patent of invention in 1443, and for twenty years no one else in Venice, Italy was allowed to build a flour mill that operated without water.2/

The importance of protecting intellectual property, especially in the context of economic development, is not accepted universally. Some people have argued that ideas are public goods that should be available for everyone to use at a zero price.3/ Advocates of this view dismiss the issue of providing a proper incentive to encourage innovative effort.

Most countries provide neither perfect appropriability for intellectual property nor complete free access to all ideas. Designing and enforcing a mechanism to protect intellectual property involves both benefits and costs. This paper addresses the benefits and costs of both the protection and the no-protection solutions. The main point is that if one considers the long-run benefits for economic growth resulting from intellectual property protection, as well as the long-run costs in terms of economic stagnation when no protection exists, the case for strengthening intellectual property protection in developed and developing countries is very strong.

BENEFITS AND COSTS

Promoting both innovative effort and innovative output is a basic requirement for economic growth. Thus, as its policy regarding intellectual property, a country must adopt a point on a scale somewhere between free access at one extreme and perfectly appropriable (monopoly) property rights at the other. The decision involves evaluating the social benefits and costs of the feasible alternatives.

The benefits of protecting intellectual property evolve from the level of innovative output available to a country. Innovative output may consist of new products, new processes, or new literary works. Both direct and indirect benefits to the country result from this innovative output even if the intellectual property protection mechanism is used primarily by foreigners.4/ Direct employment and investment benefits accrue from research and development (R&D) laboratories, new manufacturing plants, or import facilities for creating, producing, or processing the output associated with the innovative effort. Indirect benefits accrue from an increase in local market activity. For example, foreigners use many local services such as banks, insurance firms, and legal experts. If the innovative output is a book, movie, painting, or scientific article, the cultural and educational levels of the entire population increase. Furthermore, demand for this type of output in other countries with strong protection of intellectual property will generate returns for innovators in the home country and provide resources for additional expansion. This improves the prospects for economic growth of the country.

Some developing countries recognize the benefits of protecting indigenous ideas through an intellectual property protection mechanism. Several recent trends illustrate this point. In his article, "The Global Flight Over Plant Genes," Sun summarizes a meeting of the Food and Agriculture Organization (FAO) at which participants considered a resolution that all germ plasm be made freely available to all countries.5/ In 1983, developing countries voted as a block to support such a resolution. By 1985, however, many of these same countries wanted to protect the new crop varieties developed from their own research. At the 1985 FAO meeting, these countries joined the U.S. in expressing reservations about free access to the germ plasm, and the resolution did not pass.

Additional momentum for a country to protect its residents' intellectual property comes from the trend toward privatization, that is, the trend toward transferring activities from the public to the private sector, emerging in many developing nations. If a developing country wants to grow as more private firms are created, it must provide a mechanism to ensure these firms a return from any investment of resources in innovation.

Designing and enforcing laws that provide a return sufficient to make the innovative effort worthwhile are the primary costs of protecting intellectual property.6/ Secondary costs may arise due to the increased economic activity within a country. For example, new plants may require new roads or may cause environmental problems.

The intellectual property protection mechanism need not guarantee perfect appropriability for the innovator to yield net benefits to the country involved. Perfect appropriability may generate costs that exceed benefits. The optimal mechanism for a country may be one with less than perfect appropriability. The system of laws in the U.S. regarding patents, trademarks (including trade dress and industrial designs), copyrights, and trade secrets does not provide perfect protection of intellectual property.7/ Perfect appropriability is difficult to achieve because the intellectual property of each industry has unique characteristics which the protection mechanism would have to incorporate. One example of an industry-specific change in the U.S. intellectual property laws is the U.S. Drug Price Competition and Patent Term Restoration Act of 1984. It strengthened intellectual property protection in the pharmaceutical industry by restoring patent protection for time lost due to regulatory delay. The law also facilitates entry into the marketplace for drugs with expired patents.8/

Creating new types of output in such areas as biotechnology, computer software, and information transmission, heretofore not considered in intellectual property protection mechanisms, means that maintaining a degree of protection requires flexibility in the mechanism itself. Survey work by Levin et al. suggests that factors such as superior sales or service efforts are important for protecting intellectual property in some industries.9/ These factors are not attainable through legislation. Therefore, legislative solutions to intellectual property problems are not always possible to achieve.

Intellectual property protection has been the subject of major policy initiatives by the Reagan Administration (April 7, 1986), the U.S. Department of Justice in its antitrust enforcement role,10/ and the U.S. International Trade Commission.11/ These efforts increase worldwide awareness of the benefits of protecting intellectual property and demonstrate the U.S. government's commitment to protecting intellectual property rights.

Internationally, intellectual property protection is receiving more emphasis than it has in the past. The exchange of technology and other ideas is clearly a trade issue.12/ Protecting intellectual property stimulates both exports and imports. Innovators in the home country are encouraged to send their innovative output to those foreign countries that allow innovators a return for their innovative efforts (exports). Intellectual property protection in a country encourages foreign innovators to share their innovative output (imports).

Recently, policymakers have focused on the trade component of intellectual property protection. The U.S. government initiated action, under Section 301 of the 1974 Trade Act, against Korea for unfair trade practices regarding intellectual property. In July 1986, the Korean government agreed to increase the protection that it affords through patents, trademarks, and copyrights.

An emerging view in many countries is that intellectual property should be part of the General Agreement on Tariffs and Trade (GATT), so as to provide a forum for negotiating a set of minimum standards of intellectual property protection and to enhance enforcement of the basic standards.13/ Intellectual property is on the agenda for the current round of multilateral trade negotiations.

The World Intellectual Property Organization (WIPO) is the organization within the United Nations that deals with intellectual property issues. Its main objectives are promoting protection of intellectual property worldwide and ensuring administrative cooperation among the intellectual property unions.14/ The WIPO has no power to enforce any rules or regulations, but clearly has expertise in this area. Any proposal to include intellectual property in the GATT should draw on the expertise within the WIPO.

The "free access" view of intellectual property imposes costs by removing the incentive to develop new ideas and by contributing to economic stagnation. On the benefits side, this approach would allow anyone to use innovators' new ideas at no cost. Advocates of this view usually understate or ignore the magnitude of the costs. Free access to ideas does not provide innovators with exclusive rights to capture returns from their investments in creative activities. Thus, they have less incentive to allocate scarce resources to these activities.15/

Uncertainty characterizes an innovation process. For the innovator to bear this uncertainty, some possibility for a reward must exist. If innovators are not rewarded, they will not create new products, processes, or literary works. The reward is expressed most often in terms of profitability of a new product or process relative to the profitability of established products. Profitability of an R&D project is directly related to the degree of intellectual property protection. Section III contains a discussion of this relationship and its impact on the firm's decision to allocate resources to R&D.

The impact of intellectual property protection on the firm's decision to allocate resources to R&D is clearly at the core of any discussion regarding an optimal intellectual property policy. However, critics of strong protection of intellectual property are quick to point out that, especially in developing countries, those firms whose incentives to conduct R&D are preserved often are multinational corporations. Thus, some benefits of strong intellectual property protection flow out of the country. Relatively little emphasis exists regarding the developing country's own benefits of adopting strong protection of intellectual property. Therefore, Section IV cites the benefits to a developing country of protecting intellectual property and suggests topics for future work.

INTELLECTUAL PROPERTY PROTECTION AND R&D

This discussion is based on a static model of a firm's R&D decision.16/ The model provides the basis for examining the effects of changing the protection afforded any intellectual property resulting from the R&D process. The main conclusion is that the firm will devote more (fewer) resources to R&D when protection of intellectual property increases (decreases). Consequently, the expected number of new processes or products is directly related to intellectual property protection.

Assumptions and Results

From the firm's perspective, the degree of protection afforded intellectual property has an impact on its profits and therefore on the amount of money that it invests in R&D. To understand this relationship, consider a profit-maximizing firm operating in a one-period environment. The firm can maintain the status quo and earn a relatively certain level of profits from its established products, or it can invest in R&D and possibly gain greater profits. The firm's R&D decision involves the probability that engaging in research will be successful, that is, yield a profit-enhancing innovation. The probability that a firm will produce any innovation is directly related to the resources that the firm allocates to R&D.17/ However the firm incurs the cost of R&D whether or not the result is a profit-enhancing innovation.

An innovation may be either a new product or a more efficient process for producing an existing product. For simplicity, the subsequent discussion uses the term "product innovation" to refer to either type of innovation. Furthermore, the allocation of R&D resources to specific facilities operated by the firm is beyond the scope of this paper.18/

The firm's problem is to choose a level of R&D that maximizes its expected profits, defined here as the weighted average of two possible profit outcomes: (1) profits from the innovation and (2) profits from the established products. The weights are the expected probabilities of these two profit outcomes. Clearly, the firm's incentive to invest in R&D is inversely related to the profits that the firm earns on its established products. On the other hand, the firm's incentive to invest in R&D is directly related to the prospective profits that the firm will earn on new products.

Interpretation

Many existing analyses of technical advance19/ discuss the effects on the incentives to innovate resulting from changes in profits from maintaining the status quo. Because the amount invested in R&D is inversely related to the profits from maintaining the status quo, an increase (decrease) in the established or certain profit outcome will result in a decrease (increase) in investment.

To shed light on the issue of protecting intellectual property, it is necessary to examine the effect of a change in profits from successful innovation on the incentive to innovate. The firm will not invest in R&D unless it expects to earn a return on the new information. We know that as protection of intellectual property increases (decreases), the profits from an innovation increase (decrease). Since the amount invested in R&D is directly related to the expected profits from successful innovation, an increase (decrease) in such profits will result in an increase (decrease) in investment. Furthermore, the probability of discovering a new product will increase (decrease) as R&D increases (decreases). Therefore, the expected number of new processes or products will increase (decrease) as protection-afforded intellectual property increases (decreases).

The U.S. Drug Price Competition and Patent Term Restoration Act of 1984 restores patent life to some pharmaceutical products to take account of time spent undergoing regulatory review by the U.S. Food and Drug Administration. Innovative pharmaceutical firms have responded to the improvement in the U.S. intellectual property climate by increasing private investment in R&D. In 1986, R&D investment by Pharmaceutical Manufacturers Association members reached a record $4.6 billion -- more than double the R&D investment in 1980.

If the firm sells its products in many countries, it must assess the overall environment for intellectual property protection. The firm's decision to devote resources to R&D depends on the degree of intellectual property protection worldwide. The degree of protection provided in the largest market in which the firm sells its products is crucial to the R&D decision. However, the cumulative impact of the protection available in smaller markets also has an impact on the R&D decision.

The interpretation of patent laws has a significant impact on R&D decisions. For example, if the definitions of misappropriation or infringement expand to exclude certain heretofore allowed limitations, a firm engaging in R&D can expect an increase in profit. The firm will thus devote more resources to R&D. Correspondingly, firms attempting to imitate the products will devote fewer resources to this type of activity.

If the firm is a multinational enterprise and worldwide intellectual property protection is weakened by a country's or a group of countries' abolishing patents or allowing piracy and counterfeiting to increase, the firm expects a decrease in profits from successful innovation. The result is that the firm allocates fewer resources to R&D. This reduces the probability of discovering a new product or process. Thus, the expected number of technological advances decreases.

Pirated and counterfeit products in international trade markets distort trade. In 1984, Pharmaceutical Manufacturers Association members with new products protected by patents in countries such as the U.S. sold $29 million worth of those products in Korea. Patent pirates, on the other hand, sold $70 million in unauthorized copies of these same drugs in Korea. In five countries (Argentina, Brazil, Korea, Mexico, Taiwan), sales of new pharmaceutical products by patent owners in 1984 totaled $162 million, while sales of unauthorized copies of the same products totaled $192 million.20/ If such activities are not brought under control, adverse consequences will result for all research-intensive industries.

INTELLECTUAL PROPERTY PROTECTION AND ECONOMIC GROWTH

Tools for Protecting Intellectual Property

To focus on a country's benefits and costs of adopting a mechanism for protecting intellectual property, the notion of intellectual property must be made explicit. Generally, the laws regarding patents, trademarks, copyrights, and trade secrets are the traditional tools for protecting intellectual property. The mere existence of these laws does not mean that intellectual property is protected; governments must enforce these laws.

If a country adopts a rule restricting foreign ownership of the country's resources, the resulting transfer of technology to that country may weaken intellectual property protection. Local firms will gain access to valuable technology. It may be less costly to modify the technology so as to avoid violating intellectual property protection laws than it would be to discover the technology. The danger exists, however, that the notion of intellectual property will be too broad for meaningful use in any policy debate. The analysis here uses only the traditional notions of intellectual property protection.

Sources of Growth

A country has two broad choices regarding intellectual property: allowing free access (free rider)21/ or providing protection. The free access solution yields short-term benefits at best while it imposes long-term costs. The protection solution enhances the prospects for economic growth to produce long-run benefits in exchange for a grant of monopoly power to the innovator.

Protecting intellectual property improves the size, quality, and efficiency of both the labor force and the capital stock within a country. In other words, strong protection of intellectual property will tend to (1)create jobs in primary industries as well as in supporting industries, (2)create a higher-quality labor force through on-the-job training, (3)shift jobs to higher-productivity areas, (4)increase the capital stock of the country, (5)improve the quality of the capital stock through innovation, (6)improve the allocation of the capital stock, (7)expand those activities subject to economies of scale, (8)improve efficiency through a reduction in local monopoly elements, (9)provide lower-cost methods of production for existing products, and (10)provide new products. These sources of economic growth evolve by expanding the approach taken in the Harrod-Domar model, the standard used by the economists for nearly forty years.22/

Suggestions for Future Research

Advocating strong protection of intellectual property involves answering three key questions: (1)What constitutes weak or strong protection? (2)When is protection beneficial to development? (3)How can we measure the extent of the contribution of protection to economic growth? Providing complete answers to these questions is impossible at this time. Consequently, additional work should be undertaken as outlined below.

To facilitate future empirical work, researchers should develop a country-by-country index of intellectual property protection using either a survey instrument or a ranking scheme based on whether intellectual property protection mechanisms have certain characteristics. Even if laws exist, the strength of protection depends on whether (1) the laws are national or local, (2)the laws apply to all industries and/or products, (3)the laws take account of differences among industries or products, (4)the length of protection is sufficiently durable, (5)compulsory licensing requirements apply, and (6)a mechanism to settle disputes is available.

Indices may be meaningful only on an industry-by-industry basis. Some trade associations and government agencies already have identified countries particularly troublesome with regard to intellectual property protection. Table 3.1 summarizes five such lists, and Brazil, Indonesia, Korea, and Taiwan appear on all five. (It would be interesting to determine whether countries with stringent regulatory regimes for particular industries have relatively strong protection for intellectual property in those same industries.)

As discussed above, intellectual property protection tends to improve the size, quality, and efficiency of the labor force and the capital stock of a country. A case study approach is one way to determine the extent of the contribution to economic growth. However, the case study approach raises some concerns. First, determining whether the level of industrial development in a country would have been greater had the degree of intellectual property protection been changed is difficult, if not impossible. Second, intellectual property protection operates indirectly by stimulating the sources of economic growth; therefore, the contribution of such protection to growth may be difficult to quantify. Nevertheless, case studies provide a means to document the role of intellectual property protection in economic development.

Harberger and McCord23/ use the case study approach. Harberger's work was the basis for the discussion earlier in this section. McCord concluded that no single factor could explain the level of economic growth found in a number of Asian, Latin American, and African nations. Common

TABLE 3.1
Intellectual Property protection: Problem Countries

IIPA a/	NACA b/	PTO c/
Brazil	Argentina	Brazil
Egypt	Brazil	India
Indonesia	Colombia	Indonesia
Korea	India	Korea
Malaysia	Indonesia	Malaysia
Nigeria	Korea	Mexico
Philippines	Mexico	Singapore
Singapore	Taiwan	Taiwan
Taiwan	Yugoslavia	Thailand
Thailand		

PMA d/		USTR e/	
Argentina	Korea	Argentina	Singapore
Bangladesh	Mexico	Brazil	Spain
Brazil	Pakistan	Canada	Taiwan
Canada	Peru	Colombia	Thailand
Chile	Philippines	India	Venezuela
Colombia	Portugal	Indonesia	
Costa Rica	Sri Lanka	Korea	
Egypt	Taiwan	Malaysia	
Ecuador	Thailand	Mexico	
Guatemala	Turkey	Norway	
India	Venezuela	Pakistan	
Indonesia	Yugoslavia	Philippines	

a/International Intellectual Property Alliance,1985
b/National Agricultural Chemicals Association, 1985
c/Patent and Trademark Office, 1985
d/Pharmaceutical Manufacturers Association
e/U.S. Trade Representative, 1985

elements for those countries on a sustained growth path are (1)an alien influence (actual migration or through ideas), (2)progress initially in the agricultural sector, (3)progress in industrialization often aided by multinational firms, (4)investment in human as well as physical resources, (5)integration into the world economy with exports based on comparative advantage, and (6)generation of savings for reinvestment. Although McCord did not analyze explicitly the role of intellectual property protection in developing and maintaining an environment for sustained growth, it is clear such protection has an impact on the elements that he identifies. Thus, case studies that focus specifically on intellectual property protection are necessary.

Tools for protecting intellectual property include patents, trademarks (including trade dress and industrial designs), copyrights, and trade secrets. The appropriate combination of these tools to include in an intellectual property mechanism is not at all clear. Even in the absence of a patent law, a country with a relatively strong trademark law may have an overall acceptable level of intellectual property protection. Therefore, trade-offs may exist among various tools for protecting intellectual property. Further analysis on the existence and scope of these trade-offs would help in formulating an effective legal system.

Potential markets for most products are small relative to the U.S. Therefore, developing countries free ride on the intellectual property protection efforts of the more advanced countries such as the U.S. The cumulative impact of this free-riding activity produces a significant impediment to innovative activity. Government officials in these countries do not take a global view of intellectual property protection. It is necessary, then, to document that significant benefits exist for their countries if they adhere to standards for protecting intellectual property rather than pursuing a narrowly focused free-riding strategy.

A related issue concerns the costs of maintaining and enforcing an intellectual property protection mechanism. Data for assessing these costs are not yet readily available. Alternative institutional arrangements such as a multicountry patent office might achieve sufficient scale to keep costs at reasonable levels for both countries and innovators.

CONCLUSIONS

Intellectual property protection is receiving considerable attention from the academic community, the U.S. government, foreign organizations and governments, and industry groups concerned over protecting results of their R&D activities. The resulting policy initiatives will have a profound effect on the course of technological progress throughout the world.

The degree of intellectual property protection directly affects the profitability of R&D projects and thus the resources allocated to R&D. Ultimately, the degree of protection determines the expected number of new products, processes, literary works, etc., available throughout the world.

Substantial benefits to developed and developing countries evolve from individual firms' incentive to allocate resources to R&D in terms of transferring new technologies to a country and developing indigenous ideas. Policymakers in developed and developing countries should consider the long-run benefits associated with protecting intellectual property for economic growth. Measuring the net benefits of intellectual property protection is a fruitful area for future research.

NOTES

This chapter was previously printed in Contemporary Policy Issues, vol. 5, July 1987, pp. 54-65. Reprinted by permission.

1. For example, the term of a patent has been seventeen years since 1861. For a development of the modern patent system, see A.D. Lourie "Patent Term Restoration: History, Summary, and Appraisal," Food Drug Cosmetic Law Journal (1985), pp. 351-362.

2. For further details on the development of the patent system abroad, see R.A. Klitzke, "History of Patents Abroad," in Encyclopedia of Patent Practice and Invention Management ed. R. Clavert (New York: Reinhold, 1964).

3. E.V. Anderson, "Intellectual Property: Foreign Pirates Worry U.S. Firms," Chemical and Engineering News, September 1, 1986, pp. 8-14.

4. S. Greif, "Economic Growth and Patents," paper prepared for the Interpat Seminar in Taiwan, September 10, 1985. Greif demonstrates a direct relationship between patent applications of foreign origin and per capita gross national product (a measure of development). In the U.S. patent system, 42.9 percent of the 1984 patents were issued

to foreigners; F. Narin and D. Olivastro, "Identifying Areas of Leading Edge Japanese Science and Technology: Japanese Patent and Patent Citation Statistics," unpublished manuscript (Computer Horizons, Inc., April 1986).

5. M. Sun, "The Global Flight over Plant Genes," Science, January 31, 1986, pp. 445-447.

6. The Patent and Trademark Office budget in fiscal year 1987 is approximately $232 million. This is offset by $134 million in user fees and deferrals of prior-year funds.

7. Judicial interpretation of the patent laws have, at times, been antipatent. Recently, judicial decisions have taken a propatent orientation; J. Andresky, "A Weapon At Last," Forbes, March 10, 1986, p. 46. Regarding trade secrets, the legal system in the U.S. has not adapted to the increasing value of information in the technological world; G.L. Miles, "Information Thieves Are Now Corporate Enemy No. 1," Business Week, May 5, 1986, pp. 120-125.

8. Lourie, pp. 351-362.

9. R.C. Levin et al., "Survey Research on R&D Appropriability and Technological Opportunity I. Appropriability," unpublished manuscript (Yale University, July 1984).

10. R.B. Andewelt, "Antitrust Perspective on Intellectual Property Protection," Department of Justice Speech, reprinted in Patent, Trademark and Copyright Journal, July 25, 1985, pp. 319-324.

11. P. Stern, "Foreign Product Counterfeiting: Private Business Sometimes Needs the Government," International Trade Commission speech reprinted in Vital Speeches of the Day, September 1, 1985, pp. 674-677.

12. G.J. Mossinghoff, "The Importance of Intellectual Property Protection in International Trade," Boston College International and Comparative Law Review, 1984, pp. 235-249.

13. U.S. Council Task Force on Intellectual Property, "A New MTN: Priorities for Intellectual Property," U.S. Council for International Business, 1985.

14. World Intellectual Property Organization, WIPO: General Information (Geneva, 1985).

15. L. DeAlessi, "Property Rights and Privatization," paper prepared for the Academy of Political Science Conference on Prospects for Privatization, November 20, 1986.

16. The formal model underlying the discussion in this section is available from the author. For a more general model, see G.M. Grossman and C. Shapiro, "Optimal Dynamic R&D Programs," National Bureau of Economic Research, Working Paper No. 1658 (July 1985); and "Dynamic R&D Competition," National Bureau of Economic Research, Working Paper No. 1674 (August 1985).

17. "Without a doubt, on average, a direct relation between innovational effort and innovational output exists." M.I. Kamien and N.L. Schwartz, Market Structure and Innovation (Cambridge: Cambridge University Press, 1982), p. 57.

18. More than two-thirds of the R&D expenditures by U.S. pharmaceutical firms abroad from 1977 through 1883 were in Western Europe, an area where intellectual property generally is protected. On the other hand, the share of R&D expenditures in Latin America declined from 8.4 to 4.1 percent from 1977 to 1983. Latin American countries generally provide poor protection for the intellectual property of pharmaceutical firms.

19. Kamien, ibid.

20. G.J. Mossinghoff, "Intellectual Property Protection Abroad," statement of the Pharmaceuticals Manufacturers Association, November 25, 1985.

21. Those countries with little or no protection for intellectual property free ride on the relatively strong protection of intellectual property provided by nations such as the U.S.

22. A.C. Harberger, ed., World Economic Growth (San Francisco: Institute for Contemporary Studies, 1984), p. 4.

23. W. McCord (with A. McCord), Paths to Progress (New York: W.W. Norton & Co., 1986).

4

Computer Software

Protecting the Crown Jewels of the Information Economy

Anne Wells Branscomb

INTRODUCTION

Protecting the crown jewels of the information economy has become an expensive, time consuming, and frustrating experience for lawyers, software programmers, managers, venture capitalists, and users. "What" and "whether" questions plague those who must confront the dilemma of how to treat computer software in an economy whose health depends upon the existence of a flourishing software industry.

Historically, there was little concern for the value of the software in the early fifties, when it was thought by many that the big powerful machines could scarcely be replicated more than half a dozen times. Thus the programs, the design of electrical configurations used to control the applications of the computers, could easily be protected by trade secret laws as they were embedded within the hardware and licensed to users who paid very substantial sums for the privilege. Indeed, the U.S. Patent Office did not scoff at issuing patents for computers which included their operating software.

However, as computers have become much smaller and diffused among a diverse population of users, the software has been issued separately from its hardware, modified for many applications, and has become pervasive throughout the worlds of business, medicine, politics, entertainment, banking, and science. There is hardly a life in existence within the developed world which is not affected in some way by computer software, much of it tailored for the specific needs of a particular user group and some of it for the specific needs of a particular individual.

Thus computer software has become a most valuable resource for the functioning of an information-based economy which depends not only upon computer software for publishing manuscripts (the traditional province of copyright) but for operating computer-aided manufacturing (traditionally the province of patent law). Indeed, there is hardly an aspect of modern life which does not rely upon computer software -- even the fast food industry, farmers, and fishermen need reliable computer software to aid them in their daily tasks. Most significantly, the world economy now, as Walter Wriston has observed, operates on a twenty-four hour "information standard" which disseminates information widely to millions of computer terminals where the viewers make their own decisions about the value of the dollar, cruzeiro, escudo, yen, mark, franc, or pound.1/ Computer software is the intellectual capital asset upon which that information standard is based.

It is not surprising, therefore, that the scientists and computer hackers, in whose domain computer software was entrusted for development during its early years, are frustrated to discover that their electronic playgrounds have been invaded by avaricious and enterprising entrepreneurs who prefer dollars to the joy of the "great hack" or the reward of a Nobel prize. However, the strength of the scientific enterprise has been based upon a belief that sharing of information is the only way that progress can be achieved and each small step leads to the next level of performance. To wit, the clash is between the cultures of those who finance and develop the technology and those who discover and fine-tune the fundamental knowledge upon which these new technologies are founded.

APPLICABLE LEGAL REGIMES TO PROTECT INFORMATION PRODUCTS

There are basically three legal regimes under which computer software may be protected -- trade secrets, copyrights, and patents. All three are employed to provide protection to information which has value as a commodity.

Trade secrets can be used to protect information about techniques employed to market a product through the use of a contract which specifies the terms of use, including respect for confidentiality of the proprietary information. Copyrights, on the other hand, were traditionally tailored to protect the income of publishers of manuscripts from unscrupulous copiers. Thus the dichotomy within the copyright law, is that ideas may not be protected, only the explicit expression thereof. Within the copyright law the "idea" has come to be restricted in recent cases to the basic function of the program.2/ The application of that function is well within the boundaries or legal protection, so long as it is an original rendition. In other words, the idea of a program which serves the aerospace industry could not be copyrighted, but the applications software might have many different renditions each of which could be copyrighted.

Under patent law there is no idea/expression dichotomy. The information which is protected is that which is novel, original, and nonobvious. Thus the idea of a new widget as well as its design (or process) for replication may be patented so long as basic algorithms or laws of nature are not made inaccessible. In recent times, however, the Patent Office has begun to erode the boundaries for patenting of software, which were originally quite prohibitive. Today, algorithms which represent unique manners of doing business, for example, a particular way of financial accounting by computer, may be the subject of a patent.3/ One of the more troublesome recent patents is the Zimmerman patent for an "interactive teaching machine"4/ which many fear may stifle innovation in the interactive video industry until the patent expires.

All three legal regimes are currently in vogue for the protection of computer software. Each has its proponents and its detractors. Each has its pluses and its minuses. None seems to be an exact match. Sophisticated lawyers, who have mastered the arcane legal concepts of all three, seek protection for their clients under all three rubrics.5/ Some more maverick lawyers propose scrapping all three for reliance upon misappropriation law to restrain unethical competitors and/or to recover damages for unauthorized use of their clients' proprietary interests in computer software.6/ Older and perhaps wiser academics wistfully long for sui generis legislation designed to resolve the conflicting interests of the software industry with the ease of access for the users.7/ Some more imaginative legal scholars urge a more aggressive approach by the judiciary, including tailoring their decisions to the needs of the software industry for innovation rather than waiting for legislative bodies to catch up with reality.8/

In the meantime, large companies with millions of dollars of investment in software sold to their customers worldwide have turned to arbitration proceedings as a viable modus operandi for achieving certainty in their relationships within an uncertain legal environment.9/

The Office of Technology Assessment of the U.S. Congress has reported that copyright law provides unsatisfactory protection for computer software.10/ Indeed, one wonders whatever happened to the early efforts of the World Intellectual Property Organization to ascertain what the special characteristics of computer software might be which deserved special recognition.11/ Professor Pamela Samuelson, who has written extensively about the legal aspects of computer software, observes:

> It should have been obvious that when Congress decided to put software into its copyright system -- a body of law whose most fundamental tenet is the nonprotection of technologies -- that there would be considerable difficulty in integrating software into that system.12/

Which of these conflicting views will survive the political process remains uncertain. The challenge is awesome. Accommodating a hybrid technology, which is both utilitarian and literary, into legal regimes which function separately and independently will require imagination, intelligence, and perseverance. Alternatively, devising sui generis legislation which will override the objections of conflicting vested interests will require more skill on the part of legislators and lobbyists than has been exhibited in the past.

CONCERNS OF THE COMPETING INTERESTS

Too Restrictive Protection

Many of the smaller software developers look upon the industry as one of great innovation, great flexibility, and one which necessarily must take the building blocks and stack one on top of the other. Thus any legal regime which provides too stringent protection will inhibit this progressive effort which cooperatively provides the infrastructure upon which an information economy is based. The argument against patents for functionality, or structure, sequence, and organization, is that it provides a monopoly for the original inventor excluding all others for the seventeen year period.

Thus, the argument goes on the one side that, if Visicalc had obtained a patent on the "idea" of an electronic spreadsheet, the industry would have been stymied until the expiration of the patent. On the other side, it is argued that, if competitors had been required to design around the Visicalc patent, the industry would have been strengthened by superior design characteristics. As history cannot be relived, this argument cannot be resolved. However, many copyright lawyers argue vigorously for the copyright standard of originality rather than novelty for the applicability of protection to the structure, sequence, and organization (SSO) questions.13/ Others prefer the more stringent prerequisites of the patent law which leave minor modifications to be adopted freely by users and competitors alike.14/

Those who oppose copyrightability point out what they perceive to be the excessive length of protection -- seventy-five years for corporations and fifty years plus the life of the originator for individuals.15/ Indeed, some note that given the rapid rate of innovation and consequent obsolescence of software programs within the software industry, the seventeen year period afforded by patent law may be too long.16/

Those who espouse the concept of freeware, oppose both copyright and patents as placing unnecessary restrictions upon programmers. Such restrictions would require them to "make work" or duplicate efforts by either "reverse engineering" patented information based upon public knowledge and designing another way of doing the same thing, or replicating the copyrighted software through a "clean room," receiving only the design specifications of functionality of the desired software. In either case, they consider the legal requirements as excessively restricting developmental work which would necessarily be expedited by the freedom to tinker with source codes, and debug and alter programs to improve their functionality for the particular user.17/ Frank Fisher, espousing the traditional view of academic freedom points out: "Everyone gains if there is greater freedom to utilize intellectual expressions in the electronic lumberyard to build information products of the future."18/

Encouraging a Compatible User Interface

Much of the concern about the so-called "look and feel" cases is that they militate against industry standards in the user interface. Copyright infringement cases tend to preclude substantial similarities unless the similarities are dictated by the restrictions of the particular industry segment to be served (as for example, cotton growers).19/ If the needs of the user group can be expressed in a number of different ways, then substantial similarity may lead to a rebuttable assumption that actual copying did take place.20/

However, users generally desire compatibility of programs especially in a general category of programs. There is nothing more frustrating in network access, for example, than being unable to remember how you "sign off" (turn off the meter charging your account by using QUIT, OFF, DISC, SO,\Q, or whatever). Furthermore, much damage can be done by having an icon of a can or container be used as "storage" in one program and "delete" in another. Thus to have the law encourage differentiated user interfaces often frustrates users, requires programmers unnecessarily to reinvent the wheel, places higher development costs on funding sources, and inhibits the compatibility which encourages a competitive market place. The challenge is to devise a legal system which encourages standardized user interfaces while rewarding human labor devoted to innovation.

One device currently employed is called defensive patenting, whereby a company patents all of its patentable or copyrightable software in order to be able to cross license with other companies those products which are needed to serve the marketplace optimally. Another is for a group of companies to pool their patents and place them in the public domain where the subject matter covers practices which should be commonly used by the industry.21/

Large manufacturers of computer equipment also demand a right to use utilitarian interfaces for mainframe operating systems in order to enhance ease of use and to encourage competitive choices of equipment configuration.22/

The Hybrid Character of Computer Software

Part of the reason why there is still a lack of certainty concerning legal protection of computer software is historical. Originally, the patent office shied away from issuing patents, partially because of the administrative burden; whereas the copyright office accepted registrations subject to verification by the courts or by Congress that they were within their mandated authority. Thus when the Commission on New Technological Uses asked a group of copyright lawyers whether or not the law should be changed to apply copyright law to computer software, there was a warm and positive response, as they already had a large investment in this particular type of protection.

Indeed, one of the arguments put forward for retaining copyright as the legal regime of choice is that copyright lawyers have had a great deal of experience now with computer software and, therefore, retain more expertise than patent lawyers, whose arcane and especially credentialed and sequestered area of practice is without the knowledge of the software industry.23/ Patent lawyers, quite understandably, do not agree and diligently continue to pursue patents for their clients.24/ There are good reasons why neither legal regime is appropriate, as computer programs have a hybrid character which straddles the two philosophies.

Patents are issued to cover the information required to produce utilitarian articles, while copyright protection is designed to cover objects of literary, artistic, or musical merit. Of course, the distinction has not been sharp; maps were early afforded copyright protection, and compilations, catalogs,and architectural designs have been added to the roster of protectable, useful information which can be offered as market commodities.

John Hershey, the author, argued vociferously against affording copyright protection to computer software because it was machine-oriented.25/ As computer software becomes more and more machine-dependent (as in the case of artificial intelligence programs, debugging, and maintenance programs), Hershey's point of view may become more persuasive. Indeed, the recent trend toward patent protection for machine instructions which govern manufacturing processes as well as algorithms applicable to business practices, leads more and more to the conclusion that computer software is quite utilitarian. This may beg the argument; many books describing industrial practices as well as scientific experiments and technological processes, are arguably quite utilitarian. Moreover, there are many new technological applications for computer software which serve artists, musicians, and authors admirably well. Thus the creative artistic endeavor can both utilize computer technology and render its work product in machine-readable form. This is apparent in computer graphics and musical composition, as well as hairdressing, cosmetology, architectural drawings, and colorization of movie classics.

The question today becomes, quite simply, whether the role of computer software has become so critical in importance to the economic health of the nation and the world that it deserves its own system of legal protection extracting the optimum practices from all existing legal regimes.

Concern about the International Implications

Lawyers who oppose sui generis legislation or a special legal regime for computer software rely heavily upon the efficacy of international conventions which cover copyright issues. Copyright lawyers look upon the Semiconductor Chip Act as a failure because there has been so little litigation since its enactment. Patent lawyers, on the contrary, suggest that the very paucity of litigation is evidence that the act is serving its purpose because the proprietors of the "mask works" are getting the legal certainty they need to protect their interests.26/

Regardless, lawyers who favor copyrightability for computer software argue that operating within the existing framework internationally achieves compatibility of application worldwide or at least in those countries signatory of the Berne and Universal Copyright Conventions. To promote a separate convention for computer software would entail too much negotiation and haggling over the details and perhaps lead to results contrary to the best interests of some of the negotiating parties. The U.S. experience in multilateral negotiations in such fields as the Law of the Sea has not inspired confidence in the ultimate outcome.

On the other hand, there are lawyers who are apprehensive about the recent U.S. embrace of the Berne Convention. Because advances in technology are almost always achieved through incremental improvements on a knowledge base supported by research scientists, apprehensions are rampant concerning the long-term ramifications and concerning the lack of compulsory licensing applicable to copyrighted computer software. Such stringent protection to a rapidly developing technology, which is a vital underpinning of the growth industries within information economies, may hinder economic development. Membership in international conventions conferring widespread coverage may deter efforts to reach consensus on shorter periods and new ways of dealing with shared use in a more equitable manner.27/

Finding an Appropriate Public Domain

The recent ferment over patents versus copyrights, as to which is the more suitable regime for protecting computer software, leads inevitably to concern about the other side of the compromise contained within the constitutional roots of U.S. intellectual property rights. The purpose of providing legal protection was to reward productivity and public disclosure in order that society as a whole should be able to reap the benefits.

Finding the appropriate dividing line between public and proprietary use has not been so difficult within the context of a given country. The United States provides a useful historical context looking back toward both the agricultural and industrial economies which have dominated its history. As long as agricultural workers were disaggregated and could not afford to fund their own research, a research base, funded and operated by the federal government, could freely transfer information to the private sector which could then enhance the knowledge base of farmers and increase agricultural production. As long as the technological information concerning manufactured products was largely embedded in the article produced, research organizations who developed the information could be compensated from the profits of the article sold.

What has changed is the extraction of information from its cultural and manufacturing roots. It has become now a commodity bought and sold on the open market within a technological environment which provides easy access, and simple, inexpensive ways of copying or replicating. Therefore, the real challenge is to determine the appropriate boundaries between the public domain and proprietary interests. Many groups have attempted to set an appropriate expiration date for protection of computer software -- the World Intellectual Property Organization (WIPO) model legislation called for a maximum of twenty-five years,28/ the Japanese proposed ten,29/ and recently the Council of the European Communities has recommended that a copyright expire at fifty years.30/ Moreover, the Council has also addressed another troubling question of the availability of computer software in libraries (where it could be checked out and arguably copied by the borrowers) by recommending that "...the exclusive right of the rightholder to authorize rental shall not be exercised to prevent use of the program by the public in nonprofit-making public libraries."31/

Compulsory licenses, which are not favored in a market-oriented economy, are one way of setting aside a public domain while providing compensation for originators of intellectual property. This has been employed for musical recordings and cable television. Those who oppose compulsory licenses decry the practice of condemnation of private lands for public use without adequate compensation and much prefer the free market place rather than the courts or Congress for determining the value of their information products.

What is missing is long years of experience in placing value upon information as a commodity. Most analytical work has treated information as necessarily a public good, and marketplace economics for information is an area in which economists are only beginning to take an interest.32/ In time, rules will be developed. However, to develop the rules governing what constitutes the public domain for information products on the global market will necessarily be more complex and controversial than within any one country, whether it be a developed, developing, or newly industrialized economy.

CONCLUSIONS

Finding an acceptable balance between public and private use, between the sharing of knowledge and the marketing of information, has never been easy. As the value of information increases and becomes ever more a critical component in the health of nations and their economies, it will become a more and more troublesome source of controversy.

For those who argue that the legal system for the protection of intellectual property is not broken, so why fix it,33/ the unavoidable response must be, if improvements can be made in the legal infrastructure why not make them?

NOTES

1. Walter Wriston, "Technology and Sovereignty," Fortune Affairs, vol. 67, no. 4, Winter 1988/1989 pp. 63-75.

2. See, Whelan v. Jaslow, 797 F. 2d 1222 at 1238 (3d Cir. 1986); Digital Communications Association v. Softklone Distribution Corporation, 659 F. 2d 449 at 457 (N.D. Ga. 1987); Q-Co Industries,Inc. v. Hoffman, 625 F. Supp.608 at 615 (S.D.N.Y. 1985).

3. Paine Webber, Jackson & Curtis, Inc., v. Merrill Lynch and Pierce, Fenner & Smith, Inc., v. Dean Witter Reynolds, Inc., 564 F. Supp 1358 (D.C. Dela. 1983).

4. U.S. Patent No. 4,170,832, October 16, 1979. Other worrisome patents for software producers are: Hyperracks, Inc., Hypercard, No. 4,736, 308, April 1988; Advanced Software Inc., word processing comparison system, No. 4,807,182, February 1989; Quarterdeck Office Systems Inc., windowing program, No. 4,823,108, April 1989.

5. See S.W. Lundberg, M.M. Michel, J.P. Sumner, "The Copyright/Patent Interface: Why Utilitarian 'Look and Feel' is Uncopyrightable Subject Matter Under the 1976 Act," presentation to the LaST Frontier Conference of the Arizona State University Law School Center, February 13-14, 1989; D.J. Kluth and S.W. Lundberg, "The Versatility of Software Patent Protection: From Subroutines to Look and Feel," Computer Lawyer, vol. 3, no. 1, June 1986; M.A. Haynes and S.C. Durant, "Patents and Copyrights in Computer Software Based Technology: Why Bother with Patents?," Computer Lawyer, vol. 4, no. 1, February 1987.

6. C. Owen Paepke, "An Economic Interpretation of the Misappropriation Doctrine: Common Law Protection for Investments in Innovation," High Technology Law Journal, vol. 2, Summer 1987, p. 55.

7. Letters of John M Kernochan, Prof. of Law at Columbia Univ. and William J. Keating, Prof. of Law at Dickinson School of Law, to Milton R. Wessel, Director of the Center for Law, Science & Technology, ASU Law School, reprinted in Cases and Materials for LaST Frontier Conference on Software Protection, February 13-14, 1989, pp. 226-9.

8. Dan Rosen, "A Common Law for the Ages of Intellectual Property," University of Miami Law Review, vol. 38, September 1984, p. 769.

9. IBM v. Fujitsu Limited, American Arbitration Association, Commercial Arbitration Tribunal, Case No. 13T-117-0636-85.

10. Office of Technology Assessment, U.S. Congress, Intellectual Property Rights in an Age of Electronics and Information (1986), p. 81.

11. WIPO, Model Provisions on the Protection of Computer Software (Geneva, 1978).

12. Pamela Samuelson, "Reflections on the

State of American Software Copyright Law and the Perils of Teaching It," Law and the Arts, vol. 13, Fall 1988, p. 72-3.

13. Brian Kahin, Introductory Remarks of the Chairman, MIT Communications Forum on "Software Patents: A Horrible Mistake?," March 23, 1989.

14. Reichman, "Implications of Copyright Protection for Commercialized University Research," Cases and Materials for Last Frontier Conference on Software Protection (Tempe, Ariz.: Arizona State University College of Law, 1989), p. 364; Pamela Samuelson, "Is Copyright Law Steering the Right Course" IEEE Software, September 1988, p. 78.

15. Dennis S. Karjala, "Copyright, Computer Software, and the New Protectionism," Jurimetrics, vol. 28, Fall 1987, pp. 82-3.

16. Y. Braunstein, et al., "Economics of Property Rights as Applied to Computer Software and Data Bases," Report Prepared for CONTU (June 1977).

17. Richard Stallman, "Why Software Ownership Is Bad For Society," University of Texas, 1987; John Markoff, "A Battle to Make Software Free," New York Times, January 11, 1989, p. C1.

18. F.D. Fisher, "The Electronic Lumberyard and Builders' Rights," Change, vol. 21, May 1989, p. 13.

19. Plains Cotton Co-op. v. Goodpasture Computer Serv., 807 F. 2d 1256 (5th Cir. 1987).

20. Broderbund Software, Inc. v. Unison World, 648 F. Supp. 1127 (N.D. Cal. 1986).

21. Lawrence M. Fisher, "Software Industry in Uproar Over Recent Rush of Patents," New York Times, April 12, 1989, p. 1.; R. Duff Thompson, General Counsel of WordPerfect, Oral Presentation at MIT Communications Forum on "Software Patents: A Horrible Mistake?" (March 23, 1989).

22. Michael Jacobs, Presentation on Behalf of Fujitsu at the LaST Frontier Conference on Software ASU College of Law, February 13, 1989.

23. Brian Kahin, "Franchising the Information Infrastructure," Change, vol. 21, May 1989, p. 24.

24. J.P. Sumner and D. Plunkett, "Copyright, Patent, and Trade Secret Protection for Computer Software in Western Europe," Computer Law Journal, vol. 8, Summer 1988, p. 327; Ibid., "Powerful New Software Protection in Europe: The Patent Trend Continues," The Computer Lawyer, vol. 4, no. 10,

October 1987, p. 1; Ibid., "The Versatility of Software Patent Protection: From Subroutines to Look and Feel," The Computer Lawyer, vol. 3, no.6., June 1986, p. 1; David Bender, "Computer Programs: Should They Be Patentable?," Columbia Law Review, vol. 68, 1968, p. 241.

25. Library of Congress, Final Report of the National Commission on New Technological Uses of Copyrighted Works, Comm. Hershey's dissent, p. 27.

26. Oral exchange in Q&A session at the LaST Frontier Conference on Software, ASU College of Law, February 13, 1989.

27. Dennis S. Karjala, "United States Adherence to the Berne Convention and Copyright Protection of Information-Based Technologies," Jurimetrics, vol. 28, Winter 1988, p. 137.

28. WIPO, Model Provisions on the Protection of Computer Software (Geneva: 1978), p. 24.

29. Ministry of International Trade and Industry of Japan, Concerning the Legal Protection of Software, (interim report 1972).

30. European Economic Commission, Draft Proposal for a Council Directive on the Legal Protection of Computer Programs, Article 7, (December 21, 1988).

31. Ibid., Article 5(2).

32. See Christopher Burns, The Economics of Information, prepared for the Office of Technology Assessment of the U.S. Congress (January 1985); Charles Jonscher, An Economic Study of the Information Revolution (MIT/Booz Allen Hamilton, November 1987); also see recent work of Meheroo Jussawalla, Donald Lamberton, Yale Braunstein.

33. Gunter A. Hauptman, "A Perspective on 'Look and Feel' and 'SSO'," Written Presentation at the LaST Frontier Conference on Computer Software Protection, ASU Law School, February 13, 1989.

PART THREE

International Comparisons

Developing Countries

5

The Protection of Intellectual Property Rights and Industrial Technology Development in Brazil

Claudio R. Frischtak

INTRODUCTION

The objective of this chapter is to examine the system of intellectual property rights (IPR) in Brazil and its impact on industrial technology development. It will first be argued that the incentive structure for the acquisition of technological capabilities is fundamentally related to the overall economic environment and the prevailing competition policy regime. Technology policies and institutions play a complementary role that assumes increasing importance as markets become more competitive. The contribution of the intellectual property rights (IPR) regime for explaining the technological performance of Brazilian industrial firms thus should not be overstated.

In this perspective, certain key legal and administrative shortcomings in intellectual property rights protection do not appear to have a very significantly adverse impact on the current technological activities of most Brazilian firms. To the contrary, the imitative nature of these activities suggests that the firms may have in fact benefited from the gaps in the property rights system. Moreover, the tacit, uncodified character of much innovative activity suggests that the problem with the property rights regime may lie less with the lack of patent protection than with the lack of a robust legislative instrument for trade secrets protection that is effectively enforced.

However, an assessment of the property rights regime based merely on the observation that most Brazilian industrial firms do not now appear to engage in activities leading to the production of marketable inventions or major innovations would be intrinsically myopic. As firms develop their technological capabilities, effective protection of intellectual property rights assumes increasing importance for their competitive position. Moreover, the enforcement of property rights is not only necessary as a means of rewarding technological leaders; but possibly even more important, it helps induce firms to accelerate the "transition" between imitation and creation, and to acquire a greater measure of technological maturity. The trade-off between encouraging the diffusion of existing technology through unlicensed imitation and stimulating the creation of new technology becomes steeper over time.

An increasing number of Brazilian industrial firms have acquired the capabilities to generate innovations, and a growing number of agents (scientists, technical specialists) at academic and research institutions are developing patentable inventions. The challenge to policymakers is to ensure that the intellectual property rights regime does not deter producers (firms and other agents) from engaging in creative technological activities, whether major or minor innovations. Yet changes in the IPR regime are not costless; producers relying on "unlicensed" imitation will face a permanent increase in costs and may need a transitional period to adapt to stronger protection of intellectual property rights.

Clearly, Brazil faces additional trade-offs for failing to close existing gaps in the intellectual property rights regime. First, it is argued that these gaps inhibit the transfer of updated technology through direct foreign investment, licensing, or some other means. Foreign innovators consider that their proprietary technology would likely be lost to domestic imitators in the absence of strong protective barriers. Although this is a credible argument, there is no systematic evidence that the current IPR regime affects either the volume or composition of direct foreign investment in Brazil; nor is there evidence that foreign producers are engaged in transferring incomplete or outdated technology. Yet as the international trade and investment environment becomes increasingly competitive, foreign equity investors and suppliers of technology tend to pay closer attention to the IPR regime and its gaps. This is not an immaterial shift for the formulation of industrial strategy in Brazil.

Second, in the less benign international environment of the 1980s, Brazil (with a number of industrializing countries) has been targeted for countervailing actions against some of its exports on the basis that it has failed to give adequate protection for inventions and other types of intellectual property. It appears that this type of retaliatory action, irrespective of its inconsistency with GATT articles, will take effect unless there is some substantial change in the system of property rights. Here the trade-off for Brazil is clear: loss of export markets, or increased payments for foreign technology and reduced output of firms producing unlicensed goods. The key policy issue is how to modify the current property rights regime so as to stimulate the more technologically progressive firms and minimize disruption in the production activities of unlicensed imitators.

It should be stressed at the outset, however, that strengthening the IPR regime will only be effective if accompanied by policy measures that stimulate firms (and research institutions) to improve their overall technological capabilities. In addition, an adequate phasing of improved intellectual property rights protection seems critical. Initial stages of reform might offer greater protection in areas where domestic producers are already active or are likely to become engaged (with the added incentive of a reformed system) in innovative activities. Thus, the initial targets for reform would be those areas where domestic capabilities are sufficiently developed for producers to take advantage of proposed changes.

In view of growing national capabilities, chemicals (including fine chemicals) and metal alloys may be good candidates for changes in the short to medium-term (one to three years) in patent protection. A somewhat more prolonged period (three to five years) may be needed for biotechnology products and IC designs, in view of their incipient stage of development in Brazil. Pharmaceuticals is a more problematic sector where, at least in the case of product patents, a longer transition period (five to ten years) may be needed.

As in many other countries, a major national health policy objective in Brazil is to ensure that the domestic market is well supplied with low-priced, therapeutic drugs. Policymakers have attempted to attain this objective by enforcing relatively strict price controls on pharmaceutical products, denying patent protection for drugs (which is supposed to induce entry and stimulate competition), and targeting low-income consumers by subsidizing their drug purchases. Innovation in the domestic industry does not appear to be significant in view of the fact that, generally, international firms undertake their R&D activities in their country of origin -- under stronger IPR protection -- and Brazil's national producers are unable to face the costs and scale economies involved in bringing a new drug to the market.

Nonetheless a number of dynamic local producers are engaged in product development while attempting to "verticalize" by contracting out research on active ingredients to local institutions. At the same time, many international firms have a strong commitment to the Brazilian market because of its size and potential profitability. This chapter suggests that they would respond to comprehensive policy reform in the pharmaceutical industry beyond mere changes in patent protection. Such an approach might involve progressive removal of investment-constraining price controls, expanded procurement of drugs combined with technology development contracts, and introduction of patent protection with competition-enhancing, compulsory licensing requirements.

The phasing of such measures is essential. The introduction of full (product and process) patent protection might lead to market disruption and, possibly, increases in drug prices without clear benefits. A possible transitional step might be the development of a "positive list" of diseases for which new drugs would be patentable, such as tropical diseases highly prevalent in Brazil (Chagas' disease, schistosomiasis, malaria, etc.). This might be followed by allowing process patentability for all new drugs. Finally, product patentability for new drugs (other than those already eligible for patent) would be permitted under a simplified form of compulsory licensing. Progressive decontrol of prices and technology development procurement policies would function as complementary incentives. They would stimulate international and domestic firms to increase their local in-house and contracted R&D commitments for the development of drugs and active ingredients.

Improvements in patent protection need to be phased over a period that may extend up to ten years, but this need not be the case with trade secret legislation and its enforcement. Trade secrets are generally lost through labor mobility -- which carries technical knowledge with it -- and weak legal action against individuals or teams replicating proprietary technology for a new employee. Trade secret legislation should, however, be carefully crafted and judiciously enforced so as not to deter entry, or preclude average-practice firms from approaching the best-practice frontier. To minimize disruptive effects, it should not be applicable retroactively but should only be a deterrent against future offenders.

In this chapter, I will describe the system of intellectual property rights in Brazil, including the patent, copyright, trademark, and trade secret regimes. The chapter goes on to examine the impact of IPR on industrial technology development in Brazil and the connection between the property rights regime and direct foreign investment and arms-length technology transactions. The next section suggests steps to close the gaps in IPR protection, while stressing the importance of changes in other policy areas to improve the structure of incentives and strengthen the technological capabilities of Brazilian industry. The final section concludes by suggesting directions for research in assessing the relationship between IPR protection and technology development.

THE SYSTEM OF INTELLECTUAL PROPERTY RIGHTS IN BRAZIL

Brazil depends on a comprehensive system of intellectual property rights. The country was an original adherent to the Paris Convention on protection of industrial property, though it has not signed the provisions of the Stockholm text which regulates more contemporary IPR arrangements. The 1971 Industrial Property Code specifies the patent and trademark regimes, and addresses, even if tangentially, the trade secrets area; 1973 Copyright Law regulates copyright protection. The areas covered by the Industrial Property Code are in the administrative purview of the National Industrial Property Institute (INPI). INPI's mandate includes registration, protection, and assignment of patents and trademarks. Policy issues related to copyright protection are the responsibility of the National Copyright Council (CNDA), whereas copyright registration itself is decentralized to eleven entities (including INPI, in case of copyright registration for software).

Protection of intellectual property rights in Brazil is uneven. Although protection is effective in some areas, important gaps occur in the system, particularly in the protection of inventions and trade secrets. Some of these gaps are intentional, a product of policy decisions: for example, the lack of patent protection for pharmaceuticals due to public health considerations. In a number of other instances, however, these gaps result from weaknesses in the IPR administrative system -- INPI's slow processing of patent applications is a case in point. In addition, the legislators are responsible for areas where protection is insufficient or absent. Finally, time-consuming legal processes, small penalties for infringing existing legislation, and limited enforcement capabilities weaken the system of IPR protection.

Patent Protection

The 1971 Industrial Property Code states that regular inventions, utility models, and industrial models and designs are patentable if new and capable of industrial utilization. Brazil follows international convention: for a standard invention patent to be granted, an invention must be "novel" and "useful," and exhibit an "inventive step." Utility models ("petty patents") are different from regular patents in that the inventive step requirement is very weak for them. Design patents do not require an inventive step and have relatively weak usefulness requirements.1/ In accordance with international practice, standard invention patents in Brazil are for fifteen years whereas other types of patents (utility models, industrial models and designs) are for ten years.

All patent applications are filed with INPI. In the case of foreign patents (those filed first in a foreign country with which Brazil maintains an international treaty for mutual protection of patents and trademarks), applications must be filed in Brazil within the "period of priority." The Paris Convention specifies one year for patents and six months for models and designs. If not filed in Brazil within this period, the invention falls into public domain.

There are a few areas where patents either are not granted or are restricted. Most of these exceptions were outlined initially in the 1945 Patent Law, which did not allow product patenting in pharmaceuticals, chemicals, and foodstuffs. The law basically followed what was then the international pattern of denying patent privileges in areas of great social impact, where the major governmental concern was ensuring an adequate domestic supply, for example, of food and drugs. Brazil's restrictions on pharmaceuticals and other products were reiterated and extended in a 1969 law, and then made explicit in the Industrial Property Code.

Pharmaceuticals and foodstuffs are possibly the most important nonpatentable product groups, with the former being for Brazil the main source of intellectual property rights friction with developed countries (chiefly the U.S).2/ Other major nonpatentable areas are chemicals, metal alloys and mixtures, and atomic substances and materials.

In the case of chemicals, interpretation of the Industrial Property Code has not been uniform. The Code precludes patents on "substances, matter or products obtained by chemical means or processes," although the processes for obtaining or transforming such substances are patentable. Still, "composition of use" claims for chemical products were permitted in the past, even though it is not altogether different from a product patent.3/ However, the patentability of agrochemicals (and other fine chemicals) is undefined and regarded as debatable.4/

"Metallic admixtures and alloys in general" are also nonpatentable except those having "specific intrinsic qualities precisely characterized by the nature and proportions of their ingredients or by special treatment." Nonpatentability also covers atomic substances and materials and a few odd cases. Finally, in at least two areas of emerging importance, the Code is either silent or nonspecific: integrated circuit (IC) designs and biotechnology products and processes. INPI has not processed applications in either case, although it has been accepting applications for biotechnology inventions. A government review process is under way to determine if those inventions are patentable or if the view expressed in the Code that "uses or employment of means related to discoveries of varieties or species of microorganisms for a specific purpose" are not patentable should be extended to other living organisms (plants and animals).

It is argued occasionally that the system of patent protection in Brazil is weakened not only by limited coverage but by strict working requirements. According to legislation, once a patent is granted, owners must exercise patent rights within three years and without interruption for more than a year. Otherwise a patent holder faces compulsory licensing to a third party, who requests from INPI special, nonexclusive rights to exploit the patent. Compulsory licensing can also be granted if exploitation of the patent does not meet market demand.

In addition, a patent is held to have lapsed if an invention is not exploited in an "effective manner" in Brazil within four years of the date of issue of a patent or, in the event that a license was granted for exploitation of the patent, within five years of that date. Lapse of a patent also occurs when the exploitation of the patented invention has been discontinued for more than two consecutive years. A patent can be found to have lapsed either "ex-officio" or upon petition of any interested party.

Such working requirements do not appear to have significantly affected patent protection. Although guaranteed by the Paris Convention, these provisions have been applied in very few cases. Attempts at involuntary licensing tend to be legally complex, and very few applications have been filed.5/ Moreover, in most cases the information necessary in order to manufacture a product is not given in the patent but is inherent in the know-how (furnished voluntarily through technical assistance contracts). Thus, without cooperation from the technology supplier, its effective transfer of the technology would not likely take place.

Possibly more important than working requirements is that the term for patents is counted from the date a patent application is filed and not from the date patent rights are granted. Depending on how long it takes for a patent application to be processed, this may shorten considerably the period of protection. Prior to this protection period, inventors are unable to sue for violation of property rights. However, during the time an application is being processed, a patent can be licensed and produce royalties.

Data on INPI's average processing time for patent applications is unavailable. In 1980, approximately 150,000 applications were pending in the INPI Patent Directorate.6/ At the rate patents were then being processed (considerably less than 15,000 per year), average processing time would be over ten years, with effective patent protection less than five years. Between 1980-84, INPI processed applications with only a cursory review in order to decrease the existing backlog. Since 1985, applications have again been examined in greater detail, and the stock of applications has progressively increased. Thus in 1987, there were 14,474 applications and 8,825 applications processed; in 1988, the number of applications amounted to 14,561 and decisions to 11,772. To the extent that applications for most invention patents certainly take over a year to be processed, patent protection is de facto less (and sometime considerably less) than fifteen years.

Other Forms of Patent Protection

Since 1970, Brazil has operated a utility model or petty patent system. Brazilian and international experience suggests that most petty patent applications are submitted by residents (see Table 5.1). Generally such patents are awarded to individuals rather than to large corporate firms, and they are mostly focused on minor innovations of mechanical nature rather than chemical or bio-related technologies. It has been argued that the petty patent system would be a legal arrangement tailored to the needs of industrializing countries, where most innovations are of an adaptive nature, and that such a system "broadens the invention base by providing incentives to individuals and small firms to develop inventions."7/

TABLE 5.1
Utility Model Patent Applications 1975, 1980, 1988

	1975		1980		1988	
	R	NR	R	NR	R	NR
Brazil	na	na	1657	89	2289	65
W.Germany	30114	11938	26094	8153	na	na
Japan	178992	1668	190338	1397	na	na
S.Korea	7052	338	7936	622	na	na

R: Residents
NR: Nonresidents

Sources: R. Evenson, "International Invention: Implications for Technology Market Analysis," in R&D, Patents, and Productivity, ed. Z. Griliches, (Chicago: U. of Chicago Press, 1984), table 5.2; and INPI, Relatorio 1988.

In Brazil, the system of patenting models of utility (as well as industrial models and designs) appears to be working effectively as an inducement to innovation and does not seem to be hampered by major legal or administrative barriers. It is worth noting that demand for these alternative patenting systems is driven not only by the fact that minor innovations are not normally patentable, but also by what is often perceived to be the high costs versus benefits for regular patents (including the time needed for applications to be examined and the amount of technical information required).

Trademark Protection

Legislation on trademarks (Title II of Industrial Property Code) generally conforms to international standards. Registration of a mark or an advertising expression or device is granted for ten years counting from the date of issue and is renewable for identical and successive terms. A renewal of the application must be filed during the last year of each ten-year period.

There is intense trademark registration activity in Brazil. Between 1979 and 1988 over 700,000 applications were processed and 322,000 marks registered. At the beginning of 1988 there was a backlog of 88,636 applications. Considering that the average number of applications processed in 1985-87 was slightly over 63,000, the expected delay in processing time was over a year. In 1988 INPI was able to process over 123,000 applications, so that the backlog at the end of the year implied a delay of less than three months.

Two aspects of trademark protection may detract from the system's effectiveness. First, registration is on a "first-to-file" basis, so that even internationally recognized marks can be appropriated by third parties if not registered in Brazil on a timely basis. In addition, registration privileges lapse on petition from any interested party if the mark is not initiated within two years from the time of registration, or if use is discontinued in Brazil for more than two consecutive years. It has not been uncommon for these provisions to be used in bad faith and for the purpose of "greenmail" without being curbed either administratively or though the courts. (As it is costly and time-consuming to litigate, the latter alternative is not commonly pursued.)

Copyright Protection

Even critics of the Brazilian system of intellectual property rights acknowledge that Brazil has a "decentralized, relatively effective, copyright system."8/ The 1973 Copyright Law broadly protects inter alia, written works, engineering and architectural designs and plans, as well as photographs, film, music, video and other forms of creation. Collection and registration of works for copyright are undertaken by ten specialized entities ranging from the National Library (which accepts book registrations) to the Federal Council of Engineering, Architecture and Agronomy, which registers designs and plans. Although Brazilian law does not require registration as a prerequisite for obtaining protection, it is a generalized practice as a deterrent to piracy. Copyrights are valid for sixty years beyond the life of the author, or for recordings and broadcasts, sixty years after their creation.

An effective copyright-based form of protection for computer software is provided by legislation enacted in 1987 and made enforceable ("regulamentada") in November 1988. In December 1988, CNDA appointed INPI as the agency responsible for registering computer programs for copyright. Registration takes fifteen to thirty days, is valid for five years, and is renewable for twenty-five years (from the date the software was marketed).9/ The same legislation that regulates software protection also establishes the basis for its commercialization in Brazil. To be sold domestically, both national and foreign software needs to be cataloged ("cadastrado") with the Special Secretariat of Informatics (SEI). SEI's acceptance of software on its roster depends on a "similarity" test, which so far has not been an impediment to imports of either noncompeting, or competing but weakly differentiated software. In addition to a test of "similarity," local software development is protected by tariffs of up to 200 percent. There are, however, no major impediments to importing software as so-called "only copy," for personal or business use.

Protection of Trade Secrets

The current system provides weak statutory protection against disclosure of trade secrets to competitors. Although the Industrial Property Code states that "inventions and improvements thereon made during the course of a contract which is expressly directed at research in Brazil...or an invention resulting from the nature of the duties under the contract of employment, shall belong exclusively to the employer," firms acquiring trade secrets by hiring away employees cannot be sued. Firms are only liable if it can be proved that they acquired trade secrets by "unfair means" (such as through industrial espionage). The burden of protection generally falls upon the raided firm. In fact, Brazilian courts have dismissed most cases of trade secret infringement on the basis that plaintiffs failed to take adequate measures to protect their trade secrets.10/

Curbing Violations

The Brazilian judicial system does not appear to provide an effective deterrent to violations of intellectual property rights. Proceedings tend to be slow and there is a reluctance to imprison an infringer or to grant adequate damages. Neither preliminary nor permanent injunctions are available. In patent infringement cases, violators are subject to civil and criminal penalties. It has been argued, however, that de facto "the only recourse is to obtain an early decision from the court as to the fine to be imposed for continued infringement, should the patent owner prevail, and hope that the amount of the fine acts as a deterrent."11/

Copyright infringement may also lead to civil and criminal penalties. Unauthorized copies may be seized under court order, and the violator must reimburse the right holder with all the proceeds from sales. In addition, small (inflation-unadjusted) monetary fines can be imposed on violators. The only penalty that is a credible deterrent is imprisonment, with terms ranging from three months to four years. Penalties for violation of software copyrights include fines and detention for six months to two years, in addition to seizure of unauthorized copies of the software. Criminal penalties for trademark violations range from three months to one year imprisonment. There is also an assessment of losses and damages.

Civil and criminal penalties for violating intellectual property rights in Brazil are small compared to those specified in U.S. legislation and handed down in court decisions. Brazilian and American judicial standards and parameters tend to be quite distinct. In Brazil, property rights violations do not elicit public pressure demanding strong action. This reflects Brazil's public view that there is little (if anything) to gain in strengthening the system of intellectual property rights protection. But to what extent is this public perception correct when it comes to the development of industrial technology in Brazil?

TECHNOLOGY DEVELOPMENT AND THE INTELLECTUAL PROPERTY RIGHTS REGIME

What has been the impact of the Brazilian system of intellectual property rights protection on industrial technology development? Little evidence exists that the gaps and weaknesses within the system have had a substantially adverse impact on the acquisition of technological capabilities by Brazilian industrial firms. The IPR regime is one among a multiplicity of factors driving the technological activities of individual firms, and arguably not the most important.

The intensity of competition is the critical factor in firms' technological performance. International experience shows that entry, the competitive threat from a newcomer, is the force that helps generate and diffuse technological improvements by pushing managers to react and innovate.12/ Cross-country evidence also suggests that technological and managerial capabilities are acquired more rapidly when producers have to replicate the price, quality, and product performance standards of the international market. These are forced on producers as they increase their commitment to export markets and face a more open trading environment.

The proposition that competition is a major stimulus for firms to undertake technological activities is supported by a recent econometric study of the determinants of the technological behavior of Brazilian industrial firms.13/ Evidence suggests that the probability of a firm importing technology, engaging in systematic research and development, or undertaking other technological activities such as quality control is:

1. positively affected by the extent to which firms have penetrated export markets, thus confirming the notion that rivalry in those markets induces firms to adopt a more aggressive technological behavior;
2. negatively related to protection from imports,

suggesting that in sheltered environments there is less incentive for firms to allocate resources for technology development;
3. positively related to size, up to a ceiling level, after which the impact of size becomes negative, suggesting that scale economies are important for technological activities, but up to a limit;
4. positively related to concentration but negatively related to profits, suggesting that lack of competition and availability of rents have an adverse impact on technological activities.

Although the extent of competition appears to be a major determinant of Brazilian industrial firms' technological engagement, the rate of technical progress is also influenced by "supply side" considerations: (1)the science and technology infrastructure (in-house R&D centers, government institutions, and universities), (2)the size and skill composition of the human resource base, and (3)explicit government technology policies governing technology transfer, fiscal and financial incentive regimes for R&D, and the system of IPR protection.

It is also far from clear that the property rights regime dominates other factors. In fact, it could be argued that for many industrializing countries such as Brazil, there is at best a weak association between the property rights regime and the level of technological activity. If R&D expenditures as a proportion of GDP are taken as a proxy of technological activity, the pace at which firms in economies such as Korea and Taiwan intensified their technological efforts since the mid-1970s is noteworthy (refer to Table 5.2). Yet during the same period, no major actions were directed at closing the gaps in the intellectual property rights regime in those countries. Only recently (1987-88) have Korea and Taiwan reinforced patent, copyright, and trade secret protection.14/ The major driving force behind their technological "leap forward" is the need to sustain and expand their position in increasingly competitive international markets. The acquisition of technological capabilities is meanwhile facilitated by a strong institutional and human resource base.

TABLE 5.2
R&D Expenditures for Selected Countries

	1970	1975	1980	1986a/	%PEb/
Brazil	0.4c/	0.7	0.6	0.7	28
South Korea	na	0.39	0.58	1.8	60-70
Taiwan	na	na	0.8c/	1.1	na

a/ Preliminary; b/ Percentage R&D funded by "productive enterprises" or by industry in 1985 (for Brazil the year of reference is 1982); c/ estimate.

Sources: UNESCO, Statistical Yearbook, various years; the World Bank.

Brazil's R&D expenditures have remained basically flat since the mid-1970s after an initial spurt in the early part of the decade when technology development became an important part of the government's agenda. At the same time, efforts to penetrate export markets intensified. (It is estimated that R&D/GDP ratio in 1970 was on the order of 0.3-0.4.) A deteriorating economic environment and an excessively protective policy became, however, major disincentives for producers to expand their technological activities. As a result, not only did R&D expenditures fail to grow, but equally important, most of these expenditures continued to be undertaken by government (see Table 5.3). The point that should be stressed is that throughout this period, the IPR regime appears to be unrelated to the intensity of national technological efforts.15/

Evidence on the nature of technological activities being undertaken in Brazilian industrial firms also suggests that gaps in the IPR regime (particularly in the patent system) are of secondary importance for their technological performance. This evidence is drawn from the answers to a detailed questionnaire on the technological performance of the Brazilian industry from a 1980-1981 sample of 4309 industrial firms with 7156 plants. The econometric exercise by H. Braga and W. Willmore discussed earlier was based on information drawn from a "clean" subsample of this larger universe.16/ Thus:

1. Most technology in use had its origin within a firm, as an outcome of its own development efforts. That was the case, for example, with product design (70.4 percent) and plant layout projects (76.5 percent).
2. In only a relatively small proportion of firms is there a commitment to develop new products "systematically."
3. Imitation is perceived to be generalized in industry. Over 67 percent of respondents pointed out that copying of product lines from competitors is a common practice in their sector.

These findings suggest first that most technology generated in Brazilian industry consists of minor innovations, not easily codified, characterized by a high degree of tacitness, and low level of understanding. Generally, firms do not have access to well-defined production sets made up of easily replicable techniques embedded in a well-understood body of available knowledge. The replication of technologies is a resource-intensive process involving very specific and often uncodified knowledge; it does not merely involve choosing from available off-the-shelf technologies.17/

To the extent that most technology generated in Brazilian industry is minor and not easily codifiable, and that a substantial proportion is obtained through imitation (presumably through reverse engineering, or more likely, by labor mobility), gaps in the scope and administration of patent legislation would not have a substantial impact on technical change. In any case, few firms are attempting in any systematic away to produce inventions involving major creative steps.

Trade secret legislation is, however, more significant for technology development. Its impact hinges on how minor innovations are generated. If such innovations are the product of exogenous forces, or if they are the natural outcome of firms working down the learning curve (by continuously improving designs or production processes), then lack of trade secret protection could in fact be beneficial to technical progress: it would promote the diffusion of minor innovations in industry without necessarily having an adverse impact upon the generation of such innovations. If, however, such innovations are the outcome of systematic and deliberate efforts by industrial producers, then weak legislation would support diffusion (through labor mobility -- essential to the movement of hard-to-be-codified knowledge) at the expense of innovation. Case studies and anecdotal evidence suggest that innovations (even if minor) do not tend to be generated automatically.18/ In this sense, trade secret legislation might be justified to promote technical change in Brazil.

Direct foreign investment and the IPR regime

A second category of issues concerning the impact of the IPR regime on industrial development relates to the effect of weak protection on the magnitude and composition of direct foreign investment (DFI). It is often argued that weak systems of protection deter foreign investment, particularly investment involving the transfer of sophisticated but easily replicable technology. Although there is scant evidence on the impact of Brazil's IPR system on DFI flows, investor surveys have revealed that property rights protection plays a significant (in a statistical sense) but subordinate role in investment decisions.

The main factor explaining DFI flows is the "economic environment."19/ The size and growth dynamics of the domestic market, factor supply and costs, and the degree of stability of the overall macroeconomic environment are key aspects.20/ The so-called "rules of the game" -- regulatory policies and practices such as price controls, investment regulations and remittance rules -- although important, are not as influential in investment decisions. Rules that are perceived by investing firms to be arbitrary or unfair, particularly if subject to frequent changes, become a critical deterrent to investment at the margin. By increasing the cost and risk of doing business in the context of a less attractive economic climate, such rules may lower profit expectations sufficiently to cause firms to either divest or not invest in the first place.

The evolution of DFI flows in Brazil is instructive in this respect (as shown in Table 5.3): DFI grew substantially between 1970 and 1982 and fell thereafter. More recently (since 1987), investment flows have been negative as the economic crisis deepened, similar to the case in Mexico.21/ In both countries, the inflection point seems associated with the onset of the debt crisis and increasing macroeconomic instability and economic contraction. Throughout the 1970-85 period there were very few changes in Brazil's (or Mexico's) rules affecting direct foreign investment, including the IPR regime; the critical shift was in the economic environment.22/

TABLE 5.3
Direct Investment Flows in Brazil and Mexico, 1970-1985 (US$ million)

	1970	1975	1980	1981	1982	1983	1985
Brazil	145	1303	1913	2526	2922	1556	1362
Mexico	323	610	2184	2541	1644	456	503

Source: International Monetary Fund, Balance-of-Payment and International Financial Statistics, 1970-86.

Finally, it is often argued that not so much the volume but the composition of DFI is affected by the lack of an effective IPR regime, and that international firms in high-technology areas refrain from coming into countries with weak systems of protection. On a prima facie basis, the Brazilian experience does not support such a proposition. While the share of foreign firms' total sales in 1980 averaged 28.5 percent for the manufacturing industry as a whole, it was 41 percent in nonelectric machinery, 44 percent in electric machinery, 68 percent in transport material, 21 percent in chemicals, and 71 percent in pharmaceuticals. It is striking that in the least protected subsector, from an IPR perspective, the share of international firms in total sales was the second highest in industry overall (next to tobacco, which reached 73 percent).23/ It is equally noteworthy that DFI flows in pharmaceuticals (including reinvestment) grew from $113.4 million in 1971 to $300 million in 1975, $646.5 in 1979, and had reached $971 million by 1984.

Technology Flows and the IPR Regime

It is often said that the quality of technology flows is affected by the IPR regime. Indeed, a recent OECD survey on international technology licensing shows that exchange controls, government regulations (particularly prior approval), and inadequate protection of industrial property rights in developing countries were the key disincentives to licensing (see Table 5.4). Evidence on other forms of arms-length technology transfer arrangements is scant.

In the case of Brazil, there is insufficient evidence to assess the impact of the IPR regime on technology transfer. It appears, however, that the major stumbling blocks to the transfer of complete technology packages, at least in cases of licenses, are royalty payment limits and the fact that confidentiality clauses are void upon expiration of the agreement between licensor and licensee.24/ An additional constraint is the level of skill and training of local teams of engineers and technicians. In most instances, they lack the capabilities for continuously updating the technology originally supplied.

A dynamic perspective on the IPR regime. So far it has been argued that the impact of Brazil's IPR system on the technological efforts of local producers has been relatively small. It was noted that IPR protection tends to have a nondominant role among many factors influencing technical progress in industry. Among those factors, the intensity of competition stands out. In addition, it was suggested that the tacitly imitative nature of most technical change in industry underscores the secondary role of patent and similar forms of codified IPR protection. Finally, it was suggested that there is at best a weak association between DFI/technology flows and the IPR regime. Can we therefore conclude that protection of intellectual

TABLE 5.4
Disincentives to Licensing in Country of Licensee: Developing Countries a/

Nature of Disincentive	% of Respondents Citing as Significant Problem
Inadequate IPR Protection	75
Competition Laws and their Application to Licensing Agreements	21
Government Regulations:	
Prior Approval	80
Local Purchase Raw Materials	59
Local Purchase Capital Goods	55
Import Quotas	57
Export Regulations	52
Exchange Controls	88
Taxes on Licensing Income	62

a/ Based on 109 responses from executives of manufacturing or manufacturing related enterprises. Multiple responses were given.

Source: OECD, "International Technology Licensing: Survey Results," mimeo, August 1987, table 40.

property rights is of little relevance to industrial development?

The answer probably is no. The reason is that the arguments advanced so far are basically of a static nature and do not take into account the dynamics of firm growth and technology development. Although it is difficult to assess the trade-offs between the economic benefits to imitators and the disincentives to creators, they tend to become steeper over time, as a growing number of Brazilian industrial firms acquire the capabilities to develop new products and processes. A more effective

IPR system would help these firms accelerate the transition to technological maturity. It would also stimulate inventive activity among Brazil's scientists and engineers and the establishment of small, technology-based start-up ventures. If done gradually and accompanied by other measures that stimulate firms to improve their technological competence and competitive position, the process of strengthening the IPR regime in Brazil might bring large economy-wide gains.

The impact of the IPR regime on DFI and arms-length technology flows also should not be assessed from a purely static perspective. Competition among countries for direct foreign investment is intensifying, particularly for investment flows associated with the highest technological spillovers and training effects, greatest interindustry links (through suppliers' development), and strongest export orientation. Although a positive economic environment is important for attracting DFI and technology, international firms are attributing growing importance to IPR regimes and other aspects of regulatory policy.

The Brazilian experience is illustrative in this respect. In the 1970s and until the mid-1980s there was a steady flow of DFI and arms-length technology. Despite certain institutional and regulatory barriers, international firms were attracted to Brazil on the basis of locational advantages and domestic market size. Although the current (1989) low level of foreign investment is mostly explained by adverse overall economic conditions, it should not be assumed that a significant macroeconomic improvement will necessarily be followed by a reversal to the DFI levels of 1981-1982. This should not be a working assumption in an era when technical progress is diminishing the relative importance of traditional sources of comparative advantage (such as low unskilled-labor costs) and markets are increasingly globalized. As a result, regulatory issues (including the IPR regime) need to be addressed in order to attract not only significant volume of DFI but also the kind of foreign firms that have the most to offer Brazil.

The dynamics of firm development and new conditions in the international economy suggest the importance of taking a closer look at the current

IPR regime in Brazil. In addition, since the end of the last decade, Brazil has been facing a far less benign and more competitive trading environment. There is increasing pressure from its trading partners (particularly the U.S.) for the removal of nontariff barriers and a decrease in tariff protection. At the same time, there is greater emphasis on investment and intellectual property rights-related issues, linking them to access by Brazilian products to the U.S. market.

It is in Brazil's interest to move away from a defensive or reactive posture and seize the initiative by thoroughly reviewing of trade, investment and technology-related legislation, regulations, and practices. Many policy instruments are outdated, being the product of an industrial strategy of an earlier period. Since the early 1940s, the major development policy objective has been the creation of industrial capacity. Initially this strategy relied mainly on the entrepreneurial capabilities of the state and of international firms. In the 1970s, there was increased emphasis on national private firms and groups. Legislation regulating technology flows and codifying the IPR regime (including some key changes in patent protection) dates from this period and was intended to actively support the bargaining position of national firms and guide their technological choices.

At the end of the 1980s, Brazilian firms are characterized by growing financial and managerial maturity. Technologically they are in a state of transition; the acquisition of technological capabilities now depends on a movement toward a less regulated, more open and competitive economy. The challenge to policymakers is to manage the transition to a new industrial regime under which producers are neither constrained nor protected by barriers to resource mobility and competition. These barriers run counter to the imperative of timely and flexible response to shifts in demand and technology and are an impediment to the modernization of the industrial sector and its integration into the international market.25/

In principle, a shift in industrial strategy should be undertaken whether or not the position and actions of Brazil's trading partners are GATT consistent. A revision of the policy regime should be carried out because it is in Brazil's national interest. Yet, to the extent that reform removes major barriers to international competition and resource mobility, it would address many of the concerns of countries with which Brazil has extensive trade and investment relations. As such, these structural reforms would strengthen Brazil's bargaining position in bilateral and international forums for increased access to developed country markets, technologies, and investment capital. As argued earlier in this chapter, the system of intellectual property rights would be one dimension of the policy regime (though not the major one) that should be reexamined as Brazilian firms' industrial competence grows. A discussion of the scope and phasing of reform of the IPR system is the object of the next and concluding section.

THE SYSTEM OF INTELLECTUAL PROPERTY RIGHTS IN BRAZIL: AN APPROACH TO POLICY REFORM

There is a good argument for strengthening the IPR regime in Brazil. In a dynamic industrializing economy, the proportion of firms with creative potential or who are actually engaged in introducing new products and processes tends to grow over time. As firms accumulate technological capabilities and as an increasing number of agents (scientists and engineers) and institutions (universities and R&D facilities) are able to transform ideas into inventions, the trade-off between stimulating imitation and promoting innovation becomes steeper, and the economic costs of major gaps in the IPR system tend to grow.26/ In addition, rewarding the efforts of innovative firms and individuals and penalizing imitations of the proprietary stock of industrial knowledge would stimulate other producers to accelerate their transition to technological maturity.

Although the practice of imitating competitors appears to be a generalized phenomenon in Brazilian industry as discussed earlier, with only a small number of firms engaged in truly innovative activities, a much larger number have accumulated the capabilities to move beyond pure imitation. Most firms already engage in some form of minor product innovation, as well as in design, engineering, quality control, and production planning and organization activities.27/ In some areas of consumer nondurables (shoes, textiles), in certain basic intermediates (particularly metals, chemicals, cement, and pulp and paper), and in important segments of the engineering industries (such as automotive components and machine tools), these activities have been sufficient to keep producers from becoming too distant from the best-practice frontier. But they are neither pushing this frontier out nor even approaching it. A strengthening of IPR protection (with a larger emphasis on trade secrets) would bring, in the short run at the very least, a greater awareness of the importance of R&D activities. If accompanied by other policy reforms to push firms to compete in domestic and international markets, a shift in the IPR regime could contribute to firms making R&D a more systematic activity with an overall stronger commitment to innovation.

The technological capabilities of domestic firms is not as great in the more sophisticated areas, such as biotechnology, electronics and pharmaceuticals. Along with chemicals, these are also areas where firms make extensive use of patents internationally.28/ A shift in the IPR regime (particularly in patent protection) for these segments would require a transitional period during which an improved structure of incentives could be introduced and a more purposeful build-up of capabilities take place.

Improving Patent Protection

As noted earlier in this discussion, there are two key gaps in the Brazilian IPR regime: lack of patentability within certain industrial segments, and absence of effective trade secret legislation. In Brazil, producers are unable to patent, inter alia, fine chemicals (although the process for manufacturing them is patentable), biotechnological inventions, integrated circuit designs, or drugs. The technological capabilities and the potential for engaging in innovative activities in each of these areas are quite differentiated and so has to be the approach for strengthening patent protection. Before discussing individual segments, it should be stressed that a major gap in the patent regime, and one which affects all patent applications, is the de facto variable period of validity for patents. This period counts from the date the application is filed, and not from the date the patent is granted. As administrative delays in patent registration have been quite common in the past, patents tend to be valid for less than fifteen years.

Introducing patent protection for metal alloys and chemical products (including fine chemicals -- agrotoxics, pigments, catalysts, etc.) in the short to medium-term (one to three years) seems warranted. Brazil has large and diversified chemical and metals industries. In 1980 chemical/petrochemicals had the highest share of industrial value-added (14.7 percent), and value of production in 1983 was $8.5 billion or 3.2 percent of GDP. The petrochemical segment, in particular, comprises relatively large, financially strong and well-managed firms. In sum, capabilities exist for producers to undertake substantial innovation. A strong potential for innovation also exists in metal alloys for similar reasons. This area already includes a major innovator (Eletrometal).

If most metals and chemicals firms still have a weak commitment to innovation, it is due to the prevailing structure of incentives. As in many other segments of Brazilian industry, firms in metals and chemicals function in an environment protected from the forces of competition and where high returns are the norm. These returns have been strongly influenced and, in some major segments, regulated by government policy. They have been justified as a means of inducing market entry and for Brazil to attain self-sufficiency in the largest number of product segments. Managerial focus has been, as a result, on capacity creation and operation of existing plants. The emphasis on product development has been small, with most projects geared to the production of commodities based on imported process technologies.

Introducing patent protection would be per se insufficient to affect firm behavior substantially. Risk-adjusted patent rents obtained by introducing innovative products would tend to be dominated by monopoly profits on current output. Trade and regulatory policy reform would be needed to change the incentive structure, shifting profitability away from production and towards innovation. Unless competition from entrants and imports exhausts monopoly rents, high returns from current activities tend to dominate expected returns from innovative activities, and the impact of patent reform on industrial technology development is marginal. As previously suggested, to be effective, patent protection reform in Brazil needs to be part of a broader industrial policy reform.

Biotechnological inventions are not patentable yet in Brazil; there are economic and legal issues to be resolved before patents can be granted. Historically the objective of patent legislation was to stimulate so-called "industrial applications," understood as technical creations obtained through physical and chemical means. Manipulation of reproduction systems in plants and animals for example normally did not generate patentable inventions.

In Germany, a shift in this doctrine first occurred in 1922 when the concession of patents for processes employing biological means (such as for the production of immunizing substances) was permitted. In 1969, the West German Supreme Court accepted the patentability of genetic improvement of animals stating that "the relevant question, in this case, is if forces and phenomena of biological nature can be treated the same as those of technological nature.... A creation that, methodically, utilizes controllable natural forces to attain specific and predetermined ends, could be considered patentable, as long as such creation fulfills the general requirements of an industrial application, novelty, etc...." Similar conclusions were reached in 1980 by the U.S. Supreme Court and in 1982 by the Canadian Patent Appeal Chamber.29/

If international jurisprudence is a good guide, it seems that biotechnological inventions should be patentable. Even if Brazilian courts were to take a position on the issue, complex problems of interpretation and enforcement of legislation would remain.30/ A separate question concerns the economic rationale for patenting such inventions, in view of the relatively incipient stage of biotechnology development in Brazil. Most technological capabilities in this field are concentrated in major universities and government research institutes (such as Fiocruz in Rio de

Janeiro). It may be advisable to establish a moderate transition period (perhaps three to five years) before patentability is introduced.

During this period, a concerted technology development effort in this area should be undertaken, centered on training and on strengthening major research centers and their ties with industry. Firms should be encouraged to contract out research, and research centers to set up "incubators" for spinning-off new biotechnology firms. In view of long lead times in biotechnology innovation cycles, and the fact that entrants tend to be small and financially strapped, new forms of financing would be necessary. Regulatory changes may be needed to stimulate the introduction of new instruments (involving risk-sharing) and the formation of venture capital institutions.

A similar transition period of three to five years may be needed for integrated circuit designs, in which Brazil's capabilities are still incipient. At the end of 1986, there were twenty-two semiconductor producers in Brazil, half of which were foreign firms engaged just in mounting and testing discrete components (and linear circuits in a few cases). Four national firms were dedicated to linear and digital ICs. Digital IC imports are heavily concentrated in high-volume and complex-to-manufacture memories and microprocessors. Almost all application-specific integrated circuits (ASICs) are imported. Domestically, only three firms have been able so far to dominate the ASIC project cycle. An estimated thirty-eight ASIC projects were carried out between 1986 and mid-1988, of which eight have reached the production stage, though on a relatively small scale; eighteen are in progress; and the remainder were abandoned.31/ There is no question that this is a poor record, particularly in view of Brazil's potential comparative advantage in ASIC design.

The slow accretion of circuit design capabilities and the underdeveloped stage of ASIC production in Brazil are partly the result of a misguided policy focus. The first National Informatics Plan (PLANIN) not only attempted to promote too many activities in this area but, equally important, focused on the manufacture of ICs as its major policy goal in electronics. Instead, the emphasis should have been on fostering design activities by facilitating access to tools, supporting the training of design engineers and specialists, and developing a market for locally-designed ASICS. The build-up of such capabilities would be complemented by an improved incentive structure for the creation of new IC designs, including the phased introduction of patent protection. Again, patent protection should not be undertaken in isolation in the expectation that it would be sufficient to spur design activities in the microelectronics industry.

Possibly the most controversial dimension of the restrictive IPR regime in Brazil is the absence of process and product patents for pharmaceuticals. It is one of the few industries where patent protection is critical for appropriating the results of innovation. At the same time, it is the one area where patent legislation worldwide is riddled with major gaps. Indeed, most countries have patent restrictions on pharmaceuticals, but a 1978 study by the U.S. Food and Drug Administration showed that of 172 countries, only sixteen had full patent protection for drugs.32/

Restrictions on pharmaceuticals derive from the fact that this industry, like foodstuffs, is deemed essential and governments attempt to ensure an adequate supply, at accessible prices, and covering the broadest spectrum of diseases. Patent restrictions have been perceived by most countries as an instrument for spurring entry, creating capacity, and developing the production capabilities of the domestic drug industry. Full patent protection has been introduced either because the domestic pharmaceutical industry reached an advanced stage of development or in response to external pressures from trading partners.

A number of industrialized countries have "waited" for their drug industry to become verticalized and internationalized before granting full patent protection. Such was the case with West Germany, Switzerland, and Japan which only granted full protection at the mature stage of their industries. By then, West Germany had become the largest exporter of pharmaceuticals (and the third largest producer), with national firms controlling 65 percent of its domestic market; Switzerland was already the third largest exporter with 72 percent of its market dominated by Swiss firms; and Japan had become, by the mid-1970s, the second largest world producer of therapeutic drugs with national firms supplying 80 percent of the domestic market. Other countries, however, have introduced stiffer legislation in response to commercial threats, as was the case of Italy in 1978 (which introduced full patent protection as part of EEC requirements) as well as Taiwan, Mexico, and Korea, all in the 1987-88 period.

The Brazilian pharmaceutical industry comprises approximately 600 producers, of which eighty are international firms, subsidiaries of major drug companies (of the sixteen largest American drug producers, fifteen had subsidiaries in Brazil).33/ They control approximately 80 percent of total sales. Their predominance is clear: foreign firms make up eight of the ten largest producers and forty of the fifty largest. Major American, Swiss, French, and British firms compete in the Brazilian market, mainly attracted by its large population.

Despite the fact that the industry has amassed significant production capabilities for all classes of therapeutic drugs, vertical integration is limited. In 1987 the pharmaceutical industry imported 58 percent of its active ingredients. Although the value of these imports is not very significant (amounting to around $30 million), the relatively high import coefficient is an indication of insufficient technological capabilities in a key area, namely, the manufacture of raw materials. More generally, R&D efforts are limited as subsidiaries of major international producers focus on manufacturing drugs only. In view of the costs and significant scale economies in R&D, research efforts of international firms are concentrated outside of Brazil. At the same time, few national firms have the size and the associated financial means to engage in research.34/

It is unclear how the lack of patent protection has affected the technological capabilities of national firms. It does not seem to have deterred entry; to the contrary, it probably has stimulated competition in the industry. In view of relatively low imitation costs, absence of patent protection in pharmaceuticals has led to market crowding, with both incumbents and newcomers taking advantage of undeterred copying.35/ Thus, by facilitating access to drug technology and thereby promoting competition in the industry, patent policy has possibly helped the acquisition of production capabilities and the operational proficiency of national firms.

Although absence of patent protection appears to have stimulated entry and competition, there is no evidence that it has promoted local R&D efforts for either the development of new drugs or the search for new active ingredients. The moderate amount of research being conducted by national firms and research institutions is mostly in an attempt to import substitute unavailable or relatively expensive raw materials. Examples are traditional active ingredients (Codetec of the University of Campinas, for example, developed, under contract, production processes for forty active ingredients in a recent two-year period); antibiotics (those developed by Cibran -- licomycin and gentamycin); and special insulins (for which there are only four producers worldwide, Biobras being one of them). These activities suggest, however, that there are significant research assets that could be more effectively mobilized by improving the structure of incentives and further stimulating the acquisition of technological capabilities.

The issue of patent protection should not be addressed in isolation. A possible approach might be to negotiate a policy package with industry involving removal of key investment barriers (such as profit-constraining price controls) against an enlarged investment and R&D commitment by domestic and foreign firms. More specifically, progressive price decontrol could be introduced with improved targeting of the poor for free or subsidized medicine. Drug procurement could be enlarged and used on a more systematic basis to stimulate long-term technology development. Finally, a phased shift in the patent regime could be introduced against a commitment by foreign firms to license their technology on demand and undertake significant R&D locally.

The presence of major international firms in the Brazilian market should be regarded as an opportunity for cooperative R&D with national firms and contractual research with R&D centers and universities. Current patent restrictions have not significantly helped to alter the relative market position of national firms which in the last thirty years has oscillated between 15-25 percent of total sales. These restrictions have, however, been used as a justification by international firms for not undertaking R&D locally. A change in patent legislation should be undertaken within the broader context of stimulating the creative capabilities of national producers and research institutions and harnessing some of the R&D potential of international firms.

Shifts in patent legislation should be phased over a period of up to ten years. In an initial phase (within one to three years), patent protection would be introduced for new active substances and drugs developed to treat major tropical diseases which are highly prevalent in Brazil. This would stimulate firms to engage in R&D that would not normally be their priority. As a further inducement, patent protection could be combined with certain long-term, minimum purchase assurances from the government if product development efforts lead to successful results. CEME, the government agency in charge of drug procurement, already makes 11 percent of total purchases in the market. In addition to expanding its purchases and better targeting them to the poor, CEME might introduce, on a systematic basis, technology development contracts as part of its procurement policy thus minimizing the adverse social impact of progressive price decontrol.

In a second phase (within three to five years), process patents for new products would be granted. This transition period could in fact be shortened to make it consistent with the approach to product patenting outlined above. Often a drug molecule which is initially thought to be effective against one disease turns out to be effective in another area after the clinical testing is complete. Yet the patentability of that molecule should be determined as soon as possible after the initial discovery and long before the clinical testing. This timing problem could be resolved by accepting process patent applications and eventually converting them to product patents if it is determined that the molecule works for a targeted disease.

In a final phase (within seven to ten years), patents for all other new products would be accepted. To ensure that patents and cross-licensing would not be used to divide markets and deter entry by domestic firms, some form of simplified compulsory licensing on demand could be introduced. At the same time, the government might encourage international firms to commit, at the very least, their licensing proceeds to finance their R&D efforts in Brazil.

Finally, if changes in patent protection require a differentiated approach and transitional periods across industrial segments, effective trade secret legislation may be introduced on a more uniform basis. Trade secrets are particularly important for industries relying on innovative process technologies for competitive gains (generally, process parameters may be easily discovered by hiring away production workers and technicians). The absence of protection for trade secrets appears to be particularly important in view of the high degree of labor mobility in Brazil, particularly of technical and engineering specialists. The probability of losing commercially valuable proprietary information when such expertise changes jobs within the market is an element undermining R&D efforts.

Trade secret legislation in Brazil is weak and not often enforced. Its penalties fall on employees, reflecting the prevailing business culture in which the widespread practice of copying competitors' innovations is not regarded with alarm. Ironically, most innovation in industry is minor and not easily patentable; its production might benefit considerably from stronger trade secret legislation and enforcement. In order to deter the unapproved appropriation of trade secrets by third parties, legislation needs to focus not only on employees carrying away proprietary information but on firms acquiring this information. It is important, however, that legislation be crafted and applied judiciously. Experience in developed countries suggests that overly stringent protection of trade secrets -- through an excessively broad view of the scope of an innovation -- can stifle further innovation and become a deterrent to entry. The object of protecting trade secrets (and patents) should be to stimulate innovation and the acquisition of technological capabilities by Brazilian industry, without constraining entry and technological diffusion.

RESEARCH DIRECTIONS

Not much empirical knowledge has been generated on the relative importance of intellectual property rights to technology development in Brazil. Possibly the most immediate need is for a firm-level survey of the influence of IPR variables on the technological behavior of industrial managers. In particular, it would be useful to assess the relative weight of patent and trade secret protection on the intensity of the firm's technological activities and how these activities are organized. In order to establish the relationship between IPR protection and technical change, it would be necessary to define the relevant typology of firms according to size, technology, industrial segment, etc. A key objective would be to identify technological competence thresholds above which stronger IPR protection becomes an effective stimulus for firms to intensify their technological efforts.

A second area of importance where knowledge is quite limited concerns the relevance of IPR protection for research undertaken in universities and government research institutions in key areas of investigation. To what extent is the absence of patent protection in biotechnology, for example, hampering the research efforts of university investigators? Does lack of patentability influence the choice of research areas, methods, and objectives? Does it weaken potential ties with industry?

Third, not enough is known about how important IPR regimes are to the composition and quality of direct foreign investment and arms-length transfer of industrial technology. To what extent is Brazil being deprived of best-practice technology by IPR restrictions? What gaps in the IPR regime are particularly detrimental for effective technology transfer? Does the investment and technology conduct of international firms in Brazil vary according to their size, nationality, or segment of activity? Would a strengthening of the IPR regime induce these international firms to intensify their local technological efforts? These and other research issues need to be addressed if we are to have a better understanding of the impact of IPR regimes on industrial technology development. Results would be useful in the design of appropriate systems for protection of intellectual property rights in Brazil and other industrializing countries.

NOTES

1. For a useful description of patent regimes for different types of inventions, see Robert Evenson, "International Invention: Implications for Technology Market Analysis," in R&D, Patents, and Productivity, ed. Zvi Griliches (Chicago: U. of Chicago Press, 1984).

2. The Code is, in this case, quite explicit: "food and chemical-pharmaceutical substances, matter, admixtures of products and medicaments of any kind, as well as the respective processes for obtaining or modifying them" are not patentable (art. 9, item c). The English translation of the Code in found in John Sinnot, World Patent Law and Practice, vol. 2B (New York: Matthew Bender, 1981).

3. In fact, since 1980 "composition of use" applications (which by 1989 numbered some 7500) have not been processed on the grounds that time was required to establish if "composition of use" would approximate a product patent. It now appears that INPI has decided not to accept "composition of use claims."

4. See National Agricultural Chemicals Association, Piracy of American Agrochemical Technology (Washington D.C., 1985), p. 55.

5. According to INPI, two compulsory license applications were pending in December 1986. See Timothy J. Richards, "Brazil" in Intellectual Property Rights: Global Consensus, Global Conflict?, eds. R. Michael Gadbaw and Timothy J. Richards (Boulder, Colo.: Westview Press, 1988), footnote 39.

6. National Industrial Property Institute (INPI), Relatorio 1988, p. 17.

7. R. Evenson, p. 98.

8. T. Richards, p. 172. The description of the system follows this reference.

9. INPI, Relatorio 1988, p. 24.

10. T. Richards, p. 180.

11. National Agricultural Chemicals Association, p. 55.

12. P. Geroski and A. Jacquemin, "Industrial Change, Barriers to Mobility and European Industrial Policy," Economic Policy, November 1985.

13. Helson Braga and Larry Willmore, "Imports of Technology Efforts and Technological Efforts: an Analysis of their Determinants in Brazilian Firms," mimeo, 1989. The results of their study were obtained from a logit model estimated on a 1980/81 sample of 4342 industrial plants (drawn from a larger sample of 7156 plants belonging to 4309 firms).

14. Edwin Mansfield, "Protection of Intellectual Property Rights in Developing Countries," report prepared for the Economics Department of the International Financial Corporation, mimeo, February 1989.

15. This discussion, of course does not dispose of the following counterfactual: had Brazil established a stronger IPR regime, more efforts would have been devoted to R&D and the technological improvement of industry.

16. See Helson Braga and Virene Matesco, "Desempenho Tecnologico da Industrial Brasileira: uma Analise Exploratoria," Textos Para Discussão Interna no. 162, INPES/IPEA, February 1989, tables 2.1, 3.2 and 5.5.

17. Nathan Rosenberg and Claudio Frischtak, The International Technology Transfer: Concepts, Measures and Comparisons (New York, 1985). If technology is not simply a set of blueprints, producers must organize and nurture teams of engineers and technicians in order to generate technology or transfer it from a different environment.

18. Jorge Katz, ed., Technology Generation in Latin American Manufacturing Industries (New York, 1987).

19. For an excellent discussion of determinants of DFI flows see World Bank, "Direct Foreign Investment in Mexico -- Past Patterns and Future Strategy," Report no. 7146-ME, chapters I and II.

20. See, for example, the survey by the Council of Americas of U.S. multinationals with business in Latin America titled "Coping with Crisis: U.S. Investment and Latin America's Continuing Economic Crisis," January 1987.

21. In the recent period, most foreign investment in Brazil and Mexico has been associated with debt equity swaps. Since the establishment of rules allowing such operations, the volume of debt-equity related investment has grown substantially. Total foreign investment (direct and debt-equity related) reached $2.7 billion in Brazil and $2.6 billion in Mexico in 1988.

22. The case of Thailand is also suggestive. See "Thailand's Refusal to Protect Copyrights Produces Cheap Goods, Disputes with U.S.," Washington Post, March 12, 1989, p. H2.

23. Larry Willmore, "Controle Estrangeiro e Concentracao na Industria Brasileira," Pesquisa e Planejamento Economico, April 1987.

24. Technology payments range from 2 percent of net sales (in case of plastic and rubber product) to 5 percent of net sales (in case of ships and naval equipment, and material for generation of electricity and production of fuel).

25. See the World Bank report entitled "Industrial Regulatory Policies and Investment Incentives in Brazil," Report no. 7843-BR, June 30, 1989.

26. An early discussion of the differential benefits of the IPR regime to countries in different stages of industrial maturity is found in Edith Penrose, The International Patent System (Baltimore, Md: Johns Hopkins Univ. Press, 1951).

27. Braga, ibid.

28. See John Bound et al., "Who Does R&D and Who Patents?," in R&D, Patents and Productivity, ed. Zvi Griliches (Chicago: U. of Chicago Press, 1984), p. 38; and Edwin Mansfield, Technological Change (W.W. Norton, 1971), p. 131.

29. Joseph Straus, "Industrial Property Protection of Biotechnological Inventions -- Analysis of Certain Basic Issues," Doc. WIPO BIG/281, July 1985.

30. See Gary Hoffman and Geoffrey Carney, "Can Justice Keep Pace with Science?," The Washington Post, April 10, 1988.

31. Claudio Frischtak, "Specialization, Technical Change and Competitiveness of the Brazilian Electronics Industry," mimeo, May 31, 1989.

32. See E. Mansfield, "Protection of Intellectual Property Rights in Developing Countries," ibid., February 1989, p. 4.; and INPI, Revista de Propriedade Industrial, vol. 2, no. 5, 1985, supplement.

33. Data on the ranking of firms and the breakdown between national and international firms is drawn from "O Capital Estrangeiro na Industria Brasileira: Atualidade e Perspectivas," Estudos BNDES, no. 10, mimeo, 1988.

34. Between March 1986 and February 1987, twenty-one firms had annual sales over $25 million, the top firm being Merrel/Lepetit (of the Dow Chemical Group) with $70.5 million; only two Brazilian firms (Ache, with sales of $60.9 million and Dorsay, with $25.2 million) were in this group of top market performers. See BNDES, table 1.7.1, p. 77.

35. To illustrate, take the case of the anti-ulcer drug Zantac, introduced by the British company Glaxo, and that in 1987 reached worldwide sales of $500 million (the drug with the largest sales worldwide). In Brazil, there are at least five versions of Zantac: Zylium, Label, Logat, Ulcoren, and Antak, the latter being sold by Glaxo itself, and the others based on the same active ingredient.

6

Case Studies in Brazilian Intellectual Property Rights

Flavio Grynszpan

INTRODUCTION

Brazil is a country of recent industrialization. A significant part of the industrial technology is foreign and is transferred through the license of a patent, trademark, or know-how. In only a few industrial sectors have the industries developed their own technology. Since transfers of research results from universities and research institutes are not common, most industries either develop their own R&D base or rely on foreign technology.

The Brazilian debt problem exerts pressure on the national industries. In order to compete internationally in foreign markets, Brazil must develop a continuous stream of innovative products often depending on foreign technology to do so.

In areas where the R&D base is weak, most interaction between the industries and the intellectual property system is done through technology transfer agreements like the licensing of a patent or trademark or the contracting of know-how. In areas where the R&D base is stronger, some industries have developed products with local technology, but have to rely on foreign technology if they want to participate in the international market. Only a very limited number of companies have the R&D structure which can generate output to compete in both the internal and external markets.

The relationship between the science and technology institutions (universities and research institutes) and the intellectual property system is very weak mainly because of the limited transfer of research results to industrial applications. Only recently have researchers become aware of the Brazilian intellectual property system, mainly due to the use of existing patents.

The exceptions to this rule are the research institutes affiliated with government-owned companies, which dedicate a substantial number of scientists to establishing a competitive R&D environment. Since these state companies usually control the market (oil, electric energy), the technology can be transferred internally from laboratory directly to utilization. In the case of telecommunications, the government controls the specifications of the products and therefore, the results from the research of the research institutes is immediately absorbed by the industrial park. These research institutes have gradually increased their interaction with the intellectual property system either by patenting their own innovations or by maintaining an awareness of the state-of-the-art technology developments.

The new high-tech companies that are being created in the Brazilian science parks are another example. These parks transfer their research by establishing a new company. Such entrepreneurs are aware of the intellectual property system and the new products or processes are usually patented.

Finally, the industrial companies that were able to establish a convenient R&D base are becoming active participants in the intellectual property system by choosing indigenous development over transfers of technology agreements. In addition, these companies are patenting their products or processes.

This chapter will present a study of each of the mentioned groups: a large governmental company with a strong R&D base, an industrial company with the internal capability for industrial research, and a new high-tech company of a science park. The chapter will also evaluate each of three sectors of the national economy (pharmaceutical, telecommunications, and capital goods) in relation to its interaction with the intellectual property system.

CASE 1: PETROBRAS

Petrobras is the largest Brazilian company,

producing 7 percent of the gross national product. It is one of Brazil's three largest exporters and is the second largest oil producer in South America. It is the nation's largest consumer of engineering services, relying heavily on national firms. Petrobras also accounts for 20 percent of the capital goods market.

Petrobras is a holding company which controls several different firms active in all areas of the oil industry: Petroquisa (a shareholder of around eighty companies in the area of petrochemistry), Petrofertil (a controller of nine companies in the fertilizer area), Braspetro (international activities), Petrobras Distribuidora (distribution of oil), Interbras (trading), Petromisa (mineral exploration).

In 1963, Petrobras organized a research institute (CENPES) which has been located on the campus of the Federal University of Rio de Janeiro since 1973. CENPES is responsible for most of the Petrobras activities in research, development, and engineering. The research center occupies 450,000 square feet of labs and offices, in sixteen buildings. It has around 800 high-level personnel, 600 technicians, and 300 support personnel. Of these, around 800 people are involved in research and 260 in basic engineering.

Over the past twenty years, CENPES has made substantial contributions to the company's effort to master its essential technology. It has developed control over sixty different processes (in refining, natural gas, exploration, petrochemicals, fertilizers, and alternative energy). It has developed the capability to design and engineer new operational units in many of its areas of activities and has acquired skills to support Petrobras's efforts in the world market.

CENPES's technical activities are concentrated in exploration and production research (exploration, reservoir, drilling, production, equipments), industrial research (refining, fertilizers, petrochemicals, fine chemicals, polyners, catalysts), and basic engineering (exploration, refinery, design of complete products, petrochemicals, fertilizers and alcohol chemistry, natural gas, alternative energy, process equipment).

CENPES has gradually evolved from a center that provided research to one exclusive client to a center with active external relations both in Brazil and abroad. CENPES has signed contracts and cooperative technological exchange agreements with other oil companies, research institutions, and universities.

To protect the company's industrial property interests, CENPES created a division for technical information and industrial property which coordinates the efforts of the Petrobras system in those areas. Through CENPES, Petrobras can file for and maintain patents on inventions and improvements produced within the Petrobras group. It also assists the operational units in studying the possible use of patented technology.

The division for technical information has published a booklet to alert Petrobras researchers about the need for patenting their inventions and maintains a group of specialists in industrial property to collaborate in the identification of patentable items and in the filing of the respective patents. This division also examines all the patents in the related areas of development in an effort to detect technological changes, to evaluate the maturity of a technology, and to analyze the behavior of its international competitors. It is also responsible for filing oppositions to external patent requests.

CENPES already has 250 filings for patents in the country, of which 120 were granted. Of the granted patents, about 10 percent were licensed to Brazilian industries; but most of the patents are being used by Petrobras itself.

CENPES has extensive experience in technology transfers. It is one of the most active institutions in permanent contact with the Brazilian intellectual property system. The power of Petrobras generally overcomes any bureaucracy in the regulatory agencies; therefore, Petrobras has developed a great deal of independence in its foreign contracts.

Due to its size and endeavors, CENPES is an important institution within the Brazilian intellectual property system. In the opinion of CENPES, the present system is not affecting Petrobras's economic performance because the company has access to any technology needed, either from internal or external sources.

The research results from CENPES are mainly

being used by Petrobras internally. Only 10 percent of its patents have been licensed. The company does not expect a significant return from the licensing of its patents. The importance of the research is measured by the quality of the products and services that Petrobras itself can produce.

Thus, for Petrobras, the present intellectual property system does not impact its performance because:

1. Petrobras works specifically in technologically mature fields (fine chemistry, new materials, biotechnology, informatics are not major activities).
2. most of Petrobras's R&D results are incorporated into its own products and services (very little is licensed).
3. Petrobras is a state company. The investment in R&D depends not only on the economic results but also on a governmental strategy. The return on the investment of R&D is not always the determining factor.

CASE II: METAL LEVE

Metal Leve is a mid-sized company, a pioneer in the Brazilian market of pistons and bearings. Metal Leve occupies today an area of 1,000,000 square meters in Sao Paulo and is the leader on the Brazilian market for its two products.

Metal Leve has many subsidiary and affiliate companies which provide a wide variety of products and services: powder metallurgy parts, cast-iron products, high-tech machinery, programmable controllers, electromechanical products, and marketing of electronic products.

The continuous manufacturing of automotive components created an internal engineering capability which has evolved into a process of absorbing and adapting the technology to the Brazilian market. More recently, Metal Leve started to design its own products.

The indigenous design capability is a result of the establishment of a technical center in 1975, the seed of the present center. Today, Metal Leve is researching advanced areas like computer-aided design, mathematical modeling, and tribology.

Metal Leve also has technical agreements with local and foreign universities and international research institutes (Battele and Imperial Clevitte in the U.S. and Ricardo in the U.K.).

Metal Leve established a new company Metal Leve Comercial Exportadora with subsidiaries in the U.S. and Germany. Besides the commercial benefits of these foreign outposts, the company can follow the latest technological developments brought to market. Recently, Metal Leve organized a research institute in the United States to interact with American research institutes.

Metal Leve has a Department of Industrial Property, within the legal services division, which takes care of intellectual property problems. The department is responsible for filing patents, analyzing contracts, and interfacing with the governmental counterpart, Instituto Nacional de Propriedade Industrial (INPI).

Metal Leve first filed for a patent in 1955. At present, they have sixty-three requests for patents in Brazil and abroad (eight in 1988 alone). Metal Leve monitors the patents in the automotive area in order to analyze technological advancements and the activities of competitors. The information is stored in a data bank (with 2500 patent documents). The Department of Industrial Property maintains a constant watch to oppose the concession of patents which infringe on their existing patent rights.

In the opinion of Metal Leve, the present legislation concerning patents and trademarks is adequate. In relation to INPI, the company feels that the present period of analysis of a patent is very long and should be decreased.

Metal Leve is an exception because most of the Brazilian industries have little awareness of the intellectual property system. The present legislation does not disturb Metal Leve's technological development since the company's investment in R&D is aimed at the development of its own products (with a more advanced technological content), with very little interest in licensing. The only objection raised by the company was related to the bureaucratic red tape involved in the governmental analysis and review of patents and patent requests.

Since Metal Leve is one of the companies with an awareness of the importance of R&D for industrial development (with research centers in the country and abroad) it seems that for this Brazilian industrial sector (automotive parts), patents are not an effective mechanism of appropriation of R&D results.

CASE III: BIOMATRIX

Biomatrix is a start-up, small high-tech company, organized as an association of Agroceres (the leading company in seed production in the country), and Grupo Cientifico (association of researchers at the Federal University of Rio de Janeiro).

Biomatrix is a biotechnology company which emphasizes R&D that leads to innovative processes and products. Agroceres commercializes some of these new products.

Biomatrix produces hybrid seeds, common seeds, and culture media. In the future, the firm wants to branch into artificial seeds, phytochemistry, transplantation of rare human substances to plants (for mass production). However, today Brazilian legislation does not accept patents on biotechnology.

Biomatrix is quite aware of the importance of the intellectual property system as exemplified by the following factors:

1. In the production of common seeds when it is not difficult to reproduce the products, the absence of patent protection makes it impossible to guarantee a return on the investment in R&D. No one will apply capital to R&D ventures if there is not a control on the market. The patent protects the products from being copied and it is a necessary step toward ensuring future investment for R&D projects.
2. With the production of hybrid seeds there are considerable difficulties in copying the product because of the decreased productivity due to the degeneration of the hybrids. In this case, the market is protected and patents are not necessary for this control.
3. Culture media is treated as a secret. It is used internally as a media to reproduce special plants and trees. There is no interest

in protecting the technology with a patent because of the existing internal security.

4. In the new advanced areas, the investment requirements for R&D are much higher. It is not clear which will be the best way to appropriate the results. Therefore, the investors look for patent protection in order to maintain a control of the market and to guarantee a return through licensing.

Biomatrix is the leading company in its field and is incorporated in a biotechnology science park that is being created inside the campus of the Federal University of Rio de Janeiro. This same awareness of the importance of the intellectual property system exists for Biomatrix as well as for other biotechnology companies. So, it seems that for the area of biotechnology, there is an urgent need to modify existing Brazilian legislation.

The biotechnology companies formed an association (ABRABI - Associacao Brasilieira de Empresas da Biotecnologia). ABRABI has thirty-four associates to date. Due to the need for patent protection and the absence of this protection in local legislation, ABRABI is preparing a proposal for a policy of patenting in biotechnology. This proposal is based on the commercial interests of the companies and the present state of technology development. It is being assembled in conjunction with the Governmental Instituto Nacional de Propriedade Industrial.

The proposal will lead hopefully to a policy that gradually opens the possibility for patenting, in accordance with the local R&D capability. The idea is to guarantee that Brazilian industries will be able to compete with foreign companies in the areas where patents are being granted.

This case shows that in this industrial sector firms provide the leadership in the formulation of new or modifications of old legislation. The situation in the biotechnology field runs counter to the conventional view that the national legislation is shaped exclusively by national governmental agencies.

The example in the field of biotechnology is very illustrative. This is one of the areas in Brazilian industry where the results of the R&D are closely connected with the commercial uses. The need for innovative products stimulates an increase in R&D. But the investment is only possible if there is appropriation of R&D results. Therefore, the sector of biotechnology in Brazil is working to modify the existing legislation of the intellectual property system to accommodate the needs of the industry.

AN OVERVIEW OF SOME INDUSTRIAL SECTORS

Pharmaceutical Industry

Many countries have adopted national intellectual property legislation which differentiates the pharmaceutical industry from the others. The restrictions in the pharmaceutical sector are based on arguments that the needs of the public should be protected before the potential profits of the pharmaceutical companies.

On the other hand, the international companies look for a patent in order to appropriate the return from their investment in R&D. The importance of the patent to this industry is based on the effectiveness of the patent as a mean of appropriation of R&D.1/

Brazil has not permitted patents in the pharmaceutical sector since 1969. The Brazilian government argues that there has been no major change in the behavior of the multinational companies in the internal market: the foreign investment increased from $110 million (1971) to $1000 million (1984) and there was no significant delay in the introduction of new drugs.

The Brazilian decision in 1969 was based on two arguments: the defense of the interest of the public health, (the freedom to produce any drug needed by society independently of any license) and the defense of the interests of the Brazilian drug industry which do not have the R&D capability to compete with the multinational companies, (a factor that would lead to a total takeover of the market by the foreign companies).

Even though the industry was protected, the Brazilian companies decreased their share of the market (from 33 percent in 1967 to 15 percent in 1988). The local drug industries are presently limited to the production of known and tested products instead of searching for new products. The market is completely dominated by the multinational companies.

The government is planning to change the present situation. Their intention is to strengthen the national industries by stimulating the development of local R&D (either within companies or with research institutes). Access to foreign technology can be gained through joint ventures with local companies.

The idea is to change the legislation for the industry (concession of product patents) only after the Brazilian industry reaches a stage of technological and economic development sufficient to compete with the foreign companies. The concession of process patents depends on the condition of the public health sector: they must be able to offer the basic drugs to the needed population.

The expectation is that the Brazilian chemical industry (originating in the petrochemical sector) and the modern biotechnological industries will be able to influence the picture and be able to develop a strong R&D base to create a competitive industrial park.

This governmental position is supported by the industrial sector. So it seems that strengthening industrial R&D is a prerequisite for the modification of the intellectual property legislation for the drug industry.

THE TELECOMMUNICATIONS INDUSTRY

The telecommunications market is controlled by a government agency, Telebras, which defines the strategy for the services and for the industrial development of the sector. Telebras is able to specify the equipment used in the industry in accordance with the capabilities of the domestic manufacturers. Foreign participation in the market occurs through patent licensing or joint ventures with local industries.

Industrial R&D in telecommunications is still weak. Very few companies have significant research. In order to support the local industries and to create a strong R&D base in the sector, the government established a research institute (Centro de Pesquisas e Desenvolvimento da Telebras - CPqP), which is in charge of almost all innovative research in the field. The results of the research are then transferred to the Brazilian industries.

CPqP is today one of the most successful research institutes as far as technology transfers to industry go. In the past, most of the work focused on substitute imports. Today, CPqP is able to develop new products and obtain some revenue from its licenses.

During the last seven years, CPqP has transferred seventy-one products developed internally to sixty-five Brazilian industries. CPqP has applied for seventy patents (thirty-four already in use) and sixty-five trademarks (eighteen in use). The royalties are still small ($5 million) but have generated a market of $186 million for the industry in the seven year period.

So, in the telecommunications field, the main interaction between the R&D and the intellectual property system occurs within the research institute, CPqP, which acts as a research center for the industrial park.

The tendency for CPqP is to concentrate on basic research areas and to stimulate the industries to participate in the R&D process. The stronger that CPqP gets, the greater the protection for intellectual property will be thus better appropriating the results of its research.

THE CAPITAL GOODS INDUSTRY

The capital goods industry is well-developed in Brazil and has traditionally had a great deal of contact with foreign suppliers. There is no specialized governmental research institute to support the industry which must rely on its own R&D.

A recent study2/ analyzed the competitiveness of the capital goods industry and detailed the main factors that are influencing the present situation:

1. The competitiveness of the Brazilian industry is slightly better than ten years ago.
2. The local technological capability will strongly determine the competitiveness of the industry in the next fifteen years.
3. It is very important to have access to foreign technology in order to be competitive in the

next fifteen years (licensing, know-how, joint ventures).

4. The major production factors that influence competitiveness are the qualifications of personnel, investment in new equipment, product engineering, and research capability.
5. The industrial sector prefers to look for foreign technology and adapt new products instead of developing them through its own R&D.
6. The capital goods industry has stated that the Brazilian legislation is not adequate to stimulate their investment in R&D.
7. The Governmental Nacional de Propriedade Industrial (INPI) is considered an obstacle in the process of technology transfers from foreign companies to the local industries.

Thus, the capital goods industry depends heavily on foreign technology and does not have (and does not intend to create) a significant R&D effort. The sector prefers to continue to import technology from foreign sources and favors a modification of the present legislation to facilitate access to technology developed abroad.

Even though the industry is in favor of strengthening the protection of intellectual property in order to have a wider choice of new technology, it will probably not attempt to influence legislators for a dramatic change in the intellectual property system in Brazil.

CONCLUSIONS

The intention of this chapter was to analyze a few cases regarding intellectual property in Brazilian industries and research institutes, and try to reach some conclusions that could give some insights into future developments.

Even though the sample was small, it is clear that any analysis and proposal for modification of the intellectual property system of Brazil must be industry specific. The situation in each of the industries, regarding its industrial R&D and its interaction with the intellectual property system, is quite distinct.

Second, in Brazil, awareness of the importance

of the intellectual property system is very limited among business managers and scientific and technical cadre. Only the industries that have developed an internal R&D effort and the industries that depend continuously on foreign technology have an opinion that could lead to future changes in the present legislation. For most of the industrial sectors, technology development and trade are insufficient to establish a real awareness or need for an intellectual property system.

Third, the existing national legislation is supported not only by the government but also by some industries. In some cases (like biotechnology), new policies are being formulated in a joint effort between industry and the government. However, the industrial sectors that rely on foreign technologies and do not have an internal R&D capability want to reduce the legislative obstacles so that they might access external technology sources. These industries are interested in a more protected intellectual property.

Fourth, the other industries looking for a more protected intellectual property system are the ones that have reached a national or international competitiveness through a concentrated effort in R&D. The general policy stance is that once strong industrial R&D exists and the various Brazilian industries become competitive, policy makers will analyze existing legislation for possible modifications.

Fifth, in order to increase the strength of industrial R&D, there must be a transfer of the research results from universities and research institutes to industry in addition to internal development of industrial research.

Sixth, the emerging technologies that generate a substantial R&D effort and that can stimulate new start-ups (like biotechnology) are more likely to be impacted by the intellectual property protection or lack thereof.

Finally, even though the impact of intellectual property protection in the mature industries is small, the new technologies examined (like new materials and fine chemistry in the petrochemical industries) are expected to influence the behavior of the overall industrial community.

NOTES

1. R.C. Levin et al., "Appropriating the Returns from Industrial Research and Development," Brookings Papers on Economic Activity, vol. 3, 1987, p. 783.

2. Conf. Nacional Industria, "Competitividade: A visao do grupo de avaliacao da industria Brasilieira e da Ass. Bras. Ind. Maquinas," Junho, 1988.

7

A Microeconomic View of Intellectual Property Protection in Brazilian Development

Robert M. Sherwood

NATURE OF RESEARCH

This chapter reports the findings from research done in Brazil over the last twenty-four months. During nine visits, each of a week or more, interviews were conducted with over 120 people. These interviews were sought with Brazilians whose activ-ities were thought to be influenced by Brazil's intellectual property protection system. The full spectrum of intellectual property, including trade secrets, copyrights, patents, and trademarks, was addressed.

Members of the following communities were interviewed: businessmen, scientific researchers, venture capitalists, research park directors and selected government agencies. More than half of the interviews were with businessmen who represented some of Brazil's largest companies, but also included were some small and medium-sized firms. Interviews were held in Rio, Recife, Sao Paulo and its industrial suburbs, Brasilia, Belo Horizonte, Americana, and Santa Barbara de O'Este. For background information interviews were also held with academic economists, think tank researchers, and lawyers.

Interviews have typically proceeded from a general question about how Brazil's intellectual property (IP) rules influence the activities of individuals, firms, and institutions with which the interviewee was directly acquainted. No set format for the interviews was attempted. Many individuals were visited more than once and it was not unusual for additional useful information to surface in these instances.

The research was supported by a group of United States and British companies. Preparation of this paper has been assisted by the National Science Foundation and the U.S. Section of the Brazil-U.S. Business Council.

SOME GENERAL FINDINGS

Many people interviewed, including business leaders directly affected by Brazil's intellectual property rules, knew little about intellectual property. Many had given little or no thought to the ways in which Brazil's current IP system influences their patterns of activity and the structure of institutions.

Within government circles, a tiny cadre of officials were found who had given some thought to the topic and were generally knowledgeable. Indeed, they appeared to have been schooled in the thinking of twenty years ago which characterized several of the United Nations agencies.

The present system of protection for intellectual property in Brazil appears to be based on 19th century European code provisions for copyright and industrial property protection mixed with statutory innovations to preclude protection in selected areas that are of post-World War II vintage. The European statutes have since been modernized in many respects; but, Brazil has to a large degree not adjusted its system to correspond to current European IP regimes.

Administration of the IP system in practice is characterized by: (1)extended periods of severe budget restraint which leads to poorly qualified personnel at the technical levels in the National Institute of Industrial Property (INPI), (2)INPI policy decisions to deny or curtail protection in specific areas, and (3)a strong effort by INPI to broaden Brazilian public awareness of the patent system.

Brazil's intellectual property system functions within the context of the country's legal system, including the rules of civil and criminal procedure and the functioning of the courts. There appears to be room for adjusting the legal system to reflect modern economic and business realities and to improve the integrity and efficiency of the court system. On the other hand, the business culture, which is perhaps a reflection of the present IP system, appears to pay little attention to considerations of protection of intellectual property. Therefore, the net effect of the present IP system in Brazil appears to be protection which is spotty and often inadequate. There seems to be a rather widespread lack of confidence in the effectiveness of the system.

Another general finding is that there is growing awareness of the importance of IP protection, particularly among many business people. For example, at recent seminars on a variety of technological and computer software topics, discussants and attendees have spoken about the lack of protection for trade secrets.

It is common for Brazilians familiar with some aspects of IP protection to state that Brazil is an original member of the Paris Convention and to draw from that fact the conclusion that Brazil must have a sound IP system. This conclusion overlooks the fact that the Paris Convention on many points is a treaty of comity not of standards. In fact, Brazil refuses to agree to the more recent, standardized (Stockholm) amendments to the Paris Convention.

TYPOLOGY OF THE CASE STUDIES

It appears from the case studies that many facets of Brazilian economic activity are influenced by the IP system. The points of influence are principally found in arenas where technology can be generated and in the specific linkages between those arenas and the marketplace.

New technology is classically generated through in-house research and development programs in private companies. It emerges from government research centers, military programs, and space programs and from university work and research parks. Informal settings such as the garage or attic of a home has also produced new technology.

The linkages from centers of emerging technology to users and consumers are characterized by flows of both public knowledge and proprietary information. There is a wide choice of vehicles for these flows, but the ability to protect proprietary knowledge is a common denominator to most of them. They range from creation of a company centered on a new technology to a confidential conversation between a university researcher and a businessman. They also include disclosures made to a potential financial backer of a new technology and the willingness of technicians in a research park to exchange information.

Knowledge spreads in many ways. Even newspaper headlines convey valuable technical knowledge. The report that tabletop fusion had been achieved spread to scientists around the world in a matter of hours and triggered important new thinking in many locations. Knowledge diffusion occurs when products are advertized and sold. The willingness to sell these products in certain legal environments may be reduced by the lack of IP protection.1/

THE CASE STUDIES - TECHNOLOGY SOURCE POINTS

Case Study 1: Private Company Research

In interviews with over sixty Brazilian businessmen from a variety of industries, the constant report has been that their proprietary technology has been lost to competitors through the hiring away of key technical employees. Some have suffered multiple losses. This seems to be true of companies irrespective of their size; large companies are troubled by this type of loss as are small and medium-sized firms.

When asked whether something might be done about such losses, the business people tended to give one of three responses. First, they assumed that the loss is an unavoidable cost of doing business. Second, they checked with their lawyers and confirmed that nothing can be done given the present state of the law, (particularly regarding trade secret protection). Third, they assumed that departing employees always have the right to carry out any information they learned while employed with their firm.

Legal System Defects. A few of these businessmen asked how such losses are stopped in Europe and the United States. When knowledgeable Brazilian attorneys compared treatment of this issue under modern German and French laws with the current Brazilian statutory provisions, they noted apparent gaps in Brazilian law. Those in the position to compare the various systems noted that German law could be most easily introduced into Brazilian jurisprudence since much Brazilian code law has German origins.

Some businessmen commented that even if the law itself were modernized, the court system might not be able to cope with problems of esoteric technical evidence. Legal experts asked how enhanced trade secret protection would "fit" with employee rights, personal property taxes, anticompetition law, and civil and criminal procedure.

Damage Quantification. It is difficult to quantify the extent of losses caused by employee departures. Since the interviews disclosed the problem to be widespread and found in companies of all sizes, the losses are potentially significant. However, there is no accurate way to assign a monetary value to this type of loss.

Consequences. The threat of such losses appears to produce consequences which suggest greater losses than just the direct losses themselves. The adage "once burned, twice shy" comes to mind. Over half the interviewed companies reported that because of the potential loss of any research results to competitors, they are reluctant to allocate significant resources to internal company research and development. These consequences are a major economic loss to Brazil. Macroeconomic statistics for the nation seem to bear this out. In a recent year, only about .6 percent of GDP went to R&D2/ and much of this was funded by government agencies rather than by companies (see Case Study 7, below). Businesses are also reluctant to expose too much of their work force to advanced technology R&D. Therefore, training and synergy within their manufacturing units and research groups also suffers.

Another secondary consequence of the reluctance to fund private company R&D is the loss to Brazil of scientific career path opportunities in the private sector. Able young scientists emerging from graduate school can turn to government research centers or remain inside the university system to pursue research careers, but the option for on-the-job training and for satisfying research work in a private company is not widely available to serious technicians. This may cast a pall on bright students at an earlier point in the educational system as they reject science and technical careers in favor of other choices.

Yet another secondary consequence appears to be the "gypsy career" where technical employees aspire to learn the technology of a company so as to position themselves to be hired away by competitors at attractive salaries. This practice tends to bid up salaries as companies seek to both attract and retain technical people. These higher salaries reflect the cost of technology protection/acquisition rather than just worker productivity.

Case Study 2: Research Parks

Brazil, in recent years, has begun to emulate Europe and the United States in creating research parks. Like those in Nice, France, in New Haven, Connecticut, and in Research Triangle Park, North Carolina, these parks seek to cluster those working on advanced research and technology so that synergy occurs. Usually near major universities, the parks mix small start-up businesses with advanced work by large existing companies.

Interviews in Brazil have thus far focused on two research parks in Rio de Janeiro. One centers on electronics, the other on biotechnology.

The electronics park had been operating for about one year at the time of the interview. The director of this park knew the parks in Europe and the United States from first-hand observation. He reported that his park was achieving less than had been expected with respect to cooperation and exchange of information among the technical specialists working in the park. Relative to the parks of Europe and the United States his park was underachieving.

After an extended conversation, he identified the cause of the poor cooperation and information exchange as the technicians' lack of confidence in their ability to protect proprietary information developed in the course of their work in the park from loss to others who would use it without authorization. This lack of confidence came from poor trade secret protection and in some fields from a perceived lack of effective patent protection.

(The park director recommended a visit to the Instituto de Investigaciones Electricas, a state run facility in Guernavaca, Mexico. Interviews there revealed the same type of difficulty caused by lack of trade secret and patent protection. In addition, the formation of "spin-off" businesses was hampered for these reasons in Mexico.)

In Brazil, the biotechnology park, is in the process of forming an association with the Federal University of Rio de Janeiro. It will call on federal, state, and private funds. Those who are leading in the formation of the park are apprehensive that the lack of patent protection for biotechnology innovation and of trade secret protection will make the park less effective than otherwise might be expected. This factor is apparently diminishing the attractiveness of the park as an investment opportunity. Moreover, the reluctance of candidate researchers to disclose the nature of the work they are pursuing and wish to pursue within the park is making it difficult to select technicians for residence there.

Case Study 3: Government Research Centers

While valuable research is undoubtedly produced in the many federal and state-run research centers of Brazil, a visit to one center produced an interesting glimpse of difficulties which the lack of effective IP protection creates for people working in such centers. At a center funded by federal, state, and limited private sources in Minas Gerias, a mid-career technician reported that his work in metallurgy had advanced to a point where he was retained by a Canadian steel producer to help improve its Canadian facilities. In the course of his work, he came up with two advances for which he was subsequently granted patents in the United States and Canada. In the interview he reported that it did not occur to him to seek patents in Brazil, partly because of quirks in the availability of patents for metal alloys and partly because he knew that associated know-how was involved and could not be protected as a trade secret in Brazil. In addition, there are other second and third-hand reports that Brazilian inventors seek patents only abroad, sometimes leaving Brazil to finish their work and then file applications.

The Minas Gerias technician also reported that several years earlier in his career he had written a book incorporating much of what he had learned about the characteristics of steel-making. He said that his instinct had been to better inform his colleagues and young students. He had expected to recover the cost of the time it took to write the book. The book, he said, was well-received by other scholars. Sales prospered briefly, then fell off. Shortly thereafter, he discovered many unauthorized photocopies circulating among students and others. He stated that, as a result, he has no interest in writing another book, even though his career had obviously advanced to a point where he had additional valuable (nonproprietary) information to impart.

While this is only a glimpse, more research might multiply the examples to show a discouraging effect on those who work in government research centers. If such losses are common, the threat of loss probably discourages knowledge diffusion and productive activity.

Case Study 4: Military Program Losses

A few interviews suggested there is a loss to Brazilian military procurement as local companies are unable to develop or acquire best-available hardware because they have difficulty protecting advanced technology. While U.S. Defense Department unwillingness to authorize transfers of certain U.S. technology for fear of loss to "unfriendly" foreign powers is a factor, this case centers on nonprotection of IP. Foreign private companies are often unwilling to provide certain competitive technologies to Brazilian companies since they cannot safely maintain that information and know-how. The lack of in-house R&D by Brazilian private companies, as noted above, also has a negative effect on the nature of the technology available to the Brazilian military from local sources.

It seems that the military has given little thought to the effect which nonprotection is having on their own ability to acquire needed materiel. The inattention to protection may also be reflected in the lack of attention to recovery by the military of resources when the results of military research are made available to civilian industry.

In many respects, the civilian companies which supply the military are no different from other Brazilian companies. Many of them supply important non-Brazilian markets as well. However, the impact on the military may be greater because of the higher intensity of technology now required by military machines and equipment.

ROLE OF SMALL BUSINESSES IN BRAZILIAN TECHNOLOGY ADVANCEMENT

A 1982 study for the Small Business Administration3/ showed that small firms in the United States produced 2.4 times as many innovations per employee as large firms. At the same time, small firm research tends to be less costly.4/ The contribution of small new firms to the economy in terms of job creation, multiplier effect, public revenue, and technology advancement is well-known in the United States.

In looking for common sources of new technology, it has been difficult to find in Brazil a pattern of business activity in which individuals or small groups form small new businesses around a core technology. In consequence, therefore, it is also difficult to find a pattern in which small companies, harnessed to a new technology, grow to become major companies. Evidence of the pattern now emerging in the United States and Europe wherein large companies (even those conducting major in-house research programs) acquire new technology from small new businesses is also hard to find.

The absence of these business patterns in Brazil may be traceable to the lack of adequate intellectual property protection. Legal protection for new technology facilitates both the formation and financing of small new businesses and the transfer of technology from one company to another.

The presence of a large and growing underground economy or "informal sector" in Brazil may mask somewhat the effect of IP protection on small company formation, making formation difficult to discern from public records. Hernando de Soto, in El Otro Sendero, his remarkable study of the informal sector in Lima, Peru, comments on the positive role of intellectual property rights in business growth and economic development.5/ In a private conversation with the researchers, he expressed interest in researching within the informal sector to ascertain whether extralegal approximations of intellectual property protection are being created.

CASE STUDIES - LINKAGES TO SOURCE POINTS

Case Study 5: University Researchers

A leading Brazilian scientist, from her position as president of the Brazilian Society for Progress in Science, reported concern among her colleagues about the absence of effective protection for intellectual property. The Society consists of university research scientists, many working in the biological area. The example she reported is apparently sufficiently widespread to have caused the Society to form a study group on the problem.

She reports a pattern in which researchers, who may well have been pursuing research in pure science, make discoveries with unexpected commercial application. Mindful of practices now widely prevalent in European and American universities, the researchers seek to commercialize the results of their work in the marketplace. It is increasingly common for the researchers to "go outside" the university to start a new business. In doing so, they typically do not enlist the assistance of experienced technicians or businessmen, attempting instead to do everything themselves. The need to "go it alone," she explained, arises from their unwillingness to trust others with knowledge of the invention. Their lack of confidence in the ability of Brazil's intellectual property system to protect their innovations and subsequent refinements and developments leads them to choose the solitary approach. Apparently they understand from word of mouth that trade secret protection and patent protection, particularly in the biological area, are deficient.

These researchers are typically not trained to

start and run small businesses. This adds risk to an already risky undertaking. They devote time to the new business, which means their students get less of their time. Most importantly, they are not working at further research which is usually where their abilities lie. The consequent misallocation of resources undermines Brazil's scientific and technological progress to some degree.

Case Study 6: Venture Capitalists

Evidence that there are relatively few, small, new technology-based companies being formed comes from the venture capital community in Brazil. There are about ten Brazilian firms active in venture capital investing. Some are industry specific, some are geography specific and one or two are unrestricted in the breadth of their interests.

Interviews with one of the broad interest firms disclosed two patterns relevant to the impact of intellectual property protection on business growth and economic development. The first pattern observed is that there is an insufficient number of start-up firms from which to select candidates for investment. The venture capital firms prefer to examine about 100 candidates in order to choose four or five worth investing in. Because of the paucity of candidates, the interviewed venture capital firm is shifting the bulk of its portfolio into merchant banking for established firms.

The second pattern is more revealing. The interviewed firm, although shifting to merchant banking, continues to receive requests from small, new firms seeking financial backing. The applications are uniform in stipulating the amount of funding needed, in describing the location of the manufacturing facility, and in forecasting the expected sales in the early years. However, the applications for financial backing are also uniform in providing only scant information about the technology on which the new company will be based. Requests for greater detail about the technology, when made, are met with resistance. The venture capital firm finally realized that start-up companies in Brazil are reluctant to disclose much information about their new technology for fear that it will be taken by others and used in competition. The venture capital firm considered offering confidentiality agreements in an attempt to reassure the candidate start-up companies, but realized they could not, in fact, be sure that such agreements would be binding on their own employees. A secretary could easily make extra copies of the plans, specifications, and drawings and hand them "out the back door" to others. There would be no way under current Brazilian law to stop this.

Consequently, this venture capital company is rarely able to obtain enough information regarding a candidate firm's technology to enable it to make an informed investment decision. Since this is the leading venture capital firm in Brazil, the pattern disclosed appears to be indicative of a widespread phenomenon. Not reflected in this pattern is the number of instances in which deserving new businesses have not bothered to seek venture capital because of the knowledge that they would need to disclose their technology in detail. Recently, a second venture capital firm confirmed these findings.

Case Study 7: Government Financing: BNDES, FINEP, CNPq

The Government of Brazil has recognized the value of newly created technology. Three federal government agencies exemplify this concern: The National Bank for Economic and Social Development (BNDES), Financiadora de Estudos e Projetos (FINEP), and the National Council for Scientific and Technological Development (CNPq). Each in its assigned way seeks to support technological innovation. Each dispenses funds to technology source points in the country. None of the three agencies have programs which monitor the ability of its grantees to protect the results of R&D activity. In effect, each is officially oblivious to intellectual property protection.

An interview with officials at BNDES ascertained that recent applications for funding are, in some instances, being unofficially scanned for the protectability of the intellectual property content of the planned work product. Intellectual property protection is not on the official checklist of criteria examined in making funding decisions.

Likewise, an official of FINEP also confirmed that a check on intellectual property protection is not part of the examination made of applications for funding by that agency. There is also no examination made at the conclusion of the funding period to determine what technology, if any, resulted from the project. Although these aspects of the CNPq program have yet to be directly examined, casual information suggests that, here too, little thought is given to whether intellectual property protection plays a part in achieving the results sought by the CNPq program. It is interesting to consider the impact on planning were each of these agencies to require, as part of each application for funds, a statement concerning the protectability of expected intellectual property results.

It appears that in Brazil very little attention is given to who owns or is to benefit from the results of government-funded research.

Case Study 8: Foreign Source Technology

An interview with a medium-sized company in Belo Horizonte disclosed another linkage problem arising from the absence of adequate intellectual property protection. This company is active in the electronics field. They identified business opportunities for a specialized metal etching technology with electrical applications which is not practiced in Brazil. They sought this technology from a foreign source. After discussion, the technology director came to realize that if he were able to acquire the desired technology and agreed to pay for it, he stood to lose the technology to his own competitor in Sao Paulo through employee departure and yet be obligated to continue to pay the foreign supplier for it. His enthusiasm for the acquisition diminished.

Perhaps even more sweeping in its implications was an interview with a mid-level manager of one of Brazil's largest diversified, private manufacturing companies. This man manages several divisions and therefore is involved with several emerging technologies. He reported that it is not possible to count the number of times his people have considered learning about advances in their technical lines through a license or other contact with a foreign technology source; yet, they had learned from experience that the inability to protect intellectual property under Brazil's existing system, once known to a foreign technology supplier, usually precluded completing arrangements for exposure to the foreign technology. He reported that, although his people frequently estimated it would be more cost effective to learn from the foreign source than to pursue the technology by conducting internal research, they found it was usually a waste of their time even to initiate discussions with the foreign supplier. He said he understood well the reluctance of foreign suppliers to risk placing valuable technology into the Brazilian legal environment.

Further research may disclose the extent to which this paper reflects a widespread pattern in the Brazilian business community. It is hard to think of statistics which would directly support the observation. It could, no doubt, be noted that when measured in absolute payment terms, Brazil acquires less technology from abroad than countries of comparable industrial size. Other factors, such as the highly intrusive limitations imposed by the technology transfer registry of INPI, also stifle the acquisition of new technology.

The importance of foreign source technology is shown by a different type of case example. An interview with the former head of Embraer, the government-owned aircraft manufacturer, revealed what he called "the downstream effect" of foreign source technology acquisition. When his technical team was at work on the early model of the ultimately successful small Brazilian aircraft, they were able to license advanced avionics and other technology from a British aircraft manufacturer. The insights gained from the British greatly stimulated his team so that they were able to advance the state of the art. The British subsequently requested a license of the resulting, more advanced Brazilian technology.

The key point made by the former head of Embraer was that the higher the quality of the incoming technology, the greater the downstream stimulation on the Brazilian technical team and the greater the creativity released as a result. The availability of the high quality British input was facilitated in this case by license agreements assuring the greatest degree of protection for the acquired technology possible under the Brazilian system. Similar assurances were required by Embraer when the licenses ran in the reverse direction.

COMMENT: FOREIGN TECHNOLOGY ACQUISITION COST

Central Bank statistics from 1979 through 1985 show a downward trend in the cost to Brazil of imported technology from about $313 million to $175 million. On average over this period, this cost is less than 1.7 percent of the total remittances made by Brazil for services. Even if this number were to double or triple it would still be a relatively small cost to Brazil in terms of its overall external accounts.

Over that same period, Brazil exported technology with a value of roughly $1 for every $3 of technology acquisition cost. In 1979, exported technology earned Brazil $99 million. Over the period the one to three ratio stayed fairly constant and by 1985 technology export earnings had dropped to $60 million.

If the remittances for technology acquisition are netted by the revenue from exported technology, then the net technology account is about .6 percent on average over the period. This sinks to near irrelevance in the country's overall external accounts; yet it was constantly claimed in interviews that instituting adequate and effective intellectual property protection would be an insupportable burden for Brazil.

Given the "downstream effect" mentioned above, it could be supposed that paying to acquire more advanced technology would have a highly stimulative effect on Brazilian technicians, resulting in greater earnings over time from exported technology. For this to happen, however, a more effective system for protecting both imported and locally generated technology is a necessary condition.

REFLECTIONS ON THE CASE STUDIES

It appears from these case studies that the absence of an intellectual property protection system in which Brazilian's can have confidence has far-reaching effects on the patterns of business, university, financing, and research center activity. Consequently, the ability of the country to advance in the area of science and technology is hindered.

It seems that missing from Brazil's business culture, and indeed from the culture in general, is a habit of mind which assumes innovation is a possibility and is of value. When this was noted, it was frequently said that only when Brazil reaches an international level of technical ability will this culture change. The impact of Brazil's IP system in fostering this culture would appear to be significant. Upon reflection, perhaps the issue is whether the culture creates the system or the legal system creates the culture.

It appears that the absence of an effective legal system for IP protection has gone largely unnoticed. Perhaps this is because little attention has traditionally been given by developmental economists to intellectual property protection. It seems to be an unnoticed gap in the country's infrastructure.

It was often stated during interviews, particularly with economists and government officials, that even if costly problems caused by the absence of sound IP protection were corrected, the overall cost of such protection would be great for Brazil. This perspective rests on the notion that all the technology Brazil needs must inevitably come from outside Brazil. It overlooks the potential Brazil has to produce a great deal of valuable technology in the country.6/

Several interviews disclosed instances in which Brazilian companies lost export opportunities or did not seek them because they did not think to obtain patents in overseas markets which would have assisted export potential. This oversight happened because it is not part of the mental reflex or habit of mind in the Brazilian business community to obtain patent protection at home and so this tool of exporting is likewise forgotten or overlooked abroad.

Some of the misconceptions held by Brazilians about IP protection have their origin in thinking prevalent over twenty-five years ago in certain Third World circles. The context for the analysis behind these views is in part traceable to Dr. Raul

Prebisch, the great Argentine intellectual, whose work appears to have deeply influenced the formation of Brazilian policy in many regards. It is less well-known that Dr. Prebisch, in the last years of his active career, altered his basic outlook and policy advice.7/ His last views carry implications for many aspects of Brazilian policy, including intellectual property policies and technology transfer policies.

CALL FOR MORE RESEARCH

There is a remarkable paucity of research directly focused on the intersection of intellectual property protection and economic development in developing countries. Edwin Mansfield has usefully set the stage for such research in a paper delivered in November 1987, at a conference of the American Council for Capital Formation entitled "Intellectual Property Rights and Capital Formation in the Next Decade."8/

In it he notes, from the work of Robert Solow, the critical role of new technology in boosting economic growth. He also reports from his own work that the social rate of return gained from the introduction of new technology is between 56 percent and 70 percent. Finally, he suggests that, given the invitation which stronger protection of intellectual property would give to growth-inducing development of new technology, even stronger safeguarding of intellectual property would be an appropriate policy. His observations, although based on the economy of the United States, are relevant to any developing economy. Indeed, two distinguished Brazilian economists have noted that Mansfield's analysis, if transported to Brazil, would have a powerful impact and generate fresh thinking.9/ A second, more recent paper by Mansfield10/ provides recommendations for research on the role played by intellectual property protection in the economic development in the Third World.

There are several cautions worth noting in any attempts to research the role of intellectual property protection in a developing county. First is the obvious problem that public statistics which might be relevant are often of poor quality or not kept at all. Second, there is a tendency to count the number of patents granted and the nationality of the grantees as reliable indicators of who benefits from the IP system. The grant of patents is only one element, albeit an important one, in the overall system of IP protection. Often patents are virtually useless because they remain unenforceable under local juridical concepts. For example, a process patent is easily defeated as an instrument of protection because of the difficulty of sustaining the burden of proof. The question is not whether a patent has been granted but whether a given technology can be effectively protected. This may entail examination of the nature of trade secret protection, which is often a vital companion to patents in achieving effective protection.

There is a natural tendency to design economic research of intellectual property with reference to patents alone. This is understandable since good public data is usually available concerning patents. The trade secret is perhaps overlooked because of the difficulty of finding statistical evidence of its presence. More work would help to determine the importance of the trade secret in technology generation and transfer. The trade secret is vital during the weeks and months from the moment of innovation or discovery until the day a patent application can be prepared and filed. The trade secret is vital after the patent application has been filed and before the product reaches the market. This is typically when a great deal of trial and error testing is done to make the product marketable. Not all that is learned during that period is readily patentable, thus making the trade secret protection vital.

Two informal surveys of executives engaged in technology transfer licensing suggested that very roughly two-thirds of the technology that passes from one party to another is conveyed through the vehicle of the trade secret. An official of Brazil's National Institute of Industrial Property has suggested that in his experience the percentage may be as high as 90 percent.

Fruitful research could be centered on "before and after" situations. Brazil has two enticing such situations. One is provided by the institution of copyright protection for software at the end of 1987. Informal conversations suggest that Brazilian software producers are finding the new legal protection beneficial for their business planning.

The other "before and after" research opportunity arises from the elimination of patent protection for pharmaceuticals at the beginning of the period of military rule in the late 1960s. No new pharmaceutical production facilities were constructed in Brazil after the change in the law, whereas a number of facilities were built before 1968.

A Wall Street Journal article in April reported the return to Korea of many Korean scientists under a headline which spoke of a "reverse brain drain." Although not mentioned in the article, the fact that Korea promulgated modern patent and copyright protection in 1987 may be a factor contributing to the return of the scientists. This may be a promising "before and after" research opportunity.

Other research might try to correlate brain drain with weak IP systems. Still another possibility would be to run studies which would show the kind and degree of R&D expenditures in developed and developing countries in correlation with IP protection in the same set of countries. A fairly broad survey would screen out other factors.11/

If, as suggested by the case studies of this chapter, the effect of an IP protection system is all-pervasive, then to trace this effect, research will need to examine a variety of settings and use a variety of methods.

NOTES

1. M.L. Burstein, "Diffusion of Knowledge-Based Products: Applications to Developing Economies," Economic Inquiry, vol. 22, no. 4 (Western Economic Association, 1984), pp. 612-33.

2. See Edwin Mansfield, "Protection of Intellectual Property Rights in Developing Countries," unpublished (1989), p. 21, citing Hyunku Kim, 1986.

3. The Futures Group, Characterizations of Innovations Introduced on the U.S. Market in 1982 (Glastonbury, Conn.: SBA, Office of Advocacy, March 1984).

4. Small Business Administration, Innovation in Small Firms (Washington D.C.: undated).

5. Hernando de Soto, The Other Path (New York: Harper & Row, 1989), pp. 177 ff.

6. For a useful framework within which to examine the balance between costs and benefits of a sound IP system for a country like Brazil, see Carlos Primo Braga, "The Economics of Intellectual Property Rights and the GATT: A View from the South," delivered at Vanderbilt University School of Law symposium on "Trade-Related Aspects of Intellectual Property," March 24, 1989, to be published in Vanderbilt Journal of Transnational Law.

7. See, for example, his address to the 21st annual session of ECLAC in Mexico City, April 24, 1986, only days before his death, published as Annex 2 of the "Report of the Twenty-First Session of the Economic Commission for Latin America and the Caribbean."

8. Edwin Mansfield, "Intellectual Property Rights, Technological Change, and Economic Growth," Intellectual Property Rights and Capital Formation in the Next Decade (University Press of America, 1988), pp. 3-26.

9. Conversations with Annibal Villela and Julian Chacel.

10. Mansfield, "Protection of Intellectual Property Rights in Developing Countries."

11. I owe this suggestion to a conversation with Dr. Geoffrey Shepherd of the Brazil section of the World Bank. See, for example, World Development Report 1987, published for the World Bank (Oxford University Press, 1987), pp. 60 ff.

8

Intellectual Property Rights and the Management of R&D in India

Falguni Sen

INTRODUCTION

There are a number of studies on the relationship between intellectual property rights and R&D including the innovative activities of firms. These studies have primarily focused on the situation in developed countries. By and large, intellectual property rights have been viewed as conferring some degree of temporary monopoly on inventors in order to provide adequate returns on their initial developmental investment. Thus in any given country which is both a producer and user of innovations, the "social good" is not greatly compromised by conferring such a monopoly since the rate of socially useful inventive activity is stimulated. In developing countries, on the other hand, which are primarily "users" of inventions, monopolistic protection awarded to an inventor (usually from a foreign country) may not produce an incentive to innovate indigenously. When this is coupled with the fact that most licensing agreements to third world countries do not transfer patent rights to the licensee, one might question the reason for a developing country to grant any patent protection1/ unless compelled to do so by the exigencies of international trade.

India is a developing country that is fast industrializing. It has been more a user of foreign innovations than a contributor to the pool of useful innovations for international use. Although it has a large, competent, and well-established scientific and technological research base, the rate of utilization of the outputs of its R&D is very low. This is especially true of government-funded R&D which is approximately 85 to 90 percent of the total R&D effort.2/ Thus it would appear that protecting intellectual property would benefit a very small proportion of India's productive activity. However, Deolalikar and Evenson claim that "Patenting by Indian nationals has increased over all periods in many industries and the proportion of patents granted to Indian nationals has risen in all industries."3/ Further, they demonstrate that individuals and institutions have a larger share of patented innovations in 1975-78 compared to 1954-57. Bagchi et al. found that patent applications by Indian nationals have, at the least, remained reasonably steady over the last twenty years or so.4/

Intellectual property rights issues are also being reintroduced into the national debate and the government is showing some signs of willingness to reopen the issue of providing a tighter intellectual property rights regime in science and technology.5/ Thus, there appears to be a greater importance given by individuals, institutions, and firms to intellectual property rights in India. This increase in importance is probably due to a combination of the following factors: (1)an increase in international pressure, especially from the U.S. on changing India's weak intellectual property regime, (2)"liberalization" of imports by the Indian government with an expected increase in the inflow of state-of-the-art technology, (3)a recognition of the opportunity to collaborate in state-of-the-art scientific research with a number of developed countries and with a number of foreign firms, (4)some indications that imported technology is an incentive rather than an impediment to indigenous research, (5)India's emergence as a newly industrialized country seeking a greater share of international trade, (6)a changing economic scene within India with a growing middle class demanding more consumer goods, an increase in competition in some industries, and producers demanding protection for product innovations, (7)India's need for high-technology research equipment in order to maintain its state-of-the-art research in strategically critical areas of defense, space, and nuclear research, and (8)the dual role of intellectual property protection of not only conferring monopoly to the inventor but also guaranteeing the assignment of credit for scientific and technical work and thus facilitating the flow and exchange of scientific and technical information.

Most of the innovative activity which is likely to be affected by intellectual property issues is located within R&D units of the government and of individual firms. This chapter describes the structure of R&D in India and the different expectations from it. It then describes the history of intellectual property protection in India and its impact on the management of these R&D units. Finally, this chapter describes the changing role of India within the international supply of technology and knowledge and the new importance of intellectual property.

R&D IN INDIA

For a developing country, India has a massive scientific and technological research base. Its total investment in R&D was a little over 1 percent of its GNP in 1984-85, which is lower than developed countries but higher than most developing countries including Brazil and Mexico. In the last few years, the rate of government spending in R&D is believed to have increased very rapidly, and according to some estimates has gone up by almost 50 percent.6/ In terms of scientific and technical manpower, India ranks third in the world. While its research base is mostly in the government sector, there has been an increasing investment in R&D by the private sector as well as public sector industries.

Research and development in the government sector is primarily concentrated in industrial, agricultural, medical, space, atomic, electronics, defense, and more recently environmental research.7/ University research covers fundamental and applied research in various disciplines and is heavily dependent on direct and indirect government funding. Although the quality of research in some specialized areas in universities is considered to be very high, research in universities is generally viewed primarily as an aid to teaching. In particular, there is little expectation that university research will result in the development of any useful artifacts which could be commercialized.

India has a large public sector producing mainly commodities such as steel, coal, oil and natural gas, fertilizers, and heavy engineering goods. There are also public sector firms in the telecommunications and electronics industries. In many of these firms, major investments in R&D are a relatively new phenomenon. Major capital investments are being made to build an R&D infrastructure in these industries. These investments, which fall under the overall rubric of "self-reliance," are to cover a wide range of objectives from vendor development assistance to state-of-the-art research.

The private sector industries entered into R&D for a variety of reasons. Some invested in R&D only to avail themselves of the tax advantages and other government incentives. Others wanted to work on indigenization of raw materials which would give them greater control over resources, and yet others attempted to facilitate the transfer of imported technologies. The incentives provided by the government for private sector investment in R&D fall mainly into the following categories: (1)formal recognition by the government of the research activity of firms, (2)import facilities for activities of firms, (3)custom duty exemption on R&D equipment, (4)preferential treatment to firms in licensing decisions, and (5)fiscal incentives for scientific research.

There is also an informal sector which is part of the nation's scientific and technological base. This consists of voluntary agencies which work in areas of appropriate technology and rural development and which either do their own research or tap into the research base of the nation. Aside from some international funding, the major source of funding for this informal sector also comes, directly or indirectly, from government and semi-government sources.

GOALS AND OBJECTIVES OF INDIAN R&D

Expectations from R&D investments vary in the different sectors. Even within government R&D organizations, one can detect differences. For instance, the defense sector is primarily interested in reducing all possible dependence on foreign countries for production and maintenance of defense materiel and in achieving self-sufficiency in specific areas. R&D in this sector is focused on indigenization of production, quality improvements, adaptation to local needs, development of processes for indigenous production of parts, aid in the development of a defense production infrastructure, and improvements on existing generation of weapon systems. While some international sales of parts and equipment have indeed taken place, there has been little emphasis in the defense R&D for helping defense production compete in the international arms market.

Government industrial R&D is expected to reduce dependency on imports without necessarily achieving self-sufficiency. These expectations include developing new products based on import substitution, or using locally available raw materials for the domestic market, adapting existing know-how to local conditions, identifying industrial opportunities especially in areas of low industrialization, and helping in the efficient transfer of technology. Aiding domestic industry to gain or maintain international competitive advantage has never been an explicit expectation. Nor has the focus of government industrial research been on increasing the efficiency and productivity of existing industry. Increasing the productivity of existing agricultural processes has, however, been one of the major expectations from government agricultural research. Meanwhile, in the electronics field, the main expectation has been that India should not miss out on the electronic revolution; R&D should help in establishing an industrial infrastructure in this area. Thus the linkage between electronics R&D and production has been much stronger with "electronics production" having in a sense grown out of R&D. The expectation of electronics research has been, on the one hand, to put in place a production infrastructure which would be capable of absorbing the latest technologies in the field (most of which would be imported), and, on the other hand, to produce consumer electronics items indigenously which can be manufactured by small and middle-scale industries. The utilization of consumer electronics-related R&D results from government research laboratories is one of the highest in the country. In atomic and space research, the expectations in the short run have been one of national prestige. In the long run however, some results are expected to be demonstrated which have direct economic consequences.

Industrial R&D in the public sector is a relatively new phenomenon and expectations of it are not very clear. Besides indigenization and quality control, the groups are expected to set up research areas of excellence in specified industrial sectors. The focus appears to be on staffing these efforts with people who are highly trained in the state-of-the-art techniques in industrial R&D. It may be inferred that these R&D units will be expected to facilitate modernization of the technologies with as little foreign dependence as possible.

Private sector R&D in India experienced a boom due to the tax incentives provided by the government. Most R&D seems to focus on indigenization, quality control, and trouble-shooting of imported technology. To a very large extent, industrial R&D in the private and public sector works towards increasing the effectiveness of imported technologies.

Technology is imported in India by firms in the private and public sectors and by plants dedicated to defense, space, or nuclear production. In-house R&D can play a supportive role in alleviating some of the problems and inefficiencies accompanying the importation of technology. R&D groups in technology importing firms can deploy some of their resources to modify and improve the imported technologies, thereby, giving them a competitive and/or cost advantage and adapting them to the needs of the market. R&D groups can increase the bargaining power of the importing firm by working on indigenous alternatives to the technology being acquired. Finally, R&D groups in these firms can generate an innovative base to prevent the rapid obsolescence of externally acquired state-of-the-art technology.

In-house R&D can also mesh with a company's technology acquisition strategy by developing required adaptive skills which would result in improvements to the technology once it is acquired. There is a tendency for firms to invest in the development of required adaptive skills in R&D only after the technology is acquired and often as a response to troubleshooting needs of the newly acquired technology.8/ Recent results show that an early involvement of R&D units in a firm can increase the effectiveness of the technology importing process.9/ In-house R&D groups might make important contributions if they concentrate on increasing the bargaining power of their firms by raising their own technical capabilities, identifying alternative suppliers, raw materials, etc. R&D can also play a significant role in generating information and keeping in touch with developments around the world. To do this, in-house R&D might concentrate on developing pilot plants and other transfer skills as well as design strengths to facilitate adaptations and redesign needs. Finally, researchers have found that the cost of licensing out a technology is less where the importing firm has a well-developed R&D group.10/ Thus a competent in-house R&D department in the firm can act as an incentive to the source firm and result in lower costs and added bargaining power for the technology importer.

In-house R&D can also play a specifically constructive role at different stages in the process of acquiring and implementing imported technology. A large number and variety of activities which are carried out over a period of time as part of the process of acquiring and implementing external technology. These activities can be clustered into ten distinct stages. Briefly, in Stage 1 (need), there is an awareness of the need for a new technology; in Stage 2(focus), this awareness becomes better focused, which results in the identification of alternatives and an enumeration of criteria which will be used to evaluate these alternatives; in Stage 3(evaluate), the actual evaluation of alternatives takes place; in Stage 4(make/buy), a decision is made to make the technology in-house or to acquire it externally or to unpackage the technology and produce some parts in-house and acquire the rest externally; and in Stage 5(negotiate), the actual negotiations for technology acquisition take place. This completes the acquisition phase of the process. The implementation phase begins with Stage 6(receive) where the firms prepare to receive the new technology; in Stage 7(construct), the technology is installed; in Stage 8(start-up), start-up is achieved; in Stage 9 (improve), improvements are made upon the acquired technology and in Stage 10(retool/redesign), effort is expended to ensure that the acquired technology does not become obsolete.

Besides improving the effectiveness of the process of acquiring and implementing imported technology, the role of R&D includes indigenous development of technology itself. Although a number of firms have R&D units engaged in a number of the activities described above, very few engage in the development of new processes and technologies from scratch. In this, a number of firms have been successful in collaborating with government research laboratories or just commercializing the results of such laboratories through the National Research and Development Council (NRDC) which is the marketing agent of government-funded research. The discussion on the impact of intellectual property rights and the management of R&D needs to be situated within this context of the structure of R&D in India and the role it plays (and is expected to play).

THE ROLE OF INTELLECTUAL PROPERTY RIGHTS IN INDIA

Intellectual property rights are governed by a number of mechanisms in India. The Patent Act, which has been in existence since the early 1900s, was patterned after the British and is one of the major mechanisms for the protection of intellectual property. The Copyright Statute of 1957 and its regulations protect literary and artistic works and has been expanded to include computer software. The Trade and Merchandise Marks Act of 1958 provides protection for trademarks and may be expanded to include service marks. It is unclear if "intellectual goods" can be viewed as "property" under the purview of existing property laws. There are no special criminal statutes regarding intellectual property. Similarly, no codified tort law exists for protection of trade secrets. However, English common law tort protection of trade secrets, know-how, and confidential information apply in India and, in theory, "breach of confidence" action is possible. There are also the provisions of the Monopolies and Restrictive Trade Practices (MRTP) Act to restrict monopolies as well as investment and licensing aspects affecting intellectual property. Thus any protection of intellectual property that requires foreign exchange or can create conditions of monopoly will require review and can be subject to further controls. A number of government ministries are involved in coordinating policy regarding intellectual property. The main bodies are the Ministry of Industry, Department of Electronics, Ministry of Chemicals, Department of Science and Technology, Ministry of Education, Ministry of Law and Company Affairs, Ministry of Commerce, and the Ministry of Finance. Implementation of policy is primarily the responsibility of the Controller General of Patents, Designs, and Trademarks and the Registrar of Copyrights.

Despite the complexity of the mechanisms which govern intellectual property rights, the Patent Act reflects the basic philosophy guiding this issue. India would like to have a system which strongly encourages indigenous R&D. A new patent bill was introduced in 1970 whose basic philosophy was to see to it that patents were granted to encourage inventors, to secure commercial implementation within India to the fullest extent possible, and to ensure that patents were not used merely to enjoy a monopoly of importation of the patented products.

According to the findings of a number of review committees,11/ some of the major problems with the earlier patent system included its failure to stimulate indigenous invention, its low utilization of filed patents, its lack of attention to foreign exchange considerations, and its unduly limited choices for alternate sourcing due to patent protection.12/ The new patent act sought to address these issues. Briefly, this new act incorporated the following features:

1. In some critical areas, where foreign monopolies and monopoly pricing were perceived to be the norm and where foreign products had a market edge over indigenous goods, no product patents were allowed. These included pharmaceuticals, chemicals, veterinary products, pesticides, agrochemicals, alloys, optical glass, semiconductors, and intermetallic compounds. Only process patents were allowed.
2. Other areas were identified where no patents would be granted. Broadly speaking, these

include minor adaptations to existing products and processes, innovative use of existing technologies and/or processes, quality control, and process control techniques to improve efficiency, any agricultural or horticultural method, etc.

3. The duration of patent protection was considerably shortened for foods, pharmaceuticals, veterinary products, pesticides, and agrochemicals.
4. A provision was made to give the government the right to grant compulsory licenses if a price were deemed unreasonable or "reasonable requirements of the public" were not being met.
5. Licenses of right force the patentee to grant a license to any licensee after a period of three years.
6. The government gave itself broad rights to use any patent for government purposes without fear or concern of infringement. This included the use of patented items for educational purposes and for research.

By analyzing the structure of intellectual property protection in India, the following general comments may be made: (1)Intellectual property protection was considerably stronger before 1970 than it is today; (2)policy makers are primarily motivated by a desire to reduce potential for foreign monopoly; (3)some desire to increase the level of indigenous inventive activity has been expressed but except for the provision allowing patents to be used for research and education, no explicit mechanism to direct or stimulate inventive activity was implemented as part of the new patent act; (4)the broad wording of a number of provisions allows the government the flexibility to make interpretations on a case-by-case basis. Thus, if the government so desires, it can provide, within the definitions of the Act, much more complete of intellectual property for longer durations. However, the choice lies with the government, providing little bargaining power to the patentee.

A possible inference from the 1970 patent reforms is that policy makers were working under the assumption that weakening the intellectual property regime would stimulate rather than inhibit innovations. There is some evidence to suggest that, for newly emerging technologies where a dominant design paradigm13/ has not yet emerged, a tight intellectual property regime may inhibit innovations needed for the development of that technology. A weak property regime may in fact encourage a variety of innovators to develop different modifications and applications for the same technology without the fear that adequate returns to them will not be possible. However, the technologies being considered in India do not, by and large, fall under the category of newly emerging technologies for which no dominant design exists. As a matter of fact, most technologies being imported into India where patent protection is an issue are mature technologies with well-established designs. Thus a weak property regime should not offer any impetus to inventive activity in that area. Technologies imported into India may, however, require major modifications and adaptations to make them suitable to the geoclimatic and market conditions of the country. Such modification and adaptation needs may make a technology, which is otherwise considered to be mature, an evolving one where the dominant design paradigm has to be reestablished. Under these conditions it makes sense to expect that a weakened intellectual property regime would stimulate innovations. Further, Gallini and Winter14/ find that the "impact of licensing is to encourage research when the existing production technologies of firms in the market are close in costs and to discourage research in markets where firms face widely divergent production costs."15/ Since the production technologies of most Indian firms are much higher in costs as compared to the state-of-the-art technologies employed by many international firms, it is reasonable to expect that the availability of licensing would discourage research. Thus, the barriers to technology import imposed by the government could indeed be expected to stimulate indigenous research.

IMPACT OF THE 1970 PATENT ACT ON INVENTIVE ACTIVITY

In what follows, an attempt is made to evaluate the impact, if any, of the weakened patent protection in 1970 on inventive activity in India. This evaluation is based on some information on the pattern of patenting from a number of different sources and the personal experiences of this writer during his research on R&D units in India. It is important to bear in mind that there are a number of pitfalls to using patents as an indicator of inventive activity especially in a developing country. This is true because many patents are taken out without any particular productive use in mind and often to control the market protected by the patents. In addition, many innovative activities either cannot be patented (due to restrictions in the patent law discussed above) or are not patented due to fear of disclosure of proprietary information through the patent process. These limitations should be kept in mind while making inferences from the data presented below.

Figure 8.1 presents the pattern of patenting in India from 1968 to 1985. The data for the figure is derived from two sources: from 1968-1980 from Bagchi et al.,16/ and from 1980-85 from Gadbaw and Kenny.17/ While there is data on the total patents applied for from 1980-85, Gadbaw and Kenny do not break this down into "Indians" and "Foreigners." Thus, these two trends are available only up to 1980. The pattern of patenting based on "total number of applications," "applications made by Indian nationals and Foreign nationals," and "applications of Indians and Foreigners which were actually sealed" are presented in this figure. Figure 8.2 is based on data from Bagchi et al. and presents the trend in number of Indian and foreign patents in force between 1968 and 1980.

The data on total number of patent applications suggests a declining trend in patenting up to 1979 and a small increasing trend since 1980. In particular, foreign applications for patents seem to have declined rapidly after 1969 although the number of Indian applications remained steady over the period for which data is available. The number of foreign patents sealed seems to show an increase after 1981 while the number of Indian patents sealed shows a declining tendency during that period. In general, the number of foreign patents sealed up to 1980 seems to be on the decline while the number of Indian patents sealed during that same period has remained stable. According to

Figure 8.1
Indian and Foreign Patents Applied and Sealed

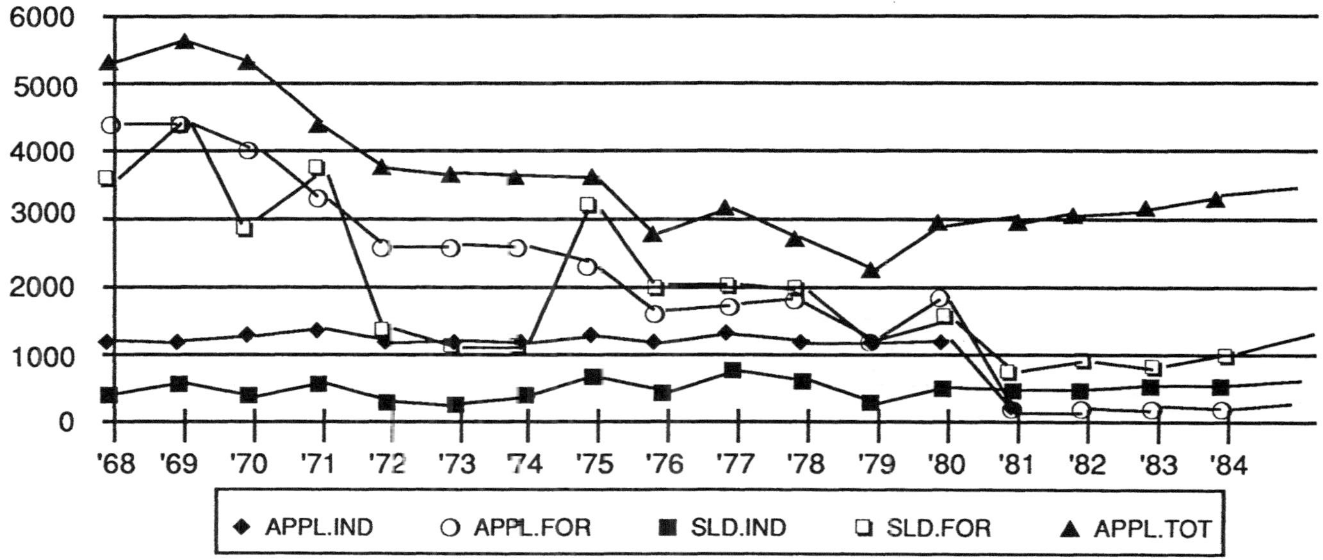

Source: A.K. Bagchi et al., "Indian Patents and its Relation to Technology Development in India," Economic and Political Weekly, Vol. 18, February 1984; and R.M. Gadbaw and L.A. Kenny, "India," in Intellectual Property Rights: Global Consensus, Global Conflict? ed. R.M. Gadbaw (Boulder, Col.: Westview Press, 1988).

Figure 8.2
Indian and Foreign Patents in Force

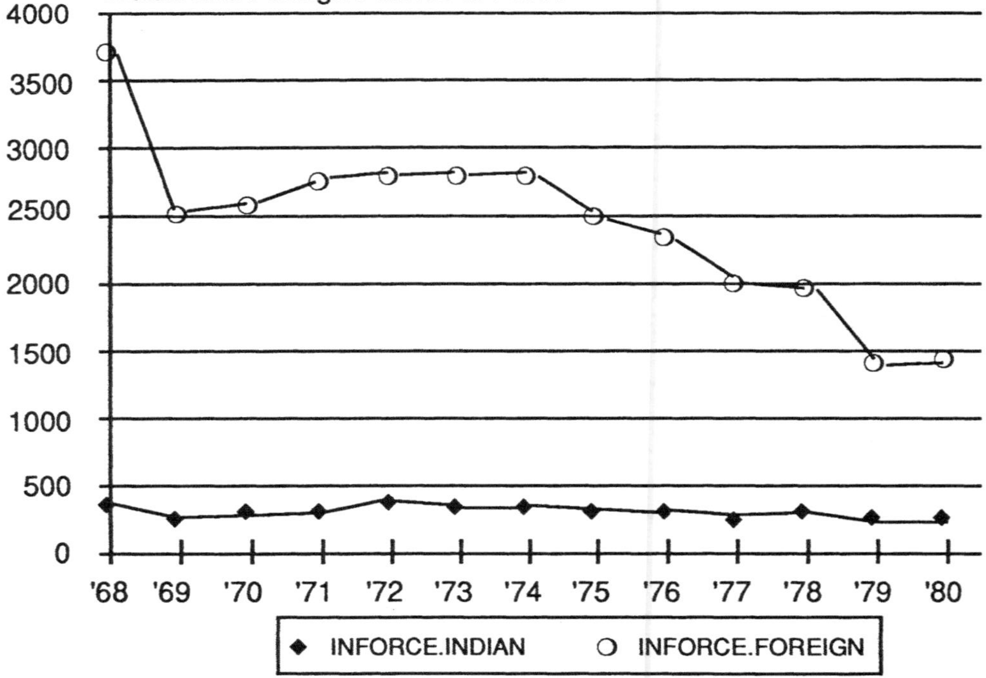

Source: A.K. Bagchi et al., "Indian Patents and its Relation to Technology Development in India," Economic and Political Weekly, Vol. 18, February 1984.

Bagchi et al., the decline in the number of patents applied for and sealed after the 1970 Patent Act can be explained by the following developments: (1)the examination procedure was made much more rigorous than before; (2)the scales of fees demanded were considerably higher and the initial grace period was reduced to two years; (3)there was a reduction in the patent period to seven years for food, medicines, and drugs; (4)"license of right" was included, and (5)only processes can be patented in chemicals, foods, drugs, and medicines which deter patentees who like to keep the products themselves secret. This is in conformity with the data provided in Table 8.1 which shows that the largest drop in the rate of patenting after 1970, even for Indian nationals, was in the food and chemicals sectors. From the data presented below, for patents granted to Indian nationals, it appears that there was a drop in the number of patents granted in some major industries in 1971-74 which picked up again. The increase in 1975-78 shows a return to the previous rate of inventive activity but no real sharp increase. Thus, it is indeed possible to conclude that there was a major drop in the patenting activity of foreign nationals after the introduction of the 1970 Patent Act but that it had little effect on the patenting activity of Indian nationals. It should be noted however, that there is no evidence to suggest that there was any appreciable stimulus to patenting by Indian nationals either. This is further corroborated by the fact that the total number of foreign patents "in force" declined sharply while Indian patents did not decline as much (See Figure 8.1).

There is no evidence from the patent data to suggest that the rate of indigenous inventive activity has been stimulated by the changes made in the Act; there is no evidence to suggest that the intensity of this activity has gone down either. Rather, there is some evidence to suggest that the importance of patenting has increased with Indian nationals and institutions in select industries. It is difficult to conclude whether this is due to the changes in the Patent Act, or a number of other factors (e.g. increased funding in R&D and other inventive activities, or an increase in foreign firms filing patents in the name of their Indian subsidiaries as a response to the changes in the

TABLE 8.1

Patents Granted to Indian Nationals in Selected Industries

	1954-57	1958-61	1962-66	1967-70	1971-74	1975-78
food processing	26	69	123	132	54	65
textiles	52	76	92	86	59	75
jute	1	2	4	3	3	0
textile products	4	6	9	19	2	7
wood products	4	5	7	8	9	16
paper & print	21	28	54	50	25	46
leather	22	13	18	23	12	9
rubber & plastic	18	33	55	59	35	53
chemicals	46	92	137	251	127	183
non-metallic	25	54	72	85	58	108
basic metals	1	2	12	7	18	38
metal products	-	-	-	-	46	124
machinery	10	37	48	74	34	70
electrical eqpt	4	26	13	16	61	156
transport eqpt	8	36	34	47	20	44
Total	242	479	678	860	563	994

Source: Deolalikar and Roller, The Journal of Industrial Economics, March 1989. Reprinted by permission of Basil Blackwell, Ltd.

Act). There is however, sufficient evidence to suggest that until recently foreign patent applications had indeed gone down. This seems to concur with the government's claim that the reformed patent act has succeeded in reducing the monopoly position of a number of foreign firms in critical industries.18/

INTELLECTUAL PROPERTY AND INDIGENOUS R&D

It is possible, however, that indigenous R&D and inventive activity have been made possible and have been stimulated in areas which cannot or are not patented. For instance, patenting has rarely been an issue with university R&D and it remains that way. Very little of the research done in the atomic energy, space, and defense sectors deals with items which are patented in India mainly due to the small size of the market and the customary one-time purchases. In the case of patented items, since these sectors are part of the government, and any use is considered government use, no patent infringement is considered. Most transfers of know-how issues are built into the licensing agreements themselves. Know-how is acquired through government-to-government relationships and an understanding on protecting intellectual property is reached. Since long-term relationships with the supplier government is sought, such commitments toward intellectual property are maintained.

The issue of protection of intellectual property becomes a critical one in the case of industrial R&D. The existing laws governing intellectual property in India provide a number of opportunities:

1. Minor improvements to existing products and processes can be made.
2. New and innovative use of patented know-how can be made.
3. Scaling down of designs becomes necessary to accommodate the smaller volumes needed in India. Patented technology can now be scaled down to provide higher efficiencies.
4. Raw material substitutions which require a modification of existing patents are possible.
5. If the patent is not a working patent for

three years it can be revoked and an indigenously developed process (or a copy of the patented process) can be put into production. Thus it is worthwhile for R&D to identify processes which have been patented and work on indigenous versions. This also increases the bargaining power of the firm in case of licensing. In short, imitative research can indeed be fruitful.

6. Spare parts and other critical "black boxes" which are often overpriced can be indigenously substituted if the patentee does not agree to a fair-price license.
7. More flexibility is available for unpackaged technologies where indigenous R&D can evaluate a total manufacturing process and determine which parts of the technology it would like to buy, which it would like to license and from whom, and which it would like to build on its own.

Comparing these "opportunities" with the potential role for in-house R&D in facilitating the import of technology, one can see that almost all the activities suggested can now be performed without fear of patent violations. Thus the weakened property regime in India has provided a mechanism for the absorption and assimilation of imported technology. The following cases may illustrate this better.

1. An engineering firm produced pressure vessels. Although the vessels were designed by the firm, the process for creating a wall for the vessel was licensed from a foreign manufacturer. It was unclear during the licensing process whether specialized testing would be required for the wall. The licensor was willing to conduct this testing with proprietary instruments at what was perceived to be excessive costs. Researchers within the firm had a general idea regarding the nature of these tests and indigenously developed them. Since the licensor was unable to patent these tests in India, the firm succeeded in saving those costs. However, all warranties pertaining to the licensed process were invalidated since it did not use specialized tests.

2. A large firm wanted to license a technology for the production of vacuum pumps. The foreign

firm was willing to license the production know-how as long as the Indian firm purchased a particular patented part to be included in each item produced. The price being asked was internationally competitive. This Indian firm had an excellent R&D base. The foreign firm withdrew at the last minute since they were not convinced that the Indian firm would not copy their patented part or that their patent would be protected.

3. Firm A produced a specialized compressor under license from a foreign firm. Firm B produced a similar item under license from another foreign firm. The R&D group in firm A did some material substitutions which reduced the cost of their item. This could not be patented and very soon firm B's product included a similar substitution. (Hypothetically a similar scenario is possible with a foreign firm providing its licensee with improvements without filing an additional patent and losing that information to its international competitors.)

4. A chemical company was reluctant to license the know-how for a particular product to India for which it had an international patent. For a number of years, it sold its product to India. A government R&D lab developed a reasonable substitute which was not as efficient nor of as high a quality but it was felt that in the Indian context it would be acceptable. The foreign firm felt that it was now in its interest to license the know-how to an Indian firm. A successful licensing agreement was reached.

Based on the opportunities for R&D created by the existing patent laws and the primary role played by industrial R&D as part of a broader technology licensing process, the existing intellectual property protection system in India seems to have been successful in meeting the objectives of indigenization. This is especially true of some industries where "The Patent Act of 1970 has helped the Indian drug industry develop, kept prices low, and brought life-saving drugs to the country quicker than they would otherwise have."19/

However, given the size of India's R&D manpower and the highly organized R&D sector, the total number of patents filed by Indian nationals is very low. This may be due to a combination of the following reasons: (1)the nature of much R&D work is irrelevant to productive activity and not many patentable ideas are produced; (2)when ideas and research results are patentable, the organization of R&D may not encourage patenting; (3)scientists do not see much point in patenting since there is a very low utilization rate of patents, and (4)patents are seen as inadequate protection of research results. Finally it is argued that the weak protection of intellectual property in India prevents state-of-the-art technology from coming in. While this may be true in some cases,20/ there is potential for great flexibility in bilateral negotiations within the framework of the current laws. However, R&D labs have often found it difficult to acquire state-of-the-art equipment for research due to this lack of faith in the protection of intellectual property.

THE CHANGING SCENE IN INDIA

Besides the difficulties facing India in the international technology market due to the perception of inadequate protection for intellectual property, a number of changes are in progress within India itself which may significantly increase the importance of protection. This progress is summarized by the following examples.

1. There is an increasing unhappiness with the quality of products, and yet imitation goods take a substantial market share and firms are compelled to compete on the basis of cost. Indian firms are demanding stronger protection of intellectual property rights and stricter implementation of existing laws in order to benefit from investments made to improve the quality of products.

2. There is more experience with long-term costs of maintenance and safety with some indigenously developed technologies which have resulted in decreasing the attractiveness of pure indigenization. Given an increased liberalization of import policies, there is likely to be a greater mixture of indigenous development, adaptations and imported technologies in some industries. Such a mixed technology development strategy will require compatibility between the indigenous, adapted, and imported aspects of the same technology. Such a compatibility will require access to proprietary aspects of the imported technology. While such

development has indeed been possible within the existing patent laws, they have been predicated upon excellent (and long-term) relations between the Indian and the foreign firm. Where such a relationship is not possible, stronger assurances through a stricter intellectual property regime may become necessary.

3. There is an increasing intensity of competition in some industries. Such competition is, in some instances, based on cost. A recent study found that in the plastichemicals and engineering goods sectors, firms that patent in India (given the weak protection) have 87.8 percent greater growth in total factor productivity than firms which do not patent.21/ It is possible to infer that such firms are better equipped for cost-based competition than others.

4. There has been a growth of the Indian middle class and increased demand for new products and product innovations. Since many product innovations cannot be patented there may be new pressure from likely innovators of new products for stronger patent laws.

5. There is new encouragement to high-tech industries. While the government has always claimed that such industries can get all the protection they want,22/ the responses of foreign high-tech firms and of foreign governments have often been skeptical. Furthermore, some foreign governments have pressured firms in their countries not to collaborate with India unless greater assurances regarding intellectual property protection can be provided.23/

6. Other countries are discovering India's great potential in scientific and technological research infrastructure and talent. Specific areas of possible collaboration between Indian and U.S. scientists have been identified.24/ A number of foreign firms see India as a low-cost alternative to in-house R&D and want to build R&D contracts within broader licensing agreements.25/ In addition, firms in some sectors see the potential for becoming a part of a larger globalized manufacturing strategy made up of a number of foreign multinationals where they could play the role of long-term suppliers of parts and components. Existing laws protecting intellectual property may prove highly inadequate in negotiating such deals.

7. Finally, there is greater demand by scientists in different research laboratories for a better system of assigning credit for work done by them. Patent application clearly identifies credit for inventive work. It is also part of an informal reward mechanism within the research laboratory. There is status associated with scientists who have a number of patents.

CONCLUSIONS

While the existing legal and cultural mechanisms to protect intellectual property have succeeded in preventing monopolies in some industries and have encouraged indigenous development in others, changes in India today may require a rethinking of existing laws. The changes described above necessitate the development of a greater sense of trust in firms who would share new technology and research, and governments who should not act as barriers. In some cases it may be necessary to do this by creating a tighter intellectual property regime. And yet, as discussed above, the existing laws have indeed succeeded in creating the conditions for better assimilation of imported technologies and for the stimulation of indigenous technology development in some industries. The question is whether India is looking for a new strategy for technology development in important industries which will address the issues raised above. Such a strategy will look for a greater integration of India's technological developments with global technological trends without providing monopolistic access to its markets. This will require creative legislation that is capable of having different intellectual property regimes in different industries based on the country's technology development objectives in that industry.

NOTES

1. A.K. Bagchi, P. Banerjee, and U.K. Bhattacharya, "Indian Patents Act and Its Relation to Technology Development in India," Economic and Political Weekly, vol. 18, February 1984.

2. G. Alam, "India's Technology Policy and Its Influence on Technology Imports and Technology Development," Economic and Political Weekly, vol. 20, Special Number 45-47, November 1985.

3. A.B. Deolalikar and R.E. Evenson, "Private Inventive Activity in Indian Manufacturing: Its Extent and Determinants," Paper presented at the Conference on Science and Technology Policy: Lessons for Developing Asia, Sponsored by the Economic Growth Center, Yale University, Washington D.C., March 23-24, 1989.

4. Bagchi et al., ibid.

5. K.S. Jayaraman and Alun Anderson, "India and United States Quarrel over Intellectual Property Rights," Nature, vol. 336, November 10, 1988, p. 102.

6. W.A. Blanpied, "Notes on the Government of India's Science Policy and Organization," Proceedings of a National Science Foundation Workshop on Indian Scientific Strengths: Selected Opportunities for Indo-U.S. Cooperation, Washington D.C., Spring 1987.

7. A.V. Desai, "India's Technological Capability -- An Analysis of its Achievements and Limits," Research Policy, vol. 13, 1984, pp. 303-310.

8. Falguni Sen and A.H. Rubenstein, "External Technology and In-House R&D's Facilitative Role," Journal of Product Innovation Management, vol. 6, no. 2, June 1989.

9. Ibid.

10. Farok J. Contractor, "The Composition of Licensing Fees and Arrangements as a Function of Economic Development of Technology Recipient Nations," Journal of International Business Studies, vol. 11, no. 3, Winter 1980, pp. 47-62; and "Technology Licensing Practice in US Companies: Corporate and Public Policy Implications," Columbia Journal of World Business, vol. 18, no. 3, Fall 1983, pp. 80-88.

11. S.S. Joshi, J.V. Rajan, and S.K. Subramanian, " The Indian Patent System and Indigenous R&D," Research Policy, vol. 3, 1974, pp. 272-306.

12. Ibid.

13. D.J. Teece, "Capturing Value from Technological Innovation: Integration, Strategic Partnering, and Licensing Decisions," Interfaces, vol. 18, no. 3, May-June 1988, pp. 46-61.

14. Nancy T. Gallini and Ralph A. Winter, "Licensing in the Theory of Innovation," Rand Journal of Economics, vol. 16, no. 2, Summer 1985, pp. 237-252.

15. Ibid., p. 238.

16. Bagchi et al., ibid.

17. R.M. Gadbaw and L.A. Kenny, "India," in Intellectual Property Rights: Global Consensus, Global Conflict?, eds. R.M. Gadbaw and T.J. Richards (Boulder, Colo.: Westview Press, 1988).

18. Jayaraman, p. 102.

19. "India Today," Eyeball to Eyeball, vol. XIV, no. 12, June 16-30, 1989, p. 103.

20. "India Today," ibid. See comment on problems with the import of a Cray computer.

21. A.B. Deolalikar and L.H. Roller, "Patenting by Manufacturing Firms in India: Its Production and Impact," The Journal of Industrial Economics, vol. XXXVII, no. 3, March 1989.

22. "India Today," ibid.

23. Jayaraman, ibid.; and "India Today," ibid.

24. Blanpied, ibid.

25. G. Paulsson, "Exporting Industrial Technology to India: Strategies and Experiences of Swedish Firms," Economic and Political Weekly, vol. XX, Special Number 45-47, November 1985.

9

Economic Development and Intellectual Property Protection in Southeast Asia

Korea, Taiwan, Singapore and Thailand

Gunda Schumann

INTRODUCTION

In recent years, the protection of intellectual property has become an issue of great concern on the national and international level. Industrialized countries claim billions of dollars in losses due to infringement of their patents, copyrights, trademarks, etc. mainly by certain developing countries. These developing countries are partly located in the South and Southeast Asian region. Some countries in this region, such as the Republic of Korea, Taiwan (Province of China), Singapore, Thailand, and others pose a threat to industrialized countries, in particular to the United States since their economies are growing fast and are predominantly export-oriented. According to some industrialized countries, developing countries including those mentioned above, have been seeking to get access to foreign technology by means of unauthorized imitation rather than by acquisition in hard currency, thereby arousing international trade disputes and creating pressure for a strengthening of intellectual property laws.

This paper tries to analyze the background of this conflict. First, it will, on a general basis, investigate the economic role of intellectual property rights in the national and international context and discuss the pros and cons of intellectual property protection for developing countries. Second, it will highlight the international dimensions of infringement of intellectual property rights. Third, it will, through the use of country case studies, investigate the economic performance and government policies on foreign investment, trade, indigenous development, technology transfer and intellectual property protection of the Republic of Korea, Taiwan, Singapore, and Thailand. Finally, it will draw some conclusions on the relationship between economic development and protection of intellectual property rights in developing countries.

INTELLECTUAL PROPERTY RIGHTS: DEFINITION AND RATIONALE

Definition

There are a variety of intellectual property rights. Within the framework of this paper, patents, copyrights, trademarks, trade secrets and sui generis rights will be discussed.

Intellectual property rights may be classified into "abstract" and "accessorial" property rights. While the former relate to properties which directly determine the value of an item, as in the case of patents, copyrights, trade secrets and sui generis rights, the latter serve as a means to further the economic process of exchange, as in the case of trademarks.1/

Patents as a form of industrial property rights are designed to legally protect the invention which must generally be new, nonobvious and commercially useful. The patent grants the patentee a monopoly right over the invention, i.e., it excludes others from making, using, or selling the invention for a period of approximately ten to twenty years. The granting of a patent requires disclosure of the invention to the public.

Trade secrets serve as an alternative to patent protection but rely exclusively on private measures, i.e., contractual arrangements. Trade secrets also protect valuable know-how which does not meet the requirements for patentability.

Copyrights traditionally protect works of literature and art and more recently, computer software programs. In contrast to patents, a copyright does not protect ideas but rather their expression if this in turn meets the requirement of originality. Copyright protection covers the use of a work, i.e., the copyright owner is protected from unauthorized use, reproduction, distribution, sale, and adaptation of his/her work for an approximate period of the life of the author plus fifty years.

Sui generis rights have been developed for new technologies which do not fit into the traditional categories. Examples are plant patents, plant breeder's rights, and semiconductor chip design rights (the last ones have similarities with copyrights).

Trademarks are labels attached to tradeable goods bearing the name (or some brand name) of their proprietors, thus identifying their source. The term of their protection is approximately ten years (with the option of renewal).

Rationale for Intellectual Property Rights

The rationale for the protection of intellectual property rights will first be discussed concerning economic and legal aspects from a national point of view and will later focus on some international issues.

National Context. Originally, intellectual property rights had been designed in the Western world to promote national technological, industrial and intellectual development. For example, the primary rationale for patents has been that monopoly rights are necessary to provide financial incentives to invent and to disclose these inventions to society, thus facilitating the generation and diffusion of new knowledge. Concerning copyrights, the original idea was to encourage the production of creative works in order to take advantage of the economic opportunities afforded by printing but also to provide society with valuable artistic and literary works.

However, economic changes and technological developments have aroused disputes over traditional economic and legal concepts of intellectual property rights or have even made them obsolete. As to patents, it has been argued that there is no simple connection between isolated innovative activity and anticipated monetary awards. What really matters is innovation, including investment, large-scale research and development, marketing and commercialization, all of which depend on expected returns.

Sufficient returns to stimulate innovation, however, would rather be guaranteed by competition itself than by patents. Moreover, lead time and learning curve advantages as to the unpatented know-how necessary for the successful use of an invention are important factors to stimulate inventive activity.2/ Furthermore, critics question whether the disclosure requirement in patents effectively promotes the diffusion of new technology and whether the benefits of increased invention outweigh the inefficiencies and anticompetitive effects associated with monopolies.3/

Legal problems associated with the concept of intellectual property rights emerged mainly with recent technological developments which have blurred some of the traditional distinctions and thereby upset the principles underlying longstanding copyright and patent laws. A good example is computer software programs which have been made subject to copyright protection in many countries. "The coverage of functional works, such as software, under copyright can only be done at the risk of undermining the original intent of the law," which was based "on the assumption that individual creativity is to be especially rewarded by society,"4/ which in turn justifies the much longer term of protection for copyrights over patents. However, creativity standards for developing computer programs are modest. At the same time, copyright protection does not require the specific patent requirements of novelty and disclosure. It therefore grants computer software programs higher protection under lower standards than patent protection would provide. "The unique character of computer program technology permits publication without disclosure of the code and creates a potential monopoly of a technology without the opportunity for related development work by others."5/

The urgency for protection of new technologies like computer software programs, semiconductor chip designs, data bases, and biotechnology, no matter whether they fit into traditional categories of intellectual property laws or not, has arisen out of a common scheme. Their creation or development is generally expensive but their reproduction or copying rather simple and relatively inexpensive; therefore the inventing/creating company is at high risk of being deprived of its expected monetary return on investment.

<u>International context</u>. Protection of intellectual property is increasingly perceived, mostly by developed market economies, as crucial to international competitiveness. Rising R&D costs require large-scale production and an open international market to recoup these costs. Intellectual property protection is viewed as an essential criterion to induce and control the flow of foreign investment and international trade, and therefore plays a significant role in the decision-making process of transnational corporations. Since new technologies are vulnerable to easy imitation and intellectual property rights are confined to national boundaries, the main concern becomes the international standard of intellectual property protection. From the investor's point of view, pirate competitors who operate in countries that reject intellectual property rights will divert their returns and ultimately lower investment in new technologies. The result will be the slowdown of technological progress worldwide even if some pirates may realize certain short-term gains.

The implication, however, that technological progress guaranteed by an intellectual property system benefits all countries equally has been questioned. "The neat theory that intellectual property rights balance short-term social costs against longer-term dynamic benefits holds only, if at all, in the closed system,"6/ i.e., in an industrially developed economy. Some developing countries argue that they lack the fundamental prerequisites that would enable them to benefit from an intellectual property rights system like monetary funds, research facilities, and scientific and technical personnel. Since they neither participate in short-term private benefits (monopoly profits) nor in the longer-term social benefit (a continuous supply of new knowledge goods), they are reluctant to recognize those rights. In their opinion, intellectual property rights give innovators a monopoly on information that is used to exact unreasonably high prices for their knowledge and to control the dissemination of knowledge-based products through unwarranted restrictions on their use. They question the assumption that royalties derived under international protection of intellectual property rights are really needed to cover development and production costs.7/

The argument made by developed countries that equal recognition of intellectual property rights of both foreigners and one's own nationals is necessary to encourage foreign technology transfer as well as indigenous technological development has not been met with great enthusiasm by developing countries. Indeed, the economic and legal history of the developed market economies seems to prove exactly the opposite. For example, product patent protection for pharmaceuticals has met fierce resistance by many developed countries until very recently. Nevertheless, recent studies have shown that there is no simple and straightforward relationship between patents and industrial development in either an affirmative or a negative way,8/ or between the introduction of a patent system in a developing country and the automatic dominance of transnational corporations.9/

Significance for a developing economy. In light of the increasing importance of advanced technologies for the economic development of all countries, an intellectual property system may, in terms of attracting valuable transfers of technology and fostering local innovation, have advantages for a developing country in conjunction with several other factors:

1. pursuing an open market strategy;
2. promoting technological collaboration between transnational corporations and local companies;
3. training of the labor force for technologically high-skilled tasks; and
4. promoting local R&D.

Some Southeast Asian nations (mainly the so-called newly industrialized countries - NICs) which had adopted more defensive strategies towards intellectual property protection have reassessed their contribution to domestic technological and creative development. In addition, they have reconsidered their need to obtain transfers of more advanced technology (including ancillary know-how) from foreign investors or suppliers. These considerations together with demands by trading partners, mainly the United States, have changed their intellectual property protection policies.

In the following section, the foundation for

these demands, namely infringement of patents, trademarks, copyrights, trade secrets, and semiconductor chip designs in Southeast Asian nations, will be presented.

INFRINGEMENT OF INTELLECTUAL PROPERTY RIGHTS

Significance

In recent years, the infringement of intellectual property rights has become an important policy issue. This issue bears special significance in the high-technology areas such as computer hardware and software, biotechnology, and pharmaceuticals since these products, processes, and services require high R&D investments but are relatively inexpensive to copy.

Definition

The term "infringement," constituting a violation of intellectual property rights, is in itself a highly debated issue within and among nations depending on the countries' intellectual property laws. For example, with regard to computer software programs, the distinction between imitation and innovation has become blurred (copying v. "reverse engineering"10/) thereby posing problems predominantly for developed nations,11/ while the basic issue of unauthorized copying is an issue between developed and developing countries. In addition, the classification of so-called gray market practices (mail order, trans-shipping, black market activities) and parallel imports as infringing activities is in dispute.

More specific terms related to infringement are "piracy" and "counterfeiting." The former refers to unauthorized reproduction of copyrighted works for commercial gain, whereas counterfeiting refers to unauthorized use of a product's trademark to give a similar appearance of a specific product.

Estimates of losses due to infringement

Since United States industry sees itself most

affected due to its large share in the world market, the U.S. government and private business associations located in the United States, the European Community, and Japan, have undertaken estimates of the losses resulting from worldwide infringement of intellectual property rights. For instance, the International Chamber of Commerce in 1986 estimated that losses incurred due to worldwide intellectual property infringement reached around $60 billion or 3-9 percent of total world trade.12/ In another study, the U.S. International Trade Commission (USITC) in 1988 reported that the aggregate worldwide losses suffered by 431 U.S. companies due to inadequate intellectual property protection reached $23.8 billion.13/ These figures reflect sales losses to the original producer. In evaluating these estimates, it has to be taken into consideration that definitions of infringement differ among countries and that it is difficult to detect infringing activities or products. Moreover, the dollar amount of infringing sales is not necessarily the same as the dollar amount of sales lost to the legitimate producer since the ultimate consumer could probably not afford the sales price of the latter. This may be particularly the case for developing country markets in Asia, which are among the primary targets of complaints about intellectual property infringement.

Regarding geographic distribution, Korea, Taiwan, Indonesia, and the People's Republic of China (PRC) have been cited most frequently as infringers by the USITC. Of these, Taiwan, Korea, and the PRC inflicted infringement losses valued at $753 million, $496 million, and $420 million respectively.14/ Recently, Thailand was cited as causing at least $240 million annually in U.S. losses due to patent and copyright infringement.15/

Infringement of intellectual property rights seems to be an ongoing issue despite efforts by some Asian countries to suppress it. In 1988, the Asia-Pacific Council of American Chambers of Commerce viewed Thailand as the worst offender, followed, inter alia, by the Republic of Korea, Taiwan, and India. The United States Trade Representative's (USTR) report on "Special 301" of May 25, 1989, determined Thailand and India as being leaders on its "priority watch list", followed by the Korea, Taiwan, and the PRC.

THE REGULATORY FRAMEWORK ON ECONOMIC, TECHNOLOGICAL AND INTELLECTUAL PROPERTY ISSUES IN ASIA: COUNTRY CASE STUDIES

This section will present country case studies concerning the regulatory framework of four Asian countries (Republic of Korea, Taiwan, Singapore, and Thailand) on trade, foreign direct investment, transfer of technology and intellectual property protection in order to investigate the linkage between economic development and intellectual property protection. First, the economic performance of these countries will be examined.

Economic performance

Within the last two decades, Korea, Taiwan, Singapore, and to a lesser extent Thailand have achieved extraordinary economic advances. The Republic of Korea, for example, has experienced a steady economic growth since 1971 (1971-1980: 8.2 percent, 1981-1987: 8.4 percent)16/. Table 9.1 presents data on growth rates from 1986-1989.

TABLE 9.1
Real GDP Growth of Asian Countries 1986-1989

	Percent Change			
	1986	1987	1988	1989a/
Korea	11.7	11.1	12.3	7-8
Taiwan	10.6	11.1	6.5	5-6
Singapore	1.8	8.8	11.0	6-7
Thailand	5.2	7.0	8.4	5.5-6.5

a/ estimated change

Source: Data derived from Business Asia, January 2, 1989, p. 1; March 6, 1989, p.79; March 13, 1989, p. 87; March 20,1989, p. 95; August 8, 1988, p.259; Business International October 31, 1988, p. 341; United Nations, World Economic Survey 1988, p. 6 (Table II.2); National Statistical Office, Statistical Yearbook Thailand (No. 35) 1987-88, p. 357.

South and Southeast Asia have a number of features that make it attractive to international direct investment (refer to Table 9.2). For instance, Thailand has a large domestic market; Singapore, Taiwan, and Korea have large, relatively cheap and well-trained industrial work forces while Taiwan, Korea and Singapore have well-developed infrastructures.

TABLE 9.2
Foreign Direct Investment Flows: Inward Investment 1986-1987

	Million US$			US share %		
	1986	1987	1988	86	87	88
Korea	353.7	1060.2	1282.7	35	24	23
Taiwan	770.4	1418.8	1182.5	20	28	15
Singapore	546.3	687.5	NA	37	38	NA
Thailand	262.6	351.7	NA	19	20	NA

NA: Not Available

Source: Own calculations based on data from: Business Asia, February 27,1989, pp. 66-67; Economic Development Board, Yearbook 1987/88, p. 17 (Singapore); Bank of Thailand data, mimeo; United States Department of Commerce, Survey of Current Business, vol. 68, August 8, 1988, pp. 63-64.

Equally important for the economic development of these countries is the role of the government, in particular its market strategy and attitude towards foreign direct investment.

While the Republic of Korea, Taiwan, and Singapore pursue a strong export-oriented trade policy, Thailand does so to a lesser extent. Concerning import trade and foreign investment, Singapore has a history of few or no restrictions, while the Korean, Taiwanese and Thai governments have been much more interventionist in protecting and promoting domestic industries. Market restrictions and/or export-oriented trade policy have led to large (but slowly declining) trade surpluses with some industrialized countries, in particular the United States.

Korea, Taiwan, Singapore, and Thailand have been introducing new economic policies that recognize the role to be played by direct investment, particularly in technology transfers. The areas of investment are changing, as far as Taiwan, Korea and Singapore are concerned, indicating industrial restructuring similar to that experienced by Japan. The weight of the services sector is tending to increase; the manufacturing sector is undergoing a change that will continually strengthen advanced-technology sectors such as information technology, electronics and biotechnology.

As these countries diversify their economies and expand manufacturing, they are being pressured by industrial countries to take on more responsibility for upholding principles generally agreed upon in industrialized countries like open markets and the protection of (foreign) intellectual property. The newly industrializing countries, having a strong economic self-interest in gaining access to industrialized country markets, have gradually come to appreciate the importance of these changes in their economic and intellectual property protection policies. However, many problems remain. In the following sections, recent trends in government policies on trade, domestic technological development, foreign direct investment, transfer of technology, and intellectual property protection in the above mentioned four Asian countries will be presented.

Government Policies: Regulation of Trade, Foreign Direct Investment, Domestic Technological Development

Republic of Korea. The Korean Government has undertaken or is planning a series of steps to liberalize import trade and foreign direct investment. A recently introduced negative import list reduces former import restrictions to thirteen (previously sixty-six) sectors. Markets which have been opened up for imports include textiles, footwear, electronic home appliances, automobiles, toys, and to a lesser extent chemical and drug imports. Furthermore, import restrictions on manufactured or processed goods including liquor, fabrics, and metals as well as agricultural imports will be lifted over the next three years.17/

Concerning foreign direct investment, the government has opened up 78.9 percent of its standard industrial sectors18/; recently, for example, it has lifted restrictions on wholesale and retail trade, insurance, banking, and shipping, and plans to do so for certain other services sectors like advertising, data base and data processing, communications, public accounting, marketing, consulting, and probably also for the chemical and petrochemical industries. Total (100 percent) foreign equity is permitted in certain sectors, but may then be linked to export requirements; however, joint ventures with local participation are preferred. In certain industries, like construction and manufacturing in twelve different areas, only joint ventures with Korean firms are permitted; joint ventures will further be allowed to manufacture defense-related industrial products; joint ventures with small and medium-sized firms are exempt from income tax. Foreign investment in "restricted areas" may be permitted, inter alia, in certain sectors like tourism or are subject to 100 percent export requirements. Performance requirements (export quotas) for transnational pharmaceutical corporations have been liberalized but are still partly applicable.19/ However, demands by the United States extend further to require easing of imports of beef and other agricultural products, lowering of duties on manufactured goods and lessening restrictions on telecommunications, legal services, commercial aviation, and construction.

With regard to indigenous technological development, Korea promotes its own high-tech industry in order to remain competitive despite increasing wages and an appreciating currency. In order to streamline efforts to become a producer and exporter of high-tech products, the Ministry of Trade and Industry in September 1988 set up a high-tech industry community consisting of several committees in order to determine investment priorities in high-tech industries. The government is also going to liberalize official approval of outward investment (automatic approval of investments up to $5 million). Korea has been most successful in the production of semiconductors, computers, fine chemicals and automobiles. It also plans to get involved in the production of robotics, aeronautics, communication equipment, biotechnology, and raw materials. Korea is the only nation among the NICs that produces very large-scale integrated circuits (VLSIs) with its own technology. The portion of total exports represented by high-tech products amounted to 13 percent in 1983 and is expected to increase to 18 percent by 1991. In 1987, semiconductors represented 20 percent of the total electronics exports, registering $2.09 billion in sales and are expected to increase by $4.1 billion in 1991. In 1988, investment in science and technology amounted to 1.99 percent of the GNP and is expected to grow to 3.8 percent in the 1990s.20/ The private sector contributed 79 percent to total R&D expenditure in 1988. Venture capital and indirect government incentives have contributed to finance these efforts. Furthermore, the government has promoted concerted R&D activities among industry, universities and government-supported research institutes. However, shortages due to low levels of domestic technology, skilled manpower, and an underdeveloped research infrastructure must still be overcome by Korea in order to fully develop a high-tech industry.

Taiwan. Taiwan, has set up import incentives in its five-year plan (1988-92) in order to change the current trade imbalance with its largest trading partner, the United States (38 percent exports to, 26 percent imports).21/ It targets an annual growth of 25 percent for imports (and only 17 percent for exports) during this period. Under the plan, tariff reductions, and liberalization of import controls will be adopted. In 1988, duties were lowered for goods including textiles, consumer goods, farm products, paper products, plastics, and marine goods. Imports of machinery and equipment for sophisticated industry are duty free. Since 1987, imports of liquor, cigarettes, and automobiles were freed. The list of controlled goods includes weapons and ammunition, drugs, farm and marine goods.

Taiwan, currently experiencing a decline in foreign investment (13.1 percent in 1988), welcomes foreign investors especially when they transfer technology. Investments in energy-intensive or environmentally offensive enterprises are not encouraged. Outside state monopolies (public services, utilities, basic industries, 28 percent of Taiwan's industry22/), no limitations on foreign equity ownership exist, but joint ventures with local participation are preferred. Recently, Taiwan has opened up export/import trade as well as the retail, shipping, insurance, and financial services sectors to foreign investors. It also dropped compulsory export quotas for them.

Regarding indigenous technological development, Taiwan is currently shifting from a labor-intensive, assembly-oriented industry to a more sophisticated, capital-intensive and high-technology production. Due to the appreciating NT dollar, the domestic market will gradually become more attractive. Taiwan's future growth will be based on the sophisticated consumer products and services sector, in particular consumer electronics and financial services, information, machinery and transport equipment. However, structural economic reforms are needed. For example, a shortage of skilled labor to operate the capital-intensive and sophisticated technology can be expected in the near future. The government has installed or expanded training programs for workers. Additional departments and courses in scientific and advanced technical fields have been set up at both public and private colleges and universities. Incentives for local (and, to a lesser extent, foreign) investment are granted by the Statute for Encouragement of Investment (due to expire 1990). Incentives include tax and tariff exemptions and are available for high-technology processing projects and scientific and technological R&D. R&D expenditures are fully deductible and imported instruments and equipment for R&D are duty free. In 1980, the government established a science-based industrial park for high-tech industry. In 1988, approximately 100 firms operated there, manufacturing computers, semiconductors, telecommunication equipment, precision instruments, machinery, and conducting biochemical engineering. Their total export amounted to $1.2 billion in January-October 1988.23/

Singapore. Since the late 1970s, Singapore has been promoting foreign investment in the high-technology industries through a high-wage, high-cost policy that would add high values to its products. After some decline in value added in the manufacturing sector due to high costs and labor shortages, the government (International Operations Division of the Economic Development Board) now promotes automation, capital-intensive investment, and investment in services; it tries to attract electronics and information technology firms and undertakes efforts to get more involved in regional countertrade business.

Singapore poses no restrictions on trade with the U.S.; however, due to its export-oriented strategy, the trade surplus will probably rise to $3 billion this year.24/

With respect to the promotion of indigenous industry, the Singaporean government has established a whole set of programs and incentives. The "Local Industries Upgrading Program" promotes business ties between local and transnational firms. Local suppliers of foreign firms are the primary target to receive training and other support since they are export-oriented and in a position to profit from new technology. Other programs are the "Joint Venture Matching Service," other local industry assistance schemes (financial, technical, and new technology assistance for small industries), skills and manpower development, research and development incentives, and a venture capital fund. In addition, the government grants incentives to Singapore residents for overseas investments in new technologies. Deduction will be given for losses suffered by the local company arising from the sale of shares in overseas investment. Furthermore, joint ventures with a 25 percent local equity participation including transfer of technology arrangements get preference in public construction contracts until local contractors have gained competitiveness with foreign firms.

Thailand. Thailand, experiencing fast economic growth in the last two years, but facing shortages of raw material, skilled workers, and an underdeveloped infrastructure, is changing its attitude towards foreign investors. It will continue to promote foreign direct investment (except in certain services sectors like insurance, advertising, leasing, construction, engineering, architectural and legal services25/), but will become more selective about the types of projects, sources of investment, and locations of proposed ventures in order to receive higher value-added equity investments. In this way, Thailand hopes to get more transfers of technology on a noncompetitive basis, thereby protecting the local producers. In the past, foreign firms, mainly Japanese producers using Thailand as an export platform for low-tech products, have dominated the Thai domestic market; 20 percent of their output is enough to dominate the Thai market (80 percent had to be exported).26/ The government will now grant incentives for investment in new technology and R&D. For example, it is planning to build a data processing zone for transnational corporations in the information and communications sector and affiliated services. These firms will be granted duty free imports and certain tax holidays. For infrastructure development projects, however, the government might offer opportunities to foreign investors, probably only if local content requirements and higher national participation in equity and management are met.

In the field of trade, some tariffs will be reduced, but protectionist policies especially on agricultural products seem to prevail. Regarding exports, the U.S. worries that Japanese and Taiwanese investors are using Thailand as a back door to its market, since exporters receive certain tax exemptions through Thailand's Investment Promotion Act. Since the trade deficit with Thailand in 1988 has amounted to $1.5 billion,27/ the U.S. in January withdrew Thailand's special trading privileges (GSP) for $165 million worth of products.

Government Policies: Legal Safeguards to Control Technology Transfer and Protect Intellectual Property

In the following section, the regulatory framework on transfer of technology (ToT) and intellectual property rights will be presented together, since they are closely intertwined as far as trade and investment in developing countries are concerned. While ToT provisions, in the opinion of several industrialized countries, would (besides import controls and limitations on equity ownership) create restrictions on *free* trade (and investment), inadequate intellectual property protection or its total nonexistence would instead hamper *fair* trade (and investment). For example, in an

OECD study28/ on international licensing, 80 percent of interviewed companies stated that prior approval of ToT contracts and/or inadequate industrial property rights protection (75 percent) would range as a strong disincentive to licensing in developing countries. Fifty-two percent reported that the difficulties which they had encountered had prevented a licensing agreement from being reached; 20 percent stated that it had led to its termination. Provisions on ToT contracts may also affect protection of intellectual property rights in a more direct way. For example, prohibition of disclosure restrictions in transfer of technology contracts might affect trade secret protection. Developing countries argue that ToT contracts have to be screened and certain contractual restrictions on the licensee's rights have to be prohibited in order to prevent abuse by transnational corporations: for example, the setting of unreasonably high prices for technology and their control over the dissemination of knowledge-based products through unwarranted restrictions on its use.

As to the quality of intellectual property protection, the Asia-Pacific Council of American Chambers of Commerce has, in 1988, evaluated Korea, Taiwan, Singapore, and Thailand. In this evaluation, the Council found Singapore to have adequate protection in the three areas of legislation, enforcement, and governmental "good faith" efforts, while Thailand needed improvement in all three areas. Korea was found to have adequate legislation but fell short in the other categories. Taiwan, conversely, had inadequate legislation and enforcement but showed adequate "good faith" efforts.29/

The U.S. Trade Representative issued a "priority watch list" as of May 25,1989 wherein the developing Asian countries are ranked. In this analysis, using the same three criteria, Thailand was found lacking in all areas. Both Korea and Taiwan fell short in only the enforcement category. Singapore did not make the list at all.30/

Republic of Korea: ToT Contracts. The Republic of Korea, today one of the leaders among Southeast Asian NICs has always carefully regulated the influx of foreign technology and the outflow of foreign currency.31/ Nevertheless, foreign licensors of technology have regarded the country as a potentially lucrative market -- even more so in the last decade. For example, of 4,692 licensing contracts concluded between 1962 and 1987, 57.8 percent were entered into within the last five years of that period. Of these 4,692 licenses, 27.2 percent belonged to the machine industry, 21.2 percent to the electronics and electrical sector, 4.0 percent to chemical fiber and 2.6 percent to the pharmaceutical industry. In 1987, the electronics and electrical sector for the first time concluded more licensing agreements than the machine industry did and paid the highest royalties in comparison to other sectors. Japanese licensors are business partners in over 50 percent of all agreements, followed by the United States, the Federal Republic of Germany, the United Kingdom, and France.

Korea's amended Foreign Capital Inducement Act (Art. 24), its accompanying Enforcement Decree (Art. 24),32/ and Public Notice No. 87-14,33/ closely regulate technology transfer agreements.

1. Approval procedure: technology imports reported to the Ministry of Finance; automatic approval granted after twenty days if no modifications have been ordered (Art. 23 Capital Inducement Act). It is expected that certain types of technology licenses (e.g., with royalty rates under $100,000 p.a.) will be exempt from government approval in the near future.
2. Territory: prohibition of restrictions on sale or export of products incorporating the imported technology to areas other than where the licensor has already registered the technology, is engaged in normal sales activities, or has granted exclusive sales rights to third parties.
3. Sales: prohibition of restrictions on sales outlets, quantities, methods, prices and/or resale prices of the licensee (except those restrictions mentioned in the foregoing item).
4. Purchase of raw materials, components, equipment etc.: so-called "tie-ins" are prohibited.
5. Term: the contract term should be kept to five years (exceptions: ten years).
6. Royalties: royalties above 2-3 percent of net

sales have to be justified, unless highly advanced technology is transferred. A royalty in excess of 5 percent of net sales will not be approved. Royalties (for advanced technology) are tax-exempt for five years.

7. Use and disclosure restrictions: The foreign licensor may not prohibit a Korean licensee from using the licensed technology itself after termination of the agreement, provided, however, that no industrial property right has been licensed. Likewise, barring the licensee, either during the time of the licensing period or for the time thereafter, from handling or using similar or competitive technologies when no intellectual property rights are involved, is prohibited. This means, unless an intellectual property right is involved, the foreign technology transferred to the Korean recipient resembles more a conditional or installment sale than a traditional license.
8. Protection of domestic firms: a contract inducing a technology for which a manufacturer of new domestic technological products is protected under the Technology Development Promotion Act (Art. 8-2) will not be approved.

Concerning intellectual property rights, Korea, in the last few years, has undertaken great efforts to strengthen its laws, partly due to successful foreign pressure stemming from Korea's dependence on its trade partners, and partly as an indication of the increasing sophistication of its own domestic industry (specifically its computer industry and its emerging biotechnology industry). This is also reflected in the percentage of patents and trademarks granted to Korean nationals. In 1986, Koreans received 24.18 percent of all patents granted (1,894 total) and 34.19 percent of all trademarks (15,086 total).34/

Nevertheless, the Republic of Korea appears on the USTR's "priority watch list" for not providing adequate enforcement of its intellectual property laws. U.S. investors complain that the Korean government forces them to take local partners (if they do not want to meet export requirements) and to transfer their technology to those who in some cases "fail to protect that technology."35/

In the following sections, some recent changes in Korea's intellectual property legislation will be highlighted and problems encountered in regard to enforcing those rights will be discussed.

Patents. Some of the most important changes introduced by the amended Patent Act 1986[36] are:

1. types of protection include patents of invention (product and process), designs and utility models.
2. protection is implicitly granted, inter alia, to chemical, pharmaceutical, and biotechnological products; patents will still not be granted for food products, beverages and nuclear inventions (Art. 4).
3. the term of patent protection has been extended from twelve to fifteen years (Art. 53(1)).
4. non-Koreans without domicile or place of business in Korea can own patents under conditions of reciprocity (international treaty) but must act through a qualified patent administrator (Art. 22).
5. the arbitration system in compulsory licensing proceedings was introduced (Art. 51(2)(8)) along with new requirements by which the holder of a dependent patent obtains a compulsory license from the holder of a dominant patent (Art. 59(2)).
6. penalties for infringers were increased (up to 20 million Won, Art. 158).
7. the burden of proof in process patent suits was reverted (Art. 45(2)).

The most important differences to the United States patent system are:

1. the first-to-file rule, i.e., foreigners may claim priority for patents that have been filed elsewhere (within one year of original filing) (Art. 11), not that have been invented elsewhere.
2. compulsory license where a patent is not used or is subject to misuse (Art. 51) and lapse of patent if it is not worked within two years after the grant of the first compulsory license.

Under the 1986 United States-Korea agreement on intellectual property rights, United States patents are retroactively protected under the amended Korean Patent Law. The bilateral agreement, however, has led to a suspension of the Republic of Korea's trade benefits in January 1988 under the EC Generalized System of Preferences (GSP) as a response to Korea's discrimination against European patents. The cost for Korean exporters amount to approximately 50 million ECUs ($64.6 million) in additional duties per annum.

Copyrights. In 1986, Korea also amended its Copyright Law.37/ It enhanced the degree of formal protection to a great extent. For example,

1. coverage (Art. 4);
2. exclusive rights of the author (Art. 11-21);
3. term of protection (fifty years) (Art. 36);
4. extension of protection to foreign works on the basis of reciprocity (Art. 3); and
5. definition of infringement (i.e., inclusion of import of infringing copies, Art. 92(1).

The Act contains the following limitations:

1. foreign works are only protected insofar as they have been created after July 1, 1987 (except United States works which are protected under the United States-Korean settlement of August 28, 1986).
2. compulsory licensing is available (Art. 47-50), for example, relatively easily for translation rights (Art. 49).

Computer Software Protection. In 1986, the Republic of Korea enacted the Computer Program Protection Act and accompanying regulations.38/ The Act follows quite closely the Copyright Act. The most important features are:

1. Coverage: no protection will be granted to program language, program rules, and algorithms (Art. 4(1)). However, no positive definition is given; in particular, it is not clear whether both source code and object code and what types of programs (application and/or operating systems program) are protected.

2. Term: fifty years is the new term starting from creation (Art. 8(3)).
3. Effective date of protection: programs created prior to the effective date of the Act (July 1, 1987) are not protected (Addenda 2).
4. Registration: ownership will not depend on registration. Registration, however, will be necessary for enforcement of a program copyright against a third party. Furthermore, the negligence of an infringer is presumed if the program is registered (Art. 8(2),24(2),27(2)).
5. Protection of foreign programs: on the basis of reciprocity, protection is only granted if the program has been published in the Republic of Korea (including programs that are published in Korea within thirty days from their original publication abroad) or if Korea is obligated by treaty to protect them (Universal Copyright Convention members) (Art. 3).
6. Exclusive rights, restrictions: ownership rights include reproduction, adaptation, translation, distribution and publication of the program (Art. 8(1)); furthermore, owners have the right to disclose and to license as well as to indicate a name and to maintain the identity of the program (moral right) (Art. 9-11, 16(1)); However, use of programs in court proceedings, for educational purposes and for private use at home is permitted (fair use) (Art. 12); compulsory licensing is provided (Art. 17); but it is not clear whether the government may approve compulsory licenses only when the copying owner is unknown (Art. 17(1) or also when he is known (see Art. 4.3 Enforcement Regulations of Computer Program Protection Act); compulsory licensing of foreign programs does not include the right to export (Art. 10(1)3 Enforcement Decree of Computer Program Protection Act).
7. Scope of infringement: besides violation of the owner's exclusive rights (Art. 8), importing of infringing copies is, among others, an infringing act (Art. 26,34). It is, however, not clear whether sublicensing without the owner's consent is deemed an infringing act (Art. 16(2),34).
8. Enforcement: the act contains penal provisions (up to three years imprisonment or a fine of

up to 3 million Won), however, minimum penalties have not been determined (Art. 34). The Act further contains provisions on the right to claim destruction of infringing copies and equipment (Art. 25(2)), and the right to claim damages (Art. 27). However, it does not elaborate further on conditions and administrative or judicial procedures relating to enforcement of copyrights on computer software programs except the provision for setting up a Program Deliberation Committee to deal with, inter alia, protection issues (Art.24, Enforcement Decree of Computer Program Protection Act.

Trademarks. In 1986, Korea amended its Trademark Act39/ and, as mentioned earlier, its Foreign Capital Inducement Act. Before 1986, trademark licenses had to be accompanied by actual transfer of technology under these acts. This requirement has been abolished (Art. 24 para. 2 Capital Inducement Act and Art. 24.1 Enforcement Decree). Important features are:

1. Validity: trademarks are protected for ten years from their date of registration and renewable for further ten years (Sec. 20).
2. Well-known trademarks: trademarks well-known overseas may be registered in the Republic of Korea only if they are not already well-known there, too. This determination is made by the Korean Patent Office (Sec. 9(1)(ix))40/.
3. Transfers: transfers of trademark rights from foreign to Korean parties are still restricted; they require an actual transfer of all the physical assets applicable to the production and sale of the designated goods (Sec. 27).

The Unfair Competition Prevention Law of 198641/ provides protection and remedies against counterfeiting for Korean and foreign nationals.

Trade Secrets. Trade secret protection is covered by torts.

Semiconductor chip designs, databases. Under the United States-Korean agreement of 1986, the Korean government promised to study the "feasibility of extending protection to semiconductor chips" and of "extending copyright protection to databases as compilations. In the meantime, the new copyright law will provide for protection of copyrightable works whether or not they are incorporated in a database." However, no action has been taken so far in regard to the latter. Concerning semiconductor chip designs, the Korean government has voted for the Treaty on the Protection of Intellectual Property in Respect of Integrated Circuits which has been negotiated at the WIPO Diplomatic Conference in Washington, D.C., May 8-26, 1989.42/

Enforcement. In spite of Korea's efforts to reform its intellectual property laws and to strengthen its enforcement measures (in 1988, it established an interministerial intellectual property enforcement task force43/), the suppression of unauthorized copying and counterfeiting of protected goods seems to be a big hurdle to overcome. Problems include the copying of pharmaceutical patents and copyrighted software and the counterfeiting of trademarks. In 1988, two United States pharmaceutical companies filed Sec. 337, 301 U.S. Trade Act suits against Korea for allowing local companies to export pirated products while closing domestic markets, and this despite the preferential patent protection given to U.S. patents in the United States-Korea agreement on intellectual property rights. Major obstacles seem to be procedural and technical difficulties as well as conflicts of legal interpretation.44/

In suits involving pharmaceutical patents, for example, where expert testimony is needed, it is very unlikely that a local expert will provide an opinion against a local company since both of them depend on each other in their business: the physicians determine the medication taken by their patients while the pharmaceutical companies in turn provide research money. Furthermore, United States companies complain about the inadequacy of the discovery process and the difficulty of proving sufficiently to collect damages. Procedural difficulties might also exist in copyright suits concerning computer software programs; as indicated above, the Computer Program Protection Act says very little about procedural details.

Technical difficulties might emerge with regard to the detection of infringing computer programs. First, extensive controls require additional human and financial resources. Second, since computer programs are made up of multitudes of other programs, there are numerous steps in processing information where "copying" is taking place, and there is no parallel to the kind of text reading with which officials are familiar. Foolproof protection of machine code, data or text is impossible with open computer systems, especially software, since it can be maintained in networks and can easily be transmitted across boundaries without detection. The main problem for enforcement therefore is monitoring the "copying" and facing a very complex evidentiary process. For a developing or a "newly industrialized" country, this might be an even more difficult process than it would be for an industrialized country. Another technical difficulty for Korea is controlling the export of counterfeit goods, since their quality "is so remarkably high."

A problem of legal interpretation, for example, exists in the area of trademarks, since translation between at least two languages is involved. The usual test for trademark infringement is whether the consumer is confused by a similar trademark in either visual or verbal form. However, if the same name has different meanings in two languages and is used for two different trademarks, the intent of the manufacturer to confuse the consumer is not so clear. For example, H.D. Lee Company, producer of "Lee" blue jeans, sued a Korean company for selling "Lee" jeans. However, "Lee" is a common Asian name and "Lee" blue jeans are known in Korea since only a short time ago. Therefore, the case could not be so easily decided as in the United States.

<u>Taiwan: ToT Contracts.</u> The licensing of foreign technology in sophisticated and heavy industries is encouraged by the government, while licensing of foreign trademarks is less welcome.45/ Between 1952 and 1988, the government approved 2,973 licensing agreements with foreign suppliers of technology, 295 in 1987 alone. The largest category was electrical and electronic equipment (26.7 percent), chemicals (25.7 percent), machinery and instruments (14.4 percent). Japanese firms account for 54 percent of the total and United

States firms for 26.6 percent. Taiwan, like Korea, also closely monitors ToT contracts. The Statute for Technical Cooperation 1962 as amended 1964 covers rights granted under patent law and know-how related to technology, management, design and administration. Important features are:

1. Approval procedure: all contracts involving foreign exchange payments require specifications (products, services, etc.) for approval. It takes about one month to get approval. The applications are reviewed on a case-by-case basis. If approval is given, production must usually begin within six months.
2. Restrictions for light industries: applications are only considered if light industries are innovative, export-oriented and can rationalize production and management.
3. Term: usually the term is five years, but longer periods are possible.
4. Renewal terms: these are possible for labor-intensive industries only if production is export-oriented or the technology will be enhanced by the licensor.
5. Restrictive clauses for licensee: restrictions on exports are prohibited; however, tying arrangements are allowed.
6. Royalties: these are usually based on net sales or sometimes on output; they range on average below 5 percent but can reach up to 10 percent if sophisticated technology is involved. If royalties are reinvested in local enterprises, the licensor will receive incentives granted to foreign investors.
7. Trademark licensing: the government policy does not favor trademark licensing. Consumer trademarks are rejected unless the firm substantially invests in Taiwan or exports all of its products. The licensor would at least have to supervise the production of the goods by the licensee.

Taiwan has recently revised its intellectual property laws and currently negotiates with the United States on bilateral copyright protection like Korea, partly due to foreign pressure, partly due to the sophistication and "internationalization" of its own economy.46/ Taiwanese business people have changed their attitudes towards protection of intellectual property since they participated more and more in international trade. When penetrating foreign markets with their own trademarks, they increasingly face infringement problems. For example, some of well-known Taiwanese trademarks have been registered by Latin American companies. When Taiwanese companies export products to those countries, they may be sued for infringing upon the registered trademarks. Copying of Taiwanese computers in other Southeast Asian countries is also widespread. The growing sophistication of Taiwan's economy is also reflected in the high percentage of patents granted to Taiwanese nationals: 55.1 percent (total:10,526) in 1986.47/

Patents. Taiwan amended its Patent Law in 1986.48/ The main changes are:

1. types of protection include patents of invention (products and processes), designs and utility models (Art. 95).
2. product patents on chemicals and pharmaceuticals are granted, but not on biotechnological inventions (i.e., new species of animal, plant and micro-organism) (Art. 4); plant patents will probably be covered in a separate law.
3. the term of protection for patents is fifteen years (Art. 6), for utility models ten years (Art. 99) and five years for designs (Art. 114) (after date of publication of the application).
4. licensing is compulsory by a product patentee in favor of the process patentee if it is, among other reasons, in the public interest (Art. 42; Art. 67 provides for compulsory licenses of patented inventions in general).
5. patents are cancelled for failure to practice or properly practice them within four years (Art. 67).
6. burden of proof has been transferred to the alleged infringer in cases of an infringement of a patented process (Art. 85(1)); however, the presumption of infringing the manufacturing process is not created if the products involved are imported (Art. 85(2)).
7. access to court by foreign patentees has been established, but only on the basis of reciprocity (Art. 88(1)).49/

8. patent tribunals will be provided to adjudicate exclusively patent disputes (Art. 88-2).
9. criteria for determining damages have been provided (Art. 82).
10. preliminary injunctions for provisional seizure of products and materials have been established (Art. 83, 84); however, the patent law does not authorize the court to confiscate the patent-infringing goods.
11. higher penalties for infringers were established (Art. 89-92; 106-108; 125-127).

Copyrights. Taiwan amended its Copyright Law in 1985.50/ The main changes are:

1. extension of scope of protected items were made to expressly include edited works, recording films, lectures, choreographic works, computer programs, maps, and scientific, technical or engineering designs (Art. 4).
2. exclusive rights of the owner include, inter alia, reproduction, public presentation, adaptation and translation of the copyrighted work (Art. 17(1)). However, copyrights of foreign nationals do not include translation rights (Art. 17(2)).
3. registration requirements for works of Chinese nationals were eliminated; however, works of foreign nationals have to be registered; registration is only permitted if the first publication of the work occurs in Taiwan, or on the basis of reciprocity (Art. 17).51/
4. the term of protection for edited works, movie films, photography and computer programs is the lifetime of the author plus thirty years (Art. 9).
5. compulsory licensing of musical works was granted (Art. 53).
6. civil and criminal remedies were strengthened (maximum fine is NT$ 150,000 and five years imprisonment, Art. 38 to 48; Art. 38 includes the rental of copyrighted material without authorization); preliminary injunctions are available; all reproduced, imitated, or copied works as well as machinery and equipment may be seized (but not confiscated), although some judges permit confiscation in practice.
7. criteria for determining damages (at least 500

times the actual retail price of the copyrighted work, Art. 33).

Trademarks. Taiwan revised its trademark law in 1985.52/ Important features are:

1. trademarks not in use for at least two years are subject to cancellation (Art. 33).
2. registration is a condition of protection; other unregistered trademarks are not protected unless the trademark owner's country has a reciprocity agreement with Taiwan (Art. 21), or unless the trademark is "famous" (Art. 37).
3. foreign nationals have legal standing to pursue trademark infringement in local courts (Art. 66(1)).
4. stricter penalties: violators face up to NT$ 150,000 and up to five years imprisonment. Individuals who knowingly or unknowingly sell, import or export copied goods or display a registered trademark in an advertisement or at a commercial exhibition in an attempt to sell copied goods face up to one year imprisonment and up to NT$ 30,000, unless the latter reveal the source of the illegal products to the authorities (Art. 62). The court can confiscate the counterfeit goods but only those that are personally owned by the defendants (not corporate property); machinery probably will not be confiscated.
5. the criteria for determining damages was outlined (Art. 62).

A Fair Trade Law has been drafted that would prohibit the use of unregistered existing or similar company or family names, brand names, containers and packaging.

Trade Secrets. Taiwan has no specific trade secret law. It has been reported that foreign companies have to release proprietary toxicological data without compensation.53/

Semiconductor chip designs. Taiwan does not provide protection to semiconductor chip designs.

Enforcement. Despite Taiwan's efforts to strengthen its intellectual property laws, infringement problems remain. It has been reported that, in particular, foreign producers of books and musical recordings, consumer products, pharmaceuticals, agrichemicals, videotape recordings and computer software54/ are confronted with unauthorized copying.

Joint efforts by the Piracy Investigation and Prevention Office of the Ministry of Economic Affairs, the private Anti-Counterfeiting Committee and the Interior Ministry have partly discouraged illegal actions. In 1987, the courts convicted 476 violators in 344 infringement cases. In addition, 142 more were sued from January to October 1988.55/

Administrative and procedural improvements are under way. For example, Taiwan's National Bureau of Standards has opened a Patent and Trademark Consulting Center to answer public inquiries about patent and trademark issues. A trademark court may be established in the near future. In May 1989, Taiwanese officials agreed to "expeditiously resolve" problems concerning the showing of motion pictures in Taiwan's "MTV" (movie television) parlors.

However, procedural and technical difficulties remain as well as problems of legal interpretation and legal loopholes. For example, potential infringers may delay judicial proceedings by filing so-called invalidation claims against a plaintiff's trademark or patent. Although the January 26, 1983 amendment of the Trademark Law provides that the suspension is indicated only if the invalidation action has been filed prior to the initiation of the infringement action, local courts, nevertheless, often suspend the infringement proceedings pending a decision of the National Bureau of Standards. The Patent Act has no parallel provision at all in this respect.

Technical difficulties are connected with tracing counterfeit goods. The Trademark Law punishes sellers of copied goods only if they display them in public. Now they present them for sale only at the request of customers. This increases the difficulties of collecting evidence and the trademark owners often have to rely on the testimony of investigators to support their claims. However, investigation and prosecution of infringing actions is not per se a public responsibility carried out by a specific government body. This has to be done by the owner of the intellectual property right itself. Furthermore, due to a lack of legal authority, the Customs Office may not (temporarily) seize suspect counterfeit goods of travelers; the consequence is that the inflow and outflow of counterfeit goods carried by individuals not living in Taiwan cannot be prevented.

Singapore. Since its separation from Malaysia, Singapore has favored free trade. Its law of contract is basically the English common law. For this reason, there are no restrictions on ToT agreements except those contained, for example, in the United Kingdom Unfair Contract Terms Act.

Concerning intellectual property protection, Singapore has strengthened its copyright law for reasons similar to Taiwan, as noted above. The government decided that in light of Singapore's steady economic development and its shift toward high-tech industries and financial services, not to mention its high export dependency, the advantages of intellectual property rights protection would outweigh any drawbacks.

Patents. Singapore grants patent protection under the U.K. Patents Act 1977. However, it does not have an own patent registry but merely reregisters U.K. patents.56/ The reregistration period is three years from the date of registration in the U.K. The government is considering the introduction of Singapore's own patent system in order to promote local R&D.

There is also a regime for compulsory licenses although it appears to be infrequently utilized. Main features of the Patents (Compulsory Licensing) Act57/ are:

1. compulsory licenses are granted on grounds of public interest for certain metallic products, glass, textiles, paper, building construction materials, foods or medicine, surgical or curative devices.
2. government use: the government may without authorization use pharmaceutical patents when making or importing drugs for distribution in government hospitals or other public medical institutions.
3. lapse of patent: two years after issuing a compulsory license, the patent may be subject to cancellation.
4. penalties, burden of proof: the Patent Act provides for preliminary injunctions and

reverses the burden of proof in cases where the defendant claims ignorance of the patent or challenges its validity.

Copyrights. In 1987, Singapore enacted its new Copyright Act and accompanying regulations.58/ The major changes are:

1. coverage includes, inter alia, computer programs, videotapes (cinematographic films) and cable television programs (Sec. 7).
2. foreign works are protected if first published in Singapore or a country to which the Act will be extended through a bilateral or multilateral treaty (Sec. 26,27,184). Singapore is not a member of the Berne Convention or Universal Copyright Convention.
3. exclusive rights are restricted by fair use provisions for private persons (Sec. 35 et. seq.) as well as for the government (Sec. 198,202). A special provision deals with backup copies of computer programs (Sec. 39).
4. compulsory licensing provisions are provided for translation and reproduction of certain works (Sec. 143 et. seq.).
5. parallel imports may be prevented upon application by the owner of the copyright (Sec. 32,142,202).
6. penalties have been sharply increased (from S$2,000 fine under the old Copyright Act now up to S$100,000, and/or imprisonment for up to five years (Sec. 136). There is an extra provision on penalties for the advertisement for supply of infringing copies of computer programs (Sec. 139); however, the provisions only contain maximum penalties, not minimum penalties and the burden is on the copyright holder to prove that the alleged infringer acted in bad faith ("... he knows or ought reasonably to know ...") before penalties will be imposed.59/
7. the remedy for such infringement is injunctive relief and either damages or an account of profits, but damages are only granted if the defendant acted in bad faith (Sec. 119).
8. no registration is necessary. The Act does, however, establish a Copyright Tribunal to adjudicate copyright-related license and

royalty disputes (Sec.149-183). This tribunal has yet to be set up. The provisions do not contain special procedures for judicial proceedings involving computer programs (Sec. 173).

Trademarks. The Singapore Trademarks Act is based on the UK Trademarks Act 1938. In addition, the Companies Act and the Business Registration Act contain specific provisions to protect corporate and trade names. The Trademarks Act provides:

1. there is coverage for registered as well as unregistered (common law) trademarks, but not for service marks.
2. trademarks are registered for a seven year period with the possibility of renewal.
3. foreign trademarks: Singapore is not a member of the Paris Convention or any other multilateral trademark agreement, it is therefore not bound to protect foreign trademarks except on the basis of a bilateral agreement.
4. nonuse for a period of five years makes trademarks subject to cancellation.
5. civil and criminal sanctions are available. Criminal actions under the Consumer Protection (Trade Description and Safety Requirements) Act are more effective than civil remedies, but cover registered trademarks only.

Trade Secrets. Trade secrets are protected under common law.

Semiconductor chip designs. Singapore does not have a specific law protecting semiconductor chip designs. It is unclear whether they are covered under the Copyright Act.60/

Enforcement. Singapore, once the third-largest producer of counterfeits (trademarks and copyrights) of United States products in the world,61/ has in the last years taken effective steps to control infringement of intellectual property rights. Under the Copyright Act, for example, the police force has broad legal authority to search and seize goods and to arrest people suspected of being involved in infringing activities (Sec. 138). Factors like the small size of Singapore (225.7 square miles) and its small population (2.6 million) make it relatively easy for the police to locate counterfeiters and undertake successful raids. Furthermore, government corruption seems to be nonexistent. Therefore, patent, copyright and trademark infringement are quite low in number. One incident, however, should be mentioned concerning conflicts of legal interpretation of copyright infringement. On January 27, 1988, the government of Singapore amended its Newspaper and Printing Press Act, permitting the copying of foreign publications (the Far Eastern Economic Review) whose circulation had been restricted in order to punish the publisher for "engaging in domestic politics." The amendment empowers the government to grant licenses to applicants, provided that copies are "made, circulated or sold" only in Singapore, that they "shall not carry any advertisements", and that "no person shall make any profit out of the production, sale or distribution" of the copies above cost.62/ As long as the licensees were public agencies working for no profit, duplication has been deemed legitimate. This legal practice, in order to be compatible with the Copyright Act, would have to be declared as "fair use" (Sec. 198 Copyright Act) -- a rather bizarre interpretation in light of the obvious purpose: hardly disguised political censorship of Western publications by economic means.

Thailand. Thailand, the fastest growing economy in Asia, does not have a deliberate control system of technology transfer like Korea and Taiwan. However, since the government is seeking more technology transfer of advanced technologies, it has been considering setting up a separate public agency to regulate technology transfers and royalty payments.63/

Thailand lags far behind the other Asian countries and faces much foreign pressure to strengthen its legal regime on patents, copyrights and trademarks.

Patents. Patents are protected under the Patent Act 1979 and accompanying regulations.64/ Important features are:

1. types of patents include patents of invention and design (Art. 5,56).
2. excluded from patent protection are food, beverages, pharmaceutical products, agricul-

tural machines, computer data systems and biotechnological inventions (products and processes) (Art. 9).

3. foreign patents are not protected since Thailand is not a member of the Paris Convention. Foreigners may apply for a "Thai patent" (Art. 37) before filing abroad or within twelve months after foreign filing (Art. 6(4)).
4. compulsory licenses may be granted after three years of patent issuance if the patentee fails to manufacture or sell the product in the domestic market or if sold at "unreasonably high prices" (Art. 46). The government may use a patent (including payment of royalties) for public purposes (Sec. 51-52). If the manufacture or sale criteria have not been met within six years from issuance, the patent may be cancelled (Art. 55).
5. goods produced and covered by a product or process patent in Thailand may not be imported without a special license (Art. 77).

Copyrights. Copyrights are protected under the Copyright Act 1978.65/ Important features are:

1. coverage includes, among others, audio-video works, broadcast and TV transmissions, and motion pictures (Sec. 4); however, it is not clear whether computer programs are covered. The Thai Juridical Council has stated that as works in the scientific domain, computer programs are subject to copyright protection, but there are no court decisions so far. Performance rights are also probably not covered.
2. no registration of copyrights is required.
3. international copyright protection is provided for member countries of the Berne Convention with certain restrictions66/; otherwise, protection is only granted to foreigners residing or first publishing in Thailand (Sec. 42,6).
4. exclusive rights of copyright owners are restricted by fair use provisions for, inter alia, research and educational purposes (Sec. 30-41).
5. civil and criminal remedies (fines up to 200,000 Baht and/or imprisonment up to one

year) are available against copyright offenders (Sec. 43-49).

An amendment to the Copyright Act, proposed in 1987, has not been enacted, since the Thai Parliament dissolved after dissenting on this issue.

Trademarks. Trademarks are given protection under the Trademark Act 1931 as amended 1961.67/ Important features are:

1. coverage is limited to trademarks. Service marks and certification marks are not included.
2. trademarks of foreign owners must be registered through an agent located in Thailand (first-to-file rule). Since Thailand is not a member of the Paris Convention, no priority right is recognized.
3. a trademark is also subject to cancellation if it has not been used for more than five years.
4. rights on trademarks may be transferred or licensed, but the Act lacks special provisions on registration of trademark licensing agreements (such agreements are, however, enforceable under the Civil and Commercial Code).
5. civil remedies (damages, injunctive relief) are only available for registered trademarks. Criminal sanctions (which are more efficient) are available for registered as well as unregistered trademarks. The proprietor of an unregistered trademark can bring a cancellation suit against an infringer with a registered mark, if he/she proves prior use in Thailand or abroad.

A Draft Trademark Bill has been submitted for Cabinet approval; it also covers service and certification marks, improves the protection of unregistered, well-known marks and adds specific provisions on trademark licensing. This bill introduces heavier penalties: counterfeiting will be punished with up to four years imprisonment (at present, 3 years) and a fine of 400,000 Baht ($15,735; at present: 6,000 Baht=$ 236). Inconsistencies between sanctions contained in the Trademark Act and Penal Code have been abolished. The Bill also recognizes Article V(2) of the Treaty of Amity and Economic Relations between Thailand and the United States, assuming national treatment.68/

Trade Secrets. Thailand does not have a special law covering trade secrets.

Semiconductor chip designs. Thailand does not protect semiconductor chip designs. It, however, voted in favor of the Treaty on the Protection of Intellectual Property with Respect to Integrated Circuits in Washington, D.C., May 1989.

Enforcement. In response to calls for trademark protection by U.S. and European manufacturers, the Customs Department has strengthened efforts to stop the import and export of counterfeit goods, but the trade ban does not include examination of goods carried by travellers. Domestic production and sale of counterfeit goods, however, are less controlled. The heavy workload of the police force, widespread corruption as well as the enormous volume of the counterfeit industry contribute to enforcement difficulties.

Foreign pressure to strengthen protection of intellectual property rights. Since its entry into the Asian group of fast-growing, export-oriented economies, Thailand's level of intellectual property rights protection has attracted international attention. The government has come under pressure from the United States to strengthen its intellectual property laws and their enforcement. Issues at stake are mainly protection of pharmaceutical products and computer software. The Thai government is considering a separate software law that, like patents, requires registration and disclosure of program construction but has a shorter period of protection than copyright law. As to patents, the Thai government wants to postpone a reform until after the end of the GATT Uruguay Round of multilateral trade negotiations, scheduled to be completed in 1990. The U.S. has asked for protection of at least new drug formulae. In order to reinforce its demands, the U.S., in January 1989, announced a cut in part of Thailand's trade privileges under the United States General System of Preferences (GSP) as of July 1, 1989, affecting Thai exports worth an estimated US$ 165 million per year (against a total of $600 million annually of Thai exports to the U.S. under the GSP system), totaling around $6 million in additional duties.69/ Furthermore, the United States Trade Representative (USTR) denied Thai petitions to reinstate or introduce duty-free treatment for jewelry, certain agricultural products, and telecommunications equipment. In addition, Thailand has been put on the USTR's "priority watch list." However, the impact of these measures is very uncertain. On the one hand, the United States is among Thailand's most important trading partners. The garment and jewelry industry will be especially affected. Furthermore, some foreign investors might start to look for other Asian GSP-privileged countries. On the other hand, only 25 percent of all Thai exports to the United States are covered by GSP provisions. And suspicion has been aroused among Thais that "GSPs are used as a stick to beat smaller countries into submission and they are likely to be withdrawn eventually."70/ The trade sanctions could probably have a negative effect on U.S. investors in Thailand, particularly pharmaceutical firms. Public opinion in Thailand is divided. Certain private sector groups like the Thai Bankers Association, the Federation of Thai Industries, and the Board of Trade are in favor of a fast approach to resolve the trade dispute. On the other side are local pharmaceutical firms (in which some influential legislators hold stakes) who oppose a patent reform, and student groups and trade unions who are against a copyright revision.71/ There might be fear among Thais that enhanced protection of intellectual property protection will drive a whole (counterfeiting) industry out of business, causing unemployment and increasing consumer prices. However, the only solution to this dilemma seems to be the development of a technologically advanced industry with the aid of foreign capital as envisaged by the Thai government. This new industry would create new employment and require higher skills thus increasing wages and per capita income which would in turn make the labor-intensive, low-wage counterfeit industry obsolete.

CONCLUSIONS

As can be seen from the country case studies, the regulatory framework of technology transfer and intellectual property protection in a particular country gains significance as it reaches a certain level of economic development, receives increasing foreign investment flows, and becomes a partner in international trade.

All countries studied have reached a considerable level of economic development; however, their regulatory framework of technology transfer and intellectual property protection differs (more v. less restrictive) depending on their economic policies towards (high-tech) foreign direct investment, indigenous development and their dependency on foreign trade partners (Singapore: least restrictive; Taiwan, Thailand: middle; Korea: more restrictive). That means that the more a country successfully promotes foreign direct investment and indigenous industrial development in the high technology field, and the more its economy is export-oriented, the more likely it is that, out of self-interest, the country will grant extensive protection of intellectual property rights (Korea, Taiwan, Singapore: patents, copyrights, trademarks). However, there is no easy causal link between these economic factors and the level of intellectual property protection. Conflicting domestic political interests especially in the early stages of fast economic growth, reluctance toward foreign pressure (for example, Thailand), and fear of foreign domination may play a role too in how intellectual property laws are designed or not designed at all.

But intellectual property protection could, in conjunction with a broader economic development policy (e.g., incentives against nonworking of patents and financial support for local research facilities):

1. attract capital-intensive, high technology foreign investment (licensing agreements, joint ventures) and
2. promote local R&D e.g., software development in the copyright area and small inventions (utility models) in the manufacturing sector in the area of patents.

In the high technology field, the potential for intra-industry specialization may be widening between developed and developing countries as well as among developing countries, thus opening the doors for the latter to develop their own resources by cooperating with foreign investors and conducting local R&D. This in turn lays the foundation for mutually beneficial intellectual property protection. A good example is the software industry: software developers in industrialized countries look to developing countries not just as markets but also as sources of software development (i.e., conversions) because of low labor costs. Developing countries could then use their experience and develop software for their own markets as well as for markets abroad by exploiting market niches and taking advantage of their low labor costs.

In pursuing an integrated economic policy with emphasis on high technology industry, possible drawbacks of enhanced intellectual property protection, like declining exports, increasing unemployment, and price levels could probably be prevented or diminished (Taiwan, Singapore: no export decline or increased unemployment after enhancing protection of intellectual property protection).

However, if the traditional concept of intellectual property does not become obsolete altogether due to the rapid progress of new technologies, its satisfactory protection based on internationally recognized standards may still not be realized today or tomorrow: it probably will not be realized until the economic gap between developed and developing countries narrows further.

NOTES

1. See, Michael Lehmann, "The Theory of Property Rights and the Protection of Intellectual and Industrial Property," International Review of Industrial Property and Copyright Law, vol.16, no.5, (1985), pp. 525, 531 (hereinafter cited as IIC).

2. Robert P. Benko, Protecting Intellectual Property Rights (American Enterprise Institute, 1987), p. 19.

3. Ibid.; and Mary E. Mogee, Briefing Paper International Issues in Intellectual Property Rights, July 1988, p. 61, mimeo.

4. Carlos M. Correa, "Changes in the Industrial and Intellectual Property System and New Technologies," paper prepared for UNCTAD, December 1987, pp. 6-7, mimeo.

5. Raymond T. Nimmer and Patricia Krauthaus, "Classification of Computer Software for Legal Protection: International Perspectives," International Lawyer, vol. 21, no. 3, 1987, p. 750.

6. Benko, p. 28.

7. Bunn Nagara in US-ASEAN Trade, Current Issues and Future Strategies, ed. Pamela Sodhy (Malaysia: Malaysian Institute for American Studies, 1988), p. 294 (hereafter cited as US-ASEAN Trade).

8. Arman S. Kirim, "Reconsidering Patents and Economic Development: A Case Study of the Turkish Pharmaceutical Industry," World Development, vol. 13, no. 2, 1985, pp. 219-236.

9. Owen T. Adikibi, "The Multinational Corporation and Monopoly of Patents in Nigeria," World Development, vol. 13, no. 4, 1988, pp. 511-526.

10. Unauthorized copying of source or object code for purposes of teaching, analyzing, or evaluating the concepts, techniques or ideas embodied in the program. Gunda Schumann, "Copyrightability of Computer Programs and the Scope of their Protection under the ITC/Apple and the Whelan Case - Part II," Computer Law and Practice, vol. 4, no. 5, 1988, p. 145.

11. See, e.g. US case law (Whelan Case), Schumann, ibid.; and Commission of the European Communities, Green Paper on Copyright and the Challenge of Technology -- Copyright Issues Requiring Immediate Action (Brussels: June 1988), p. 183.

12. ICC Business World, July 1986, cited in Helena Stalson, Intellectual Property Rights and US Competitiveness in Trade (Washington D.C.: National Planning Association, 1987), p. 43.

13. US International Trade Commission, Foreign Protection of Intellectual Property Rights and the Effect on United States Industry and Trade (Washington D.C.: January 1988), p. viii (hereafter cited as ITC).

14. Ibid., p. xi.

15. "Thai Copyright War Divides Washington," Financial Times, February 27, 1989, p. 5.

16. United Nations, "Current Trends and Policies in the World Economy, World Economic Survey 1988 (New York: 1988), p. 142 (table VIII.2).

17. Nontariff Barriers, "Trade Licensing Rules Set to East in Korea," *Business Asia*, March 20, 1989, pp. 90-91; and Ministry of Finance, Republic of Korea, *Guideline for Foreign Investment*, December 1988, pp. 4-5, mimeo.

18. United States Trade Representative, *1989 National Trade Estimate Report on Foreign Trade Barriers* (Washington D.C.: 1989), p. 121 (cited as *Foreign Trade Barriers*).

19. *Business Asia*, ibid.; and "Korean Opportunities, Taiwanese Uncertainties Govern 1988 Investment," *Business Asia*, February 27, 1989, p. 66.

20. Lho Joo Hyoung, "Korea Seeks Quantum Leap," *Korea Business World*, November 1988, p. 42.

21. Office of the U.S. Trade Representative, *Fact Sheet "Special 301" on Intellectual Property* (Washington D.C.: May 25, 1989), p. 4.

22. USTR, *Foreign Trade Barriers*, p. 167.

23. See also, Business International Corp., *Investment, Licensing, and Trade - Taiwan*, March 1989, pp. 1-26 (now cited as *ILT*; *Business Asia*, January 25, 1988, p. 30; *Business Outlook Taiwan*, August 8, 1988, p. 258; *The 1989-90 Business Outlook for 14 Asia/Pacific Countries at a Glance*, January 9, 1989, pp. 12-13; ibid., February 27, 1989, p. 67; "Foreign Investment Allowed in Export/ Import Business," *East Asian Executive Reports*, September 1987, pp. 8-9.

24. *Business Asia*, March 20, 1989, p. 94; GSP benefits were withdrawn in 1988.

25. USTR, *Foreign Trade Barriers*, p. 172.

26. See also, "MNCs Looking at Thailand May Sense a Slight Chill in the Investment Climate," *Business Asia*, October 24, 1988, p. 345.

27. USTR, *Foreign Trade Barriers*, p. 169.

28. OECD, *International Technology Licensing: Survey Results* (Paris: 1987), pp. 32, 36.

29. Asia-Pacific Council of American Chambers of Commerce, reprinted in *Business Asia*, November 28, 1988, p. 1.

30. USTR, *Fact Sheet*, pp. 4,6-8.

31. See also, T.H. Lee, "Korea Licensing -- Past, Future," *Les Nouvelles*, March 1989, pp. 11-15; and "Licensing Regulations in 18 Nations," *Business International*, March 7, 1988, p. 69.

32. Law No. 1802 of August 3, 1966 as last amended by Law No. 3691 of December 31, 1983, and the Enforcement Decree of the Foreign Capital Inducement Act of September 24, 1966 as last amended June 25, 1987.

33. Public Notice No. 87-14 (September 12, 1987) issued by the Economic Planning Board.

34. R. Michael Gadbaw and Timothy J. Richards, Intellectual Property Rights, Global Consensus, Global Conflict? (Boulder, Colo.: Westview Press, 1988), pp. 297, 302.

35. "South Korea Raises Limit on Overseas Investment," Wall Street Journal, April 12, 1989, p. A8.

36. Law No. 2505 of February 8, 1973 as last amended by Law No. 3891 of December 31, 1986 (effective: July 1, 1987) [all articles cited hereafter are those of the Copyright Act].

37. Law No. 432, January 28, 1957 as amended by Law No. 3916, December 31, 1987 (effective: July 1, 1987) [all articles cited hereafter are those of the Copyright Act].

38. Computer Program Protection Act (No. 3920 of December 31, 1986; effective: July 1, 1987); Enforcement Decree of Computer Program Protection Act (No. 12,218 of July 24, 1987; effective on date of promulgation); Enforcement Regulations of Computer Program Protection Act (No. 328 of August 25, 1987; effective on date of promulgation) [all articles cited hereafter are those of the Computer Program Protection Act, unless otherwise indicated].

39. Law No. 71 of November 28, 1949 as last amended by Law No. 3892 of December 31, 1986 (effective July 1, 1987).

40. "Korea's New Trademark Law: Some Practical Considerations," East Asian Executive Reports, July 1987, p. 19 [all sections cited hereafter are those of the Trademark Act, unless otherwise indicated].

41. Law No. 3987 of 1986 (effective Jan. 1, 1987).

42. The United States and Japan, however, voted against the treaty since it contains quite favorable provisions for developing countries in regard to compulsory licensing, term of protection, and dispute settlement.

43. USTR, Fact Sheet, p. 4.

44. See also, Dae R. Chang, "Barriers to Enforcing Intellectual Property Right Legislation: The Case of Korea and the ASEAN Nations," in US-ASEAN Trade, pp. 296-309. See also, Gadbaw, pp. 298, 302-4, 307; ITC, pp. 3-2 to 3-12.

45. ILT, pp. 10-13.

46. One agreement probably to be concluded soon concerns a "Berne-type" copyright approach and the other one deals with copyright enforcement of performance rights of motion pictures, see, USTR, Fact Sheet, p. 4. In order to monitor the enforcement of those laws and bilateral agreements, Taiwan has been set on the USTR's "priority watch list" under the "Special 301" provisions of the US Trade Act 1988, ibid., p. 8.

47. Gadbaw, p. 359.

48. Patent Law of 1949 as last amended December 24, 1986 (effective: December 26, 1986) [all articles cited hereafter are those of the Patent Act].

49. Since Taiwan lacks diplomatic recognition by most countries and therefore is not a member of the Paris Convention, only nationals from countries having a bilateral agreement with Taiwan enjoy legal standing in Taiwanese courts. The US-Republic of China Friendship, Commerce and Navigation Treaty provides these rights for US nationals.

50. Copyright Act of 1928 as last amended July 10, 1985 (effective July 12, 1985) [all articles cited hereafter are those of the Copyright Act].

51. Currently, only the US, the UK, and Spain have copyright reciprocity with Taiwan. Taiwan is not a member of the Berne Convention or Universal Copyright Convention.

52. Entry into force: November 29, 1985 [all articles cited hereafter are those of the Trademark Act].

53. USTR, Foreign Trade Barriers, p. 166.

54. Apple Corporation filed several successful patent and copyright suits in Taiwan in recent years, see, Apple's Worldwide Product Protection Program, 1988, mimeo.

55. ILT, p. 12.

56. Registration of United Kingdom Act, 6 Sing. Stat., Ch. 206 (1976).

57. Act No. 12 of 1968.

58. The Copyright Act 1987 (Act No. 2 of January 26, 1987; entry into force: April 10, 1987); The Copyright (Records Royalty System) Regulations 1987 (No. S112 of 1987; entry into force: April 10, 1987); The Copyright Regulations 1987 (No. S117 of 1987; entry into force: April 10, 1987); The Copyright (Import Restrictions) Regulations 1987 (No. S118 of 1987; entry into force: April 10, 1987) [all sections cited hereafter are those of the Copyright Act].

59. The burden of proof is also on the copyright holder in case of infringing imports, see Sec.32. For further comments, Gadbaw, pp. 332-333.

60. Gadbaw, pp. 337-338.

61. US International Trade Commission, The Effects of Foreign Product Counterfeiting on US Industry, USITC Publ. 1479 (January 1984), p. 82.

62. "Singapore steals the Headlines," The Wall Street Journal, March 30, 1988; see also, Chang, in US-ASEAN Trade, pp. 304-305.

63. Business Asia, October 24, 1988, p. 345.

64. Patent Act B.E. 2522 (1979) (effective: September 12, 1979), and Ministerial Regulations B.E.2522 (effective: November 5,1979) [all articles cited hereafter are those of the Patent Act].

65. Copyright Act B.E. 2521 (1978), promulgated on December 11, 1978 [all sections cited hereafter are those of the Copyright Act].

66. Thailand's last accession to the Berne Convention for the substance part is the Berlin Act of 1908 and the Berne Additional Protocol of 1914; therefore, Thailand is bound to protect only copyrights of members of the Berne Convention who acceded to those early acts; under the national treatment clause of Art. 4 of the Berlin Act 1908, Thailand is bound to grant equal treatment to foreign copyrights of those selected members only; see, Sophon Ratanakorn (WIPO), The Judiciary and the Intellectual Property System in Thailand, WIPO doc. IP/ISB/86/14 (November 6, 1986), pp. 6-7.

67. Trademark Acts B.E. (1931) as amended by B.E. 2504(1961).

68. "Thai Moves to Beef up Outdated Copyright Law are Raising a Ruckus," Business Asia, June 1, 1987, p. 170.

69. *Financial Times*, January 27, 1989, p. 5 and "Country Monitor - Thailand," *Business International*, January 30, 1989, p. 32.

70. *Financial Times*, January 27, 1989, p. 5.

71. *Business Asia*, June 1, 1987, p. 170.

PART FOUR

International Comparisons

Developed Countries

10

New International Environment for Intellectual Property Rights

Ashoka Mody

INTRODUCTION

In the 1960s and early 1970s, many developing countries charged that the international intellectual property system was biased against them. Critics of the system argued that it gave monopoly rights to foreign holders of intellectual property without benefiting developing countries in any significant way. They demanded the rolling back of protection in selected areas.1/ Some countries (India, Brazil and Argentina) passed laws restricting the scope of intellectual property protection. The international system of protection was partially strengthened during the 1970s as more countries joined the two main conventions for intellectual property protection (the Paris Convention for patents and the Berne Convention for copyright protection). However, developing countries continued to attempt a reduction in standards of protection in the Paris Convention, though without any success. In the 1980s, the United States, with some support from other developed countries, has criticized the system as being too lax and has demanded substantial increases in protection. With all sides adopting inflexible positions, the stalemate is being resolved de facto by the unilateral trade actions of the United States.

It is common to ask whether developing countries might actually gain by increasing protection of intellectual property. Given that they are primarily users of technology, the answer is, at best, "perhaps." Short-term international pressures are such that developing countries have increased protection of intellectual property in recent years and will probably continue to do so. The phasing and extent of future protection, along with possible negotiating positions in international forums, are matters of importance.

However, these are not the issues considered in this paper. The focus here is on the underlying forces that have generated the demand for increased protection of intellectual property, the strength of the institutional mechanisms implementing increased protection, and an assessment of whether the demand for and supply of protection could become counterproductive.

Discussions centered on the North-South divide have become prominent. However, they deal with issues that are not the most important for the evolution of the world system of intellectual property protection. The central question is whether the system can protect the rights of an innovator without stifling the creativity of other innovators. This paper argues that the system so far has responded to some genuine (and other more questionable) needs for greater protection. However, the levels and mechanisms of protection are already becoming counterproductive in some areas. In the short run, actions stimulated by the North-South perspective are having real effects on developing countries' access to technology. In the long run, all countries will experience reduced growth if creativity is indeed stifled by current developments. At the present time, there is neither a theoretical basis nor an institutional capability for forging a worldwide consensus on appropriate levels and mechanisms of protection. Strangely, very little discussion has focused on the need to ensure a global productivity increase.

Chemical products, namely drugs and pharmaceuticals, have been the main source of contention in the past and continue to be important in the current debate. However, the intellectual property issues have attained prominence because of their encroachment into new areas: information technology and biotechnology.

The significance of intellectual property protection in the area of information technology and services goes well beyond the narrow confines of the sectors in which these services are produced. Particularly, information services will be most relevant as critical inputs in the production of other goods and services. Existing and emerging technologies -- artificial intelligence, computer-aided design and manufacture, shared networks, compact disk memories, desk-top publishing and computer editing of graphics and sound -- will all be relevant to numerous applications in developing countries.

Current protection trends could retard technical progress in information technology which depends upon a series of interrelated innovations. Access to complementary technologies is critical to developing new products and processes. Increasingly, the emerging system of intellectual property protection is being used to protect key technologies, and in some instances, the industry standard. Both of these factors limit access to complementary technologies. Questions addressed in this paper and their outlined answers are:

1. Why have perceptions regarding intellectual property changed, and how real are the changes? The major factor driving the change is the increasing research intensity of production.
2. Has intellectual protection become more effective and what are the mechanisms being used? Courts and governments are according greater affirmation to protection, particularly in the United States. The level of protection has almost certainly increased. Major firms have become active in policing infringements and taking legal action.
3. Have other forms of protection become less effective? Keener competition has shortened the period of advantage for the innovator. Japan and the East Asian industrializing countries in particular have shown themselves adept at copying and at reverse engineering. It is also no coincidence that the industries most stridently demanding intellectual property protection, pharmaceuticals and information industries, are also those experiencing an extremely high degree of competition.
4. Do internal brakes in the system limit the extent of protection accorded to innovations? Some brakes probably are just beginning to manifest themselves.

WHY THE HIGH PROFILE?

Intellectual property protection has acquired a high profile partly because of the dramatic stand-off between the United States and developing countries caused by U.S. trade actions. However, real issues are also involved. Investment in research and development (R&D) has accelerated worldwide; product life cycles have become shorter; protection of intellectual property by being a first-comer in the market or by being further along the learning curve has become more difficult as copying has become easier. The imperatives for privatizing information have extended beyond private individuals and firms to government agencies. Intellectual property protection is being sought not just for chemicals and pharmaceuticals but for electronics, information technologies, and biotechnology.

Rising Importance of R&D

In the past decade, production has become progressively more R&D intensive in the sense that the use of R&D relative to capital and labor inputs has increased sharply. This may be inferred from two pieces of evidence. First, since 1979, R&D expenditure has grown much more rapidly than gross domestic product (GDP) in all major OECD countries (Table 10.1). In the United States and France, the rise follows a decade of decline in the R&D/GDP ratio. The share of R&D being funded by the private business sector also has risen in all countries.2/

Second, at the same time, total factor productivity (TFP) growth in the United States has accelerated.3/ An increase in TFP growth implies that GDP in the United States has grown since 1979 at an increasingly rapid rate relative to capital and labor inputs. Although there is no firm evidence on acceleration of TFP growth in other OECD countries, the increase in the R&D/GDP ratios and positive TFP growth implies that production has become progressively more R&D-intensive in those countries also.

TABLE 10.1
National Expenditures on R&D a/ as a Percent of GNP b/

Year	France	West Germany	Japan	United Kingdom	United States
1970	1.91	2.06	1.85	2.07	2.57
1971	1.90	2.19	1.85	NA	2.42
1972	1.90	2.20	1.86	2.11	2.35
1973	1.76	2.09	1.90	NA	2.26
1974	1.79	2.13	1.97	NA	2.23
1975	1.80	2.22	1.96	2.19	2.20
1976	1.77	2.15	1.95	NA	2.19
1977	1.76	2.14	1.93	NA	2.15
1978	1.76	2.24	2.00	2.24	2.14
1979	1.81	2.40	2.09	NA	2.19
1980	1.84	2.42	2.22	NA	2.29
1981	2.01	2.44	2.38	2.41	2.35
1982	2.10	2.59	2.47	NA	2.51
1983	2.15	2.54	2.61	2.25	2.56
1984	2.25	2.52	2.61	NA	2.59
1985	2.31	2.67	2.77	2.42	2.69
1986	2.41	2.74	NA	NA	2.72
1987	NA	NA	NA	NA	2.77

Note: NA = Not available.
Note: The latest data may be preliminary or estimates. The figures for West Germany increased in 1979 in part because coverage as small and medium enterprises not surveyed prior to 1977.

a/ Gross expenditures for performance of R&D including associated expenditures for the United States where total capital expenditure data are not available. U.S. estimates for the period 1972-80 show that the inclusion of capital expenditures would have an impact of less than one percent of the R&D/GNP ratio.

b/ Gross domestic product is used for France.

Source: National Science Board 1987. Science & Engineering Indicators - 1987, Washington, D.C. - U.S. GPO.

Increase in the relative importance of R&D inputs could result from two factors: (1) increase in productivity of knowledge relative to other inputs such as capital and labor (Figure 10.1); and (2) increase in cost of producing knowledge (Figure 10.2). An increase in productivity leads to greater demand (an upward shift in the demand curve), resulting in more use of the knowledge input (k) relative to output (q) and a greater shadow price (p_k) of knowledge. When costs rise, the supply curve shifts up and the shadow price rises. In this case, the knowledge input will decline, but the total value of R&D expenditure (kxp_k) could increase if the demand for R&D is relatively inelastic.

It is likely that both these forces have been at work. In information technology sectors (computers, communication, and software) the marginal product of knowledge probably has risen, as the synergies between computer and communication technologies are being exploited and as greater availability of software is making better utilization of hardware possible. Englander, Evenson and Hanazaki have estimated the elasticity of output with respect to R&D capital for different sectors and subperiods. Their estimates show that elasticity increased in 1980-83 for machinery, instruments and equipment; these sectors encompass the information technology industries.4/

Table 10.2 shows that the share of "other manufacturing" in total U.S. R&D expenditure fell by 5 percent between 1979 and 1985. Electrical equipment (which includes telecommunications) and the machinery sector (which includes computers) have increased their shares. These increases are not dramatic, partly because the categories are very aggregated. However, the National Science Foundation has forecasted that even at this level of aggregation, the electrical equipment sector will further increase its share, particularly in R&D financed by private firms.5/ In addition, these estimates do not include expenditure on software development, which has grown at a rapid rate in the last decade. Patel and Soete argue that software development is similar in nature to conventional R&D and serves a similar purpose (principally product development but in some cases also process technology development).6/

FIGURE 10.1
Increased Demand for Knowledge because of Increased Knowledge Productivity

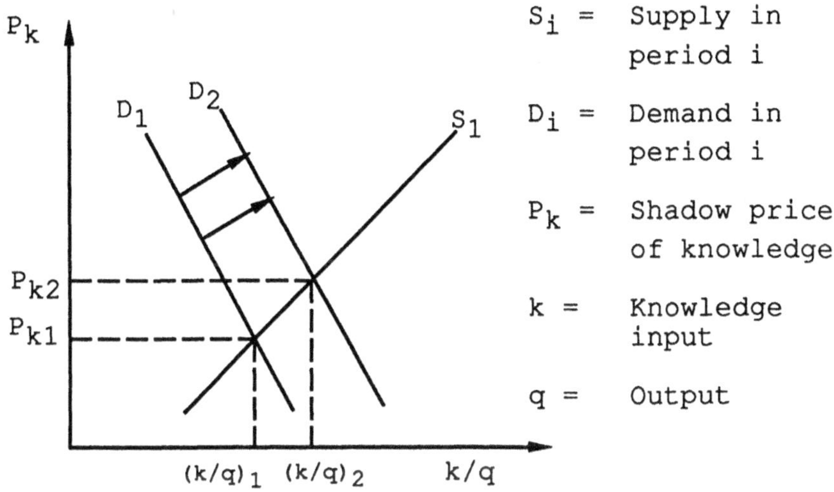

FIGURE 10.2
Increase in R & D Costs of Knowledge Production

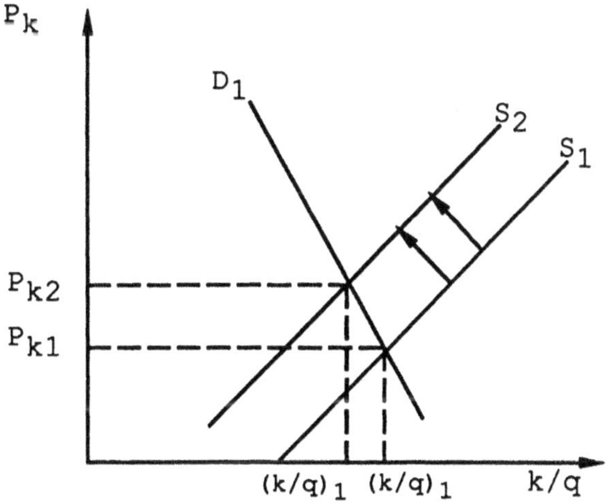

TABLE 10.2
Sectoral Shares in U.S. R&D

YEAR:	1975	1979	1981	1983	1985
CHEMICALS	11	11	11	12	11
MACHINERY (COMPUTERS)	13	13	13	13	14
ELECTRICAL EQUIPMENT	21	20	20	22	22
AIRCRAFT & MISSILES	24	21	23	22	23
INSTRUMENTS	5	7	7	7	7
OTHER MANUFACTURING	23	25	22	21	20
NON MANUFACTURING	3	4	4	3	4

Source: National Science Board 1987. Science & Engineering Indicators - 1987, Washington D.C. - U.S. GPO.

In contrast, in the chemical industry the principal change has been the increased cost of knowledge production, shifting the supply curve upwards.7/ Since new knowledge of products and processes is critical to maintaining profitability and market share, firms have been forced to increase R&D expenditures.

To summarize, the role of R&D has increased significantly over the last decade in all major manufacturing sectors. The reasons and their relative importance have varied across sectors. The area of information technology, defined to include computers, communications and software development has offered relatively high marginal returns to R&D and therefore has attracted greater R&D expenditures. The chemical industry has faced increasing costs of knowledge production, and firms have had to expend more funds for R&D to remain competitive. Both patterns have led, however, to a higher "price of knowledge."

Ease of Imitation

The price of knowledge is easy to define conceptually but is hard to measure empirically. When knowledge is sold embodied in a product, the price is not observed directly. Competition in the product market limits the returns to R&D. Flamm notes that in the past benefits of technical progress in the computer industry have been largely passed on to consumers.8/ Competition results from the independent research efforts of the different firms and also from the ability of competitors to imitate. Protection of intellectual property in products is a means of reducing such competition. The force of competition can also be weakened if a firm possesses technology that is a step ahead of its rivals.

When knowledge is sold as knowledge, it is difficult to realize the appropriate shadow price. One study concluded that the licensor of technology could only hope to get between one-third and one-half of the shadow price.9/ A well-known difficulty arises because the seller has to convince the buyer of the value of the technology; in doing so, the seller risks revealing the key innovations of the technology. Another problem arises because the value of the technology changes over time as complementary and substitute technologies appear. If the buyer and the seller have different perceptions about the evolution of the value of the technology, extraction of the shadow price becomes even more difficult.

Given the inherent difficulties in realizing the price of knowledge, either through sale of products or directly through sale of knowledge, the problem is compounded when potential competitors are also good "imitators." When imitation is swift, being first in the market is not a major advantage. Research by Mansfield shows that "...information concerning development decisions is generally in the hands of rivals within about twelve to eighteen months, on the average, and information concerning the detailed nature and operation of a new product or process generally leaks out within about a year."10/ The ability to use this information depends upon the competence of the imitator such as can be found in a number of Western and Japanese firms. South Korea and Taiwan have demonstrated that they can imitate efficiently. Other countries with significant industrial literacy (Brazil, India, Indonesia, China, Mexico, Thailand) are potential imitators.

With knowledge becoming a more important input, with imitation being relatively easy and more widespread as the number and competence of potential imitators increases, and with product cycles becoming shorter, it is no surprise that firms are seeking new ways of protecting their intellectual property. Recent evidence shows that firms are increasingly resorting to so-called alliances to share technology.11/ In such alliances often no money changes hands. Firms pool complementary technologies to exploit synergies (particularly in the early phases of the product cycle). They also form joint ventures or merge to exploit economies of scale in R&D (particularly during the later phases of the product cycle).

In addition, firms are seeking greater intellectual property protection through legal mechanisms. The Conference Board questioned 164 firms (130 U.S., 5 Canadian and 29 European) regarding their attitudes to intellectual property protection. Their responses were as follows:

1. Half said that they were engaged by themselves or through industry groups in strengthening domestic and international intellectual property protection mechanisms.
2. Two-thirds were engaged in intellectual property litigation.
3. Two-thirds use noncompetition or nondisclosure contracts to prevent employees from carrying away valuable company secrets.12/

It is possible and likely that the sample of firms that responded to the survey was biased. However, the responding firms were all large (median sales were $2 billion) and hence likely to be influential in mobilizing industry support toward their viewpoints. In the discussion below it is shown that a few key firms are having a major influence on the evolution of the intellectual property regime.

Privatization of Information

A related trend is the movement towards privatization of information once provided freely or at low cost to firms and individuals. The privatization, in turn, is leading either to lack of availability of technology or higher costs. Bell Laboratories, part of AT&T, was a significant source of "free" technology until 1984. The transistor and the UNIX operating system are two examples of major technologies to emerge from Bell Laboratories and made available at very low cost to anyone who sought them. Bell Labs acted as a major public laboratory providing a public good.

Since the breakup of AT&T in 1984, the situation has changed.13/ Research at Bell Labs has focused increasingly toward the internal needs of AT&T. Major innovations are controlled to a much greater extent for potential commercialization. An example is AT&T's attempt to privatize further developments of UNIX. Another example is the manner in which "Karmakar's algorithm" has been handled. As is well known, Karmakar developed a potentially revolutionary method of solving linear programming problems. Many of the details of this algorithm have not been made public because AT&T is developing its own applications that use the algorithm.

The significance of Bell Labs' privatization probably goes beyond the technology it has generated; as a major supplier of technology, Bell Labs also influenced the price at which others could sell their technology. For many years, the royalty rate payable in the electronics industry was 1 percent of the sales value of the product.14/ It is speculated that the 1 percent rate had become a "focal point" in the industry partly because that was the rate charged by Bell Laboratories. As described below, royalty rates have increased significantly since 1984.

Government agencies, which traditionally supplied data at low cost, are beginning to seek larger compensation for their data. "'Government agencies are getting greedy with their data'" according to Robert Gellman, staff director of the Government Operations Subcommittee on Government Information, U.S. House of Representatives.15/ The State of New York makes available its paper printouts of legal statutes relatively cheaply but charges a high price for computer access. Similarly the National Institutes of Health allow free access to bibliographic databases on paper but charge royalties for electronic access. The National Technical Information Service and the National Library of Medicine have been mandated to become self-supporting through user fees. The U.S. Federal government is prohibited from copyrighting its data, a situation that could change, but many state governments have recourse to copyright protection. Since the federal government is a large generator of data, any change in copyright prohibition is a matter of special concern both to users and to private providers of information services.

MECHANISMS FOR INTELLECTUAL PROPERTY PROTECTION IN THE UNITED STATES

Mechanisms to protect intellectual property have evolved in response to the forces described. The United States' domestic patent laws and their implementation processes have been strengthened. The U.S. has also seen the development of case law in the area of information technology (software and databases) which has proved particularly difficult to protect. Although case law has evolved in an uncoordinated manner, the general direction of change has been towards substantially increased protection. Trends in the United States do not necessarily create international legitimacy -- in the past, the United States has been a "technology pirate" of significance.16/ However, since the United States is such a large technology market, current U.S. trends have implications for the international system. In many areas, U.S. case law is not only the most developed but is the only case law.

For the United States, the spillover from the domestic to the international arena of tougher intellectual property protection is highly desirable since it continues to be a net exporter of technology. Hence, both in defining the internationally acceptable "minimum standards of protection" and in evolving legislation for specific sectors, the U.S. has taken the lead. In particular, the U.S. has used trade policy instruments with some effect. The next section focuses on developments in the U.S.; the following section treats the use of trade policy for protecting intellectual property.

Patent Protection in the United States

Antitrust considerations held priority in the U.S. for many decades while judicial process viewed intellectual property with suspicion. Only between 30 and 40 percent of patents challenged in courts were upheld.17/ Restrictive practices to protect intellectual property were regarded as inadmissible per se. This has given way to the "rule of reason" and hence a more liberal interpretation of the rights of intellectual property holders.

Further, in 1982 a new Court of Appeals for the Federal Circuit (CAFC) was set up to decide on patent cases. Previously, appeals were heard in eleven Circuit Courts of Appeal. Decisions were inconsistent among the eleven courts, some regarded as especially biased against intellectual property holders. As a result, much effort was expended in determining the "right" court in which to have one's case heard. Decisions often took as much as three years out of the seventeen year life of a patent.

The CAFC has created a unified patent case law. The CAFC has also been basically pro-patent. The grant of a patent requires that the discovery be nonobvious and novel; the CAFC has lowered the standards required to establish novelty. The CAFC also has awarded high damages to patent holders. It has shown a willingness to permit criminal rather than civil cases against intellectual property offenders (IBM v. Hitachi). In at least one instance, the CAFC has required the infringing firm (Kodak) to exit the industry rather than merely pay royalties to the patent holder (Polaroid). The effect of these decisions has trickled down to lower courts which are using the criteria and precedents set by CAFC. Recent estimates are that 70 percent of patents are now being held valid, increasing the value of the patent to the patent holder.18/

Finally, administrative rulings of the U.S. Patent and Trademark Office also have extended patent protection on intellectual property, especially in the area of biotechnology and information technology.

Protection of Information Technology

Two information technology areas of special interest to developing countries are databases, especially those relying on compilations of non-copyright materials and software. Information technology has proved difficult to protect through existing mechanisms. Patents traditionally have been the most important mechanism for protecting commercially useful technology. The requirements for patenting have proved to be too stringent for some newer technologies, however. Computer programs, databases, and semiconductor layouts are not sufficiently novel or sufficiently nonobvious to be patentable. A broad consensus developed that neither programs nor databases could be protected adequately by patents; trade secrets were similarly thought to be ineffective. Almost by default, therefore, copyrights became the chosen form of protection. To the software developer, copyrights have considerable appeal over patents since the process of obtaining a copyright is shorter, cheaper, and requires no disclosure of the underlying method or procedure. However, recent rulings by the Patent and Trademark Office have raised once again the possibility that patents could be used to protect some aspects of information technology.

Copyright case law has evolved to give increasing protection to databases and software. Copyrights were designed primarily to protect creative expression (i.e., how an idea or a thought is stated) and not the underlying idea. If it is determined that idea and expression are inseparable, protection by copyright becomes unavailable. Therefore, protection by copyright requires ingenuity in defining "expression" and "idea."

Expression in the computer context was initially considered to be the computer program and the contents of a database. Recent judgments have become increasingly liberal in interpreting what constitutes expression. These judgments (Williams v. Arndt 19/ and West Publishing Company v. Mead Data Central Inc. 20/) have noted the need for protecting and rewarding the investment of the intellectual property holder. They have moved case law toward greater protection of methods and concepts, thus bringing copyright law closer to patent law.

In a key case, Whelan v. Jaslow 21/, the reach of copyright law has been extended. Whelan produced a computer program to manage Jaslow's dental laboratory. Jaslow then developed a new version of the program and sold it to dental prosthetic firms. The court ruled that Whelan's copyright had been infringed. In this case, although the computer instructions had not been copied, the file structures, screen outputs and key subroutines performed in a very similar manner. The court ruled that "structure, sequence, and organization" of the computer program constituted expression. The "idea" was ruled to be "the efficient organization of a dental laboratory."

At the same time, many firms are seeking protection of their innovations through patents. Here also, a relaxation of criteria, such as the nonobviousness requirement, has been occurring. The number of patent applications for protecting software has grown several-fold in recent years. In 1980, the Patent Office started granting patents to software programs that were considered part of a process. It is not difficult to make the case that the program is part of a process and the applications apparently reflect that.22/ In 1989, the Patent and Trademark Office has issued a large number of software patents, suggesting the possibility that in the future patents may be easier to obtain than in the past. A spate of new patent applications has followed.

The relative role of patents and copyrights in protecting information technology in the future is unclear. Patents provide greater protection; however, as described above, copyright case law has evolved to provide strong protection also. Patents have been harder to attain, a situation that also seems to be changing. Under either method, protection for information technology has substantially increased over the years in the U.S. The question now is whether protection has become excessive.

U.S. TRADE POLICY AND INTELLECTUAL PROPERTY PROTECTION

The United States has tied the intellectual property issue to international trade. The strength of the U.S. commitment to intellectual property protection derives from the perception that it has a comparative advantage in technology generation. The U.S. has for many years been by far the world's largest exporter of disembodied technology (measured by the royalties from patent and knowledge licensing). In surveys conducted by the United States International Trade Commission (USITC), U.S. producers have reported large losses from intellectual property infringement by foreigners; in 1986, over $40 billion in losses were reported. These reports reflect subjective evaluation of losses and are not entirely believable. However, the industry distribution of these losses (Table 10.3) is interesting because it is largely consistent with the pattern associated with the productivity and cost of R&D, as described earlier and illustrated in Table 10.2.

TABLE 10.3
Industry Distribution of Losses due to Intellectual Property Infringement Reported by U.S. Firms, 1986

	PERCENT=100
SCIENTIFIC AND PHOTOGRAPHIC GOODS	21
COMPUTERS AND SOFTWARE	17
ELECTRONICS	10
MOTOR VEHICLES AND PARTS	9
PHARMACEUTICALS	8
OTHERS	38

Source: U.S. International Trade Commission 1988, Investigation No. 323-245, Washington D.C., USITC, p. 4-2.

Two aspects of U.S. trade policy are relevant to the intellectual property discussion. In the last decade, but particularly since 1984, the United States has broadened its definition of the foreign policies and actions considered unfair to the U.S. both under U.S. trade law and under GATT articles.23/ At the same time, the U.S. also has moved toward settling its trade disputes through bilateral discussions and unilateral actions.24/

The broader interpretation of domestic and international trade laws to include remedies for intellectual property infringement is consistent with this general trend. Specifically, violation of U.S. intellectual property is viewed as "unfair trade" and is liable to retaliation under Section 301 of the Trade Act (1974) and Section 337 of the Tariff Act (1930). (As will be described shortly, U.S. interpretation of GATT articles in this context has been less successful.)

Section 337 is designed to protect U.S. firms from unfair competition from imports. Despite its mandate to cover the broad area of unfair competition, it has been used primarily for protection against infringement of intellectual property (Table 10.4). Section 337 comes into play when products imported into the United States violate the intellectual property held by U.S. firms or individuals.

Section 301 is more broad-based. Under this section, the U.S. administration can take action against inadequate protection of its intellectual property in other countries. No import into the United States is required for taking action under Section 301.

The Trade and Tariff Act of 1984 created formal tools to improve intellectual property protection by other countries. The Trade and Tariff Act strengthened Section 301 actions by explicitly designating weak intellectual property protection as an appropriate basis for withdrawing concessions under the General System of Privileges (GSP) and increasing tariffs on goods imported from the offending country. The GSP is a means by which the U.S. and other developed countries may waive duties on certain imports from selected developing countries. Four countries, Korea, Mexico, Brazil and Thailand, have been affected by this legislation.

TABLE 10.4
Outcome of Section 337 Cases

Year of Initiation	Total No. of §337 Cases	No. of Patent & Copyright Infringement Cases	Decision (% of total no. of cases)			
			No Infringement	§337 Violation	Settlement	Ongoing
1974	16	13	25.0	18.8	56.3	0.0
1975	5	4	0.0	0.0	100.0	0.0
1976	7	5	57.1	28.6	14.3	0.0
1977	11	10	27.3	36.4	36.4	0.0
1978	23	19	43.5	34.8	21.7	0.0
1979	14	12	28.6	21.4	50.0	0.0
1980	18	17	5.6	22.2	72.2	0.0
1981	17	14	11.8	35.3	52.9	0.0
1982	22	17	40.9	18.2	40.9	0.0
1983	44	37	27.3	31.8	40.9	0.0
1984	33	27	18.2	12.1	69.7	0.0
1985	25	19	28.0	16.0	56.0	0.0
1986	24	22	25.0	4.2	62.5	8.3
1987	18	14	16.7	16.7	66.7	0.0
1988	11	9	9.1	0.0	45.5	45.5
1989*	6	5	0.0	0.0	0.0	100.0

*Jan.-Feb.

Source: Compiled from U.S. International Trade Commission §337 Investigations since the Trade Act of 1974, Washington, D.C.

The Omnibus Trade and Competitiveness Act of 1988 has further increased the importance of intellectual property in U.S. trade legislation. Essentially, the United States Trade Representative (USTR) is now required to be more of an activist than in the past; timetables for investigations and actions have been clearly specified. Under the so-called "super-301" the U.S. Trade Representative will be required to identify foreign countries that have inadequate and ineffective intellectual property regimes and that deny market access to firms and persons whose intellectual property is protected. Such countries are to be declared "priority" countries; negotiations with the countries and suitable actions are required within short time periods.

Section 337 of the 1930 Tariff Act has been strengthened also. The requirement to prove injury to a domestic industry claiming patent infringement has been eliminated. Although the existence of a domestic industry will still be a requirement for excluding imports that infringe domestic patents, the definition of what constitutes an industry has been expanded.

Actions Under Section 337

Section 337 has in the past been used primarily by small U.S. firms against small foreign firms, particularly when it was difficult to identify the offending firm. Section 337 cases are filed before the United States International Trade Commission (USITC), which is required to take no more than twelve months (no more than eighteen months in more complicated cases) to reach a decision. The provisions of Section 337 were strengthened in 1979, and the Section was used often in the early 1980s (Table 10.4). Reliance on Section 337 fell in 1987 and 1988 in anticipation of strengthened provisions. Judging from the first two months of 1989, Section 337 has become popular again.

A U.S. firm appealing under Section 337 has less than a one-third probability of losing its case (see column for "no infringement" in Table 10.4). A violation under Section 337 results in exclusion of the foreign product from the U.S. markets unless the infringing firm enters into a licensing agreement with the intellectual property holder. In recent years, foreign firms generally have preferred to settle directly with U.S. firms by paying royalties for the use of the patent or copyright before the USITC hands down a decision.

Firms cited in Section 337 cases have originated most often from Japan and Taiwan, followed by West Germany, Canada, and Great Britain. Firms from these five countries can imitate effectively -- even a "technology pirate" needs certain technological capabilities. Other developing countries, including India, Mexico, and Brazil, have not been cited for significant violations which are worth noting. The number of Korean firms cited in intellectual property cases under Section 337 is not large (14); however, two recent cases have resulted in a significant Protection of Information Technology setback to major Korean companies. These actions are part of the trend for big U.S. firms to use Section 337 against large foreign firms.

Investigations of Foreign Property Systems

The United States is reported to have held discussions with more than sixty countries on intellectual property protection. The only developed country that has raised U.S. concerns is Japan. Discussions are initiated by the United States Trade Representative (USTR) who is a part of the executive office of the President. Actual investigations under Section 301 have been undertaken in Korea, Brazil, and Thailand. Brazil has been subject to two investigations: one initiated in 1985 dealt with the larger issue of Brazil's computer policy but included copyright protection of software and a second initiated in 1988 on inadequate protection of pharmaceuticals. The former USTR, Clayton Yeutter, has claimed that in addition to these three countries, intellectual property protection improved in Taiwan, Singapore, Indonesia, and Chile as a result of informal discussions.

The main objectives of the United States have been to: (1) increase the minimum level of protection; (2) protect software through the copyright mechanism; (3) change procedures that create risks in applying for patents; and (4)phase in the needed changes rapidly. The United States has also steadfastly refused to grant any quid pro quo for increased intellectual property protection in a developing country. In effect, the U.S. attitude has been close to regarding intellectual property protection as a natural right.

A major concern of the U.S. has been that, in addition to processes, products should also be patentable. If only the process is patented, a competing firm can claim that it has "reverse engineered" the product by developing an alternative process. A product patent blocks this avenue for reverse engineering; an alternate process becomes insufficient because the product concept itself is protected. The U.S. has also been pressing for elimination of compulsory licensing clauses which require the patent or copyright holder to license the intellectual property when it is considered of special importance or when it is not being used for production.

Regarding patent protection of products, compulsory licensing, and software protection through copyrights, no internationally accepted standards exist. Compulsory licensing requirements are a common feature in many countries, including Japan.25/ Japan also resisted protection of software through copyrights, before giving in to U.S. pressure.

Many U.S. firms have claimed that the Japanese patent system is unfair to innovators. Under the Japanese system, the patent award procedure can be long because objections to the patent from interested parties are considered very seriously. However, eighteen months after the patent application, the substance of the application (and hence the concept, plus an outline of its implementation) is made public without any assurance of a patent award. U.S. firms have argued that this procedure makes patenting in Japan very risky.26/

Many developing countries have agreed on the need for according greater protection to intellectual property-holders. They have argued, however, that a gradual phasing in of protection would be appropriate to balance the conflicting interests of innovators and consumers, the assumption being that most innovators currently are foreign but that over the years domestic innovation will increase. The

U.S. has not been convinced and has taken the stand that foreign intellectual property systems should be remedied quickly. Confrontation with Mexico in 1986 centered on this question.27/

Penalties for noncompliance with U.S. requirements have included the withdrawal of Thailand's GSP privileges (resulting in a 5-10 percent import duty increase on $165 million worth of Thai exports) and imposition of 100 percent duties on $39 million worth of Brazil's exports. These exports are not related to products or sectors in which infringement of intellectual property is alleged. Punitive tariffs on $105 million worth of Brazilian exports were also proposed as sanctions against the Brazilian computer policy; however, a series of concessions, including the passing of a law that made software protectable by copyright, resulted in suspension of that action. Exporters in Thailand and Brazil have said they can live with the increased duties, which are not high. However, in Brazil, the duties could dampen the future growth of consumer electronics, a sector in which Brazil was hoping to make a major effort. In Thailand, the cost of the loss of GSP has been political tension contributing to the change of government. Of the three countries investigated under Section 301 (Korea, Thailand and Brazil), only Korea was not penalized. Korea changed its laws quickly to satisfy U.S. criteria. However, the conclusion of the Section 301 investigations has not meant an end to U.S. friction with Korea. Complaints from U.S. firms about claim interpretation, possible discrimination, and inadequate sanctions against violators have continued. U.S. companies have requested further Section 301 investigations of the inability to enforce patent rights in Korea. These complaints are actually being investigated under Section 305 of the 1974 Trade Act.

The use of "super-301" under the Omnibus Trade and Competitiveness Act of 1988 has been initiated. Japan, Brazil, and India have been named "priority" countries, though intellectual property was not used as a consideration in their being so designated. However, twenty-five countries have been placed on the "watch" list, with eight being on "priority-watch." Negotiations with these countries are expected to be concluded before the end of 1989. Intensive negotiations are likely even with countries such as Korea and Taiwan, which have made changes in their legal systems.

Multilateralism v. Bilateralism

In the short-run, bilateralism is proving more effective than multilateral efforts in furthering U.S. interests. Bilateralism is quicker and allows more focused and tailored responses.28/ Using its domestic laws, the U.S. is pushing a series of changes in the intellectual property legislation of a number of countries. In other areas of trade policy also, the United States has found bilateral (and even plurilateral) actions more effective than cumbersome multilateral efforts.

If the primary effect of U.S. initiatives is movement toward greater specialization in accordance with comparative advantage, everyone should be better off. That would be the case if the U.S. and other industrialized countries were assumed to be proficient in the production of technology and if the less developed countries were users only. If greater protection of intellectual property led to increased productivity and new products, the producers and users would all gain.

The main argument against bilateralism is its arbitrary and discretionary nature. By deciding on its own which countries to punish and how to punish them, the U.S. could well be distorting international trade. The initial Korean reaction to the Section 301 investigations was to grant protection to technology originating in the United States but deny it to all others. Since then, under the pressure of the European Community, protection has been extended to European firms, though some differences in retroactive protection still remain. More serious, however, is the U.S. imposition of standards and modes of intellectual property protection that have not been established as either the most effective or the most desirable methods of protection. If bilateralism is a mechanism for setting standards and precedents that could be used for an eventual multilateral accord, the inefficiency of these standards will be perpetuated. The short-term U.S. viewpoint is that some form of protection rather than none is desirable. But it is not necessarily good for everyone and is perhaps counterproductive for the U.S. in the long-run (as will be discussed later).

CORPORATE FIGHT AGAINST COPYING

Small and large companies have become equally aggressive in fighting alleged infringement of intellectual property. In some ways small firms with high dependence on innovative technology have more to lose from infringement than larger, better-established firms. (However, it is the actions of large firms that are sending signals on the competitive importance of intellectual property.) These same firms also have considerable influence on the setting of royalty rates. For example, IBM has taken a very strong stand on protection of its intellectual property.

IBM Leads the Crusade

IBM is establishing that it will pursue defense of its intellectual property vigorously. IBM has initiated and won cases against both large and small competitors. In terms of dollars, IBM's greatest success has been against Fujitsu of Japan. The Japanese company infringed on IBM's copyrighted software programs in the 1970s to develop mainframe computers compatible with those produced by IBM. In 1982, IBM initiated legal action. After a protracted process, it has been determined that Fujitsu should pay $833 million for infringement up to the present time (Fujitsu has already paid $437 million). However, the arbitration process also determined that Fujitsu should be allowed continued access to IBM's software. The access will be limited to knowing "what IBM's new software does, but not how it does it". For this privilege, Fujitsu will pay IBM between $26 and $51 million every year, the exact amount depending upon the precise use of the facility.29/

The royalty payments from Fujitsu to IBM are large in absolute amounts but modest in relation to the sales of the two companies. The implication for the future lies in the signals to other companies planning on a strategy of copying and in the potential decline in competition.

IBM is the world's largest producer of mainframe computers and by virtue of that position also sets the standards for the operations of these machines. By partially sharing its future software development with Fujitsu, IBM has reduced its monopoly control over the market. However, the agreement with Fujitsu will further strengthen the IBM standard and IBM will, therefore, continue substantially to determine the pace of technical progress in the area of mainframe computers. Entry barriers for other computer manufacturers will continue to be high. The other major mainframe producer, Hitachi of Japan, has not been included in the IBM/Fujitsu agreement. Similarly, many U.S. producers will continue to be denied access to IBM system software.

As the world's largest computer company, IBM dominates the mainframe market but also holds key technologies relevant for very different types of computers. In a statement unlikely to win high marks for modesty, IBM recently announced: "anybody who is developing an information-handling system probably needs to use an IBM patent."30/ IBM has "informed" several companies of its patent claims in personal computers and RISC (reduced instruction set computer) systems. Both are areas of high growth. IBM claims it holds twelve key patents on RISC technology and has applied for 100 more.

IBM has also been extremely aggressive toward small companies both in the United States and abroad. It has initiated numerous infringement cases from which it can expect very little immediate compensation in the form of royalties. For example, by the end of 1987 IBM had been involved in eighty court and police actions in Taiwan and earned damages of only $650,000; on the conservative assumption that each case cost $10,000 to prosecute, IBM suffered a net loss on these cases. IBM has also taken several court actions for copyright infringement in Singapore and Hong Kong.31/ In Europe, IBM has traditionally not resorted to court action but has relied on persuasion. However, in mid-1988, as a part of its general intellectual property protection drive, IBM sued Bit Computers, the fourth largest supplier of IBM PC-compatible machines in Italy, for copyright infringement. The case was decided in favor of IBM.32/ The purpose of these cases is more to send a signal about the seriousness with which IBM is going to protect intellectual property than to collect royalties. For small companies such threats are becoming increasingly credible. A number of firms in East Asia and Europe have closed down or significantly modified their business as a result of IBM actions. Thus far Korea has been the least affected of the newly industrializing East Asian economies because large Korean firms have had to comply with internationally acceptable protection norms in order to sell their products through major retail channels in the United States and Europe. However, IBM's new patent policy is likely to have a significant impact on the Koreans.

IBM has substantially increased royalty rates and extended its patent claims. Royalty rates have been raised from a maximum of 1 percent to a maximum of 5 percent. The current royalty rate on IBM's AT machines is 3 percent, but royalties on PS/2 machines are likely to rise to 5 percent.

Most infringement cases in the past have been for copying application software, the Basic Input-Output System and IBM cabinets. Now IBM is also seeking to define more clearly its rights on the new PS/2 series of microcomputers. IBM has kept proprietary the micro channel architecture (MCA) of the PS/2 and is using that leverage to demand royalty payments from potential "clone" producers.

More intriguingly, IBM is demanding retroactive royalty payments on the venerable IBM-PC.33/ It seems that firms are paying IBM an MCA initiation fee based on past PC sales. The PC was designed using standard, off-the-shelf components. Since these components were not designed by IBM and were widely available, a number of clone producers emerged who created the industry standard. However, the question now being raised is whether "cloning" constitutes intellectual property infringement despite ready availability of individual, underlying components. If that turns out to be the case, IBM would have succeeded in having its cake and eating it too. Cloning helped create an international standard from which IBM benefited enormously; now that the standard is established and many "cloners" are producing PCs more advanced than IBM's, royalty receipts are clearly welcome.

Korean Experience with Technology Acquisition

In the 1970s, Korea sought steel technology for its Pohang Iron and Steel Co. (POSCO). The initial purchase of technology was from Japanese firms; however, when POSCO showed signs of international success, the Japanese refused to sell any more technology. Korea was strategically well-positioned and managed to play the major international firms off each other. In the end, POSCO gained know-how from several firms, including Japanese firms.

The current situation is different. Korea is looking for technology in areas such as electronics. Semiconductor production has received a particular boost in Korea. The leading Korean semiconductor producer, Samsung, bought the basic process technology from Micron Technology of the United States. However, Samsung was sued by Texas Instruments, another U.S. firm, for violation of several patents.34/

The Samsung/TI case contains two points of interest. First, Texas Instruments also sued seven Japanese companies on the same charges at the same time. These seven companies have reportedly paid a total of $200 million, an average of less than $30 million per firm. Samsung paid over $90 million.35/ The Japanese firms had several patents of their own and were able to negotiate cross-licensing agreements and thus lower the amount of royalty payments to Texas Instruments.

Second, it is no longer easy to play one company off another. Samsung had been clever in going to the financially weak Micron Technology for its original infusion of technology. However, the protection of intellectual property in this area is very extensive and is covered by literally thousands of patents. It is, therefore, not possible to license technology from a single firm. Besides Texas Instruments, Samsung has also been sued by Standard Microsystems, which has won a temporary injunction preventing Samsung from seeking new customers for certain kinds of chips.36/

At the same time, a few large firms control substantial blocks of patents and hence exercise considerable power over the terms on which technology is available. Texas Instruments has stated: "We think it is pretty impossible to make DRAM chips without using one of our patents."37/

DANGERS AND RESTRAINTS

As noted, the pendulum in the United States has moved away from antitrust towards greater intellectual property protection. Driven largely by the actions of U.S. firms and the U.S. government, the international pendulum also is moving steadily towards greater intellectual property protection and away from controlling excessive monopoly power. In the national context, the pendulum is perhaps an appropriate metaphor because self-correcting forces eventually reverse the direction of the swing.38/ No obvious mechanism for such a reversal exists in the international context. However, some restraints are emerging.

Main Danger

Monopoly of key technologies, private ownership of industry standards, and deliberate uncertainty created by firms about the extent of their current and future holding of intellectual property are the main dangers of the current system. As noted above, emerging technologies in the information sector are characterized by strong interdependencies. When a single firm monopolizes critical technologies (such as IBM in RISC technology, TI in DRAM technology, Intel in microprocessors) both the nature and speed of technical change can be affected. The pace of change can slow if the firm holding the technology refuses to license it or licenses it at very high royalty rates. The pace can also slow if the firm holding the critical technology develops a strong, vested interest in the technology and limits its efforts in generating or releasing superior technology.

A closely related problem arises when a technology owned by an individual firm becomes the de facto industry standard. In the so-called "look and feel" cases, Apple Computer and Lotus Corporation are trying to privatize what has become the de facto industry standard. At issue is the computer interface. Apple has claimed that the screen displays and icons used in its Macintosh computers are copyrighted and that similar interfaces used by Microsoft and Hewlett Packard are illegitimate. Lotus has claimed that the program menus, commands, and file structures used in its spreadsheet programs are copyrighted. In neither case is the actual source code (the expression of the computer program) being defended. Rather, protection is being sought for the end result of the program, its "look and feel."

Neither case has been decided so far. In the meantime, a relatively unknown firm, Quarterdeck Office Systems has been issued a patent for a method of implementing user interface technology. A rapidly growing conventional wisdom in the industry holds that, in fact, "look and feel" can also legitimately be protected through copyright.39/

The uncertainties created by the lack of decision on the Apple and Lotus cases and the award of a patent to Quarterdeck have resulted in considerable confusion in the industry and have slowed down development plans in many firms.

If indeed "look and feel" becomes protected in a well-defined manner, there will be two further implications. First, protecting the "result" rather than the process by which the result is achieved would restrict the scope for legitimate reverse engineering. Such a development, however, would not be inconsistent with the evolution of intellectual property protection laws in other areas. Schumann has noted that although reverse engineering is technically permissible under the new semiconductor protection law, the protection provided to the end product circumscribes the possibilities.40/ (As noted earlier, a similar tension exists in the debate between product and process protection in the chemicals and pharmaceuticals industry.) Second, unless Apple gains a monopoly on all graphical user interfaces for personal computers, the number of new standards for graphical interfaces will proliferate. Besides increasing the difficulty of communication, this would also mean waste in R&D. If in the unlikely event Apple gains monopoly on all graphical interfaces, a significant though unseen impact on innovation and technology diffusion would affect the whole area of microcomputer software. Much creativity in this industry depends upon "niche players," and their activity could well be stifled. Legislators and courts face the unenviable task of balancing these conflicting objectives without the benefit of precedent.

Similar tensions will arise if Ashton-Tate, the producer of database programs, is successful in protecting its computer language. At present Ashton-Tate is testing the legal waters. If protection is granted, development of applications using the database programs will presumably require licenses from Ashton-Tate for the use of its language, possibly reducing the activity of software producers who now use the language for customizing computer programs.

A final problem with the emerging intellectual property regime is the scope it allows for strategic game playing which has no welfare increasing effects. The level of litigation related to intellectual property protection has increased substantially over the years. Firms litigate to protect their intellectual property from infringers. They also use litigation or the threat of litigation to restrict potential competition. In the new generation of PS/2 personal computers, for example, IBM holds proprietary the key technology (micro channel architecture). IBM's refusal to divulge the details of the technology has naturally drawn criticism from others in the industry:

> To rivals, IBM's reluctance to detail its new technology, coupled with its eagerness to warn that others will have a hard time legally matching it, is an effort to stir doubts about clones and thereby prod customers into buying Big Blue (IBM). High-technology marketers speak of the FUD factor, or "Fear, Uncertainty and Doubt." Says Dell's (Dell Computer Corporation's) Mr. Beachum, "If you take it from any other perception but IBM's, its really nothing else but pure FUD."41/

While it is not possible to ascertain the motivations of firms involved in this particular case, it seems very probable that such concerns are genuine.

Restraints

As noted, protecting intellectual property has led to considerable litigation, which some will argue has become excessive. To reduce the costs and uncertainties of the process, more firms are using arbitration as a substitute for litigation. Since an arbitrator does not have to abide by the rule of law, greater emphasis is placed on give and take. As a result, intellectual property-holders give up some rights in return for quicker judgments and lower litigation costs.

Concern for consumer rights has also had an effect. In 1988, the U.S. Supreme Court upheld the right to sell legitimately imported products such as cameras, batteries, and perfumes, without the permission of the trademark or copyright holder. Previously, brand-name firms kept domestic prices high to finance their advertising expenses, and then prevented discount stores from selling the brand names at prices much lower than the full-value retail stores.42/ Challenges to U.S. trade policy and decline in its influence will also restrain growth in intellectual property protection. Both Section 337 and Section 301 have been challenged in the GATT. A GATT dispute panel, set up in response to a complaint from the European Community, found the Section to be illegal under GATT articles. The European Community argument, which was upheld by the dispute panel, said that forcing a foreign firm to appear before the USITC discriminated against foreign firms. Foreign firms would prefer to have their cases tried in the slower and more cumbersome court system.

Brazil has complained to GATT that the imposition by the U.S. of duties under Section 301 violates the standstill commitment under the Uruguay Round and has asked for a review by a disputes panel. Under the standstill agreement, governments undertook not to introduce restrictive trade measures or measures to improve bargaining positions during the duration of the round. After initially blocking the move, the U.S. has agreed that a GATT disputes panel could hear a Brazilian complaint against the import sanctions.43/

The withdrawal of GSP privileges will probably become a blunt instrument from the U.S. point of view. Not only have many important trading partners lost these privileges already, but the U.S. is reducing them in response to the more general trade deficit problem.44/ Finally, although the U.S. is a net technology exporter at present, it could well become a significant importer of technology in the next decade. A lot of technology of relevance to

U.S. firms is generated outside the U.S. In the auto industry, U.S. firms have teamed up with Japanese firms to learn better manufacturing methods. In steel, U.S. firms are importing technology from Japan and Korea. Given the declining competitiveness of many segments of the U.S. industry, a case could be made for importing more technology. If U.S. dependence on foreign technology increases, the incentive to protect intellectual property may well decline. When, in the past, it was still a major technology importer, the U.S. had weak laws for protection of intellectual property.

CONCLUSIONS

Although intellectual property protection is not principally a North-South issue as it is often made out to be, developing countries have an important stake in the evolution of an intellectual property system for three reasons.

1. Protection levels are being set so as to restrict the scope of legitimate reverse engineering. These levels are being applied to new technologies and to conventional and mature products.
2. The price of technology is being raised and access to it is being restricted as innovators seek greater rents, particularly from key technologies such as information technology, biotechnology, and new materials technologies.
3. Lastly, the larger concern for developing (and developed) countries is that methods of protection for information services technologies are evolving in an ad hoc manner without a good understanding of the global implications. Although any form of intellectual property protection must by definition retard the diffusion of the technology, poor systems of protection can aggravate this problem.

Developing countries can also gain by increasing protection. The main benefit for some of the newly industrializing countries (NICs) is the credibility they need to continue participation in world trade. Less developed countries (LDCs) also gain from increased credibility. China's recent decision to increase trademark protection and to include software protection under copyright laws reflect that need. Indonesia has also been guided by similar concerns.

However, current trends suggest that low-income countries will have to live through a more stringent technology transfer environment than did the NICs. Successful U.S. trade actions to promote intellectual property protection have produced effects that will very likely last for at least the next decade. The actions of U.S. firms suggest that they are taking more seriously the task of entry deterrence than in the past. The refusal to license key technologies and the energetic challenge to alleged offenders shows that they are not going to lose control over technology as easily as they have in the past. Low-income countries need to respond to the U.S. challenge in two ways. First, they need to improve the efficiency of their technology acquisition policies. Better information-gathering institutions and mechanisms will be required to identify alternative sources of technology, particularly small and innovative firms that may be willing to license technology. Greater emphasis will be required on acquiring technology embodied in capital goods. The link between suppliers of inputs and buyers of outputs will also need to be stressed in order to acquire technology. Flexibility in the terms of payment and in relationships with foreign suppliers of technology will also be required.

Second, developing countries stand to gain by using international forums to highlight the global implications of current protection trends. These forums include the World Intellectual Property Organization and the GATT. This effort may enlist Japan and even the European Community as allies. Japan has made no secret of disliking current trends in protection.45/

NOTES

1. These views were articulated through the United Nations Conference on Trade and Development (UNCTAD).

2. Surendra Patel and Luc Soete, "Measuring the Economic Effects of Technology," STI Review,

vol. 4, 1988, pp. 121-166. In the United States, federally funded R&D has increased faster than privately funded R&D since 1984; however, more of such R&D is being done in the private sector.

3. Martin N. Baily and Robert J. Gordon, "The Productivity Slowdown in the Services Sector: Can it be Explained by Measurement Errors," The Service Economy, vol. 2, no. 4 (1988), pp. 1-7.

4. A. Steven Englander, Robert Evenson, and Masaharu Hanazaki, " R&D, Innovation, and the Total Factor Productivity Slowdown," Yale University, 1988, mimeo. Strictly, their estimate measures the combined effect of costs of knowledge production and productivity of knowledge. There is no evidence that the costs of knowledge production have declined.

5. National Science Board, Science and Engineering Indicators - 1987 (Washington D.C.: National Science Board, 1987).

6. Patel and Soete, ibid.

7. Martin N. Baily and Alok K. Chakrabarti, "Innovation and U.S. Competitiveness," The Brookings Review, Autumn 1985; and Englander et al. ibid.

8. Kenneth Flamm, Targeting the Computer: Government Support and International Competition (Washington D.C.: The Brookings Institution, 1987).

9. Richard E. Caves, Harold Crookell, and J. Peter Killing, "The Imperfect Market for Technology Licenses," Harvard Institute for Economic Research, Discussion Paper 903, Cambridge, 1982.

10. Edwin Mansfield, "How Rapidly Does Industrial Technology Leak Out?" The Journal of Industrial Economics, vol. 34, no. 2, 1985, pp. 217-223.

11. Deigan Morris and Michael Hergert, "Trends in International Collaborative Agreements," Columbia Journal of World Business, vol. 22, no. 2, pp. 15-21.

12. Ronald E. Berenbeim, Safeguarding Intellectual Property (New York: The Conference Board, 1989).

13. The Labs have been rechristened as AT&T Bell Laboratories.

14. Ashoka Mody and David Wheeler, "Technological Evolution of the Semiconductor Industry," Technological Forecasting and Social Change, vol. 30 (1986), pp. 197-205.

15. Journal of Commerce, November 16, 1988.

16. Office of Technology Assessment (OTA), Intellectual Property Rights in an Age of Electronics and Information, OTA-CIT-302 (Washington D.C.: U.S. Government Printing Office, 1986), p. 215.

17. David Henry, "Patent Absurdity No More," Forbes, September 10, 1984, p. 163; and Kevin McDermott, "Owning Ideas: A Better Bet in the '80s," D&B Reports, vol. 34, 1986, pp. 36-43.

18. Gary M. Hoffman, "Response," in "A Written Panel Discussion on Patent Issues," IEEE Technology and Society Magazine, ed. John Osepchuk, September 1988, pp. 14-21.

19. 626 F. Supp. 571 (D. Mass. 1985)

20. 616 F. Supp. 1571 (D. Minn. 1985), aff'd, 799 F.2d 1219 (8th Cir. 1986)

21. 797 F.2d 1222 (3rd Cir. 1986) cert.den 107 S.Ct 877 (1987).

22. Wall Street Journal, March 14, 1989, p. B1.

23. Catherine L. Mann, "Protection and Retaliation: Changing the Rules of the Game," Brookings Papers on Economic Activity, vol. 1, 1987, p. 330.

24. John H. Jackson, "Multilateral and Bilateral Negotiating Approaches for the Conduct of U.S. Trade Policies," in U.S. Trade Policies in a Changing World Economy, ed. Robert M. Stern (Cambridge: MIT Press, 1987), p. 384.

25. Compulsory licensing is almost never used in Japan; its use in developing countries is equally rare.

26. U.S. Congress, The Effect of the Japanese Patent System on American Business (Washington DC: U.S. Government Printing Press, 1988), hearing before the Subcommittee on Foreign Commerce and Tourism of the Committee on Commerce, Science, and Transportation, U.S. Senate, 100th Congress. What is not clear in this discussion is why the same features do not create similar problems for Japanese firms, which have a very high propensity to patent.

27. R. Michael Gadbaw and Timothy J. Richards, Intellectual Property Rights: Global Consensus, Global Conflict (Boulder, CO: Westview Press, 1988).

28. Another advantage of bilateralism is that free riding by countries not providing reciprocal

concessions is eliminated. However, this consideration does not apply here since the U.S. view has been that intellectual property protection by other countries does not require quid pro quo from the U.S.

29. Financial Times, November 30, 1988, p. 1.

30. Financial Times, June 29, 1988, p. 21.

31. Asian Computer Monthly, July 1988, p. 1.

32. Asian Wall Street Journal, July 28, 1988, p. 4.

33. B.K. Electronics, August 1988, p. 26.

34. Texas Instruments later alleged that Micron was also infringing many of TI's patents. The suit covered 256K and 1M dynamic random access memories (DRAMs). Micron reached a settlement with TI by agreeing to a cross-licensing agreement in which TI netted $38 million. Electronic Engineering Times, May 8, 1989, p. 10.

35. Asian Wall Street Journal, November 14, 1988, Section 3, p. 7.

36. Asian Wall Street Journal, February 21, 1989, p. 2.

37. Financial Times, November 23, 1988, p. 26.

38. Stephen M. Hudspeth, "Recent Developments in the Patent/Antitrust Interface - Response to a New Reality," The Journal of Law and Commerce, vol. 3, pp. 35-64.

39. Microsoft's claim that Apple had in fact licensed the relevant technology to Microsoft has not been upheld by the court. However, the court has yet to decide whether the "look and feel" of the Macintosh computer is protectable by copyrights. The Broderbund v. Unison World case is being partially cited as evidence that courts will protect "look and feel": in that case two computer printing programs were held to be similar in "appearance." The Whelan v. Jaslow case is also a useful precedent possibly supporting the protection of "look and feel."

40. Gunda Schumann, "Copyrightability of Computer Programs and the Scope of their Protection under the ITC Apple Case and the Whelan Case - Part II," Computer Law and Practice, vol. 4, May-June 1988, pp. 141-147.

41. Wall Street Journal, August 24, 1987, p. 6.

42. <u>Business Week</u>, June 13, 1988 p. 30.

43. <u>Financial Times</u>, February 2, 1989, p. 6.

44. Mexico lost $200 million of GSP in 1987 as part of the U.S. deficit reduction drive. Singapore was promised continuation of GSP privileges in return for better intellectual property protection but lost them soon after it changed its laws. South Korea also lost GSP privileges after its sweeping changes in intellectual property laws.

45. Although the European Community and Japan have expressed some support for U.S. positions, real differences continue to exist among the Big Three. There continue to be restrictions and ambiguities in Japanese law for the protection of software and databases. For example, Japan does not permit the protection of computer languages, syntax and mathematical algorithms. If languages become protected in the United States, this matter would have to be resolved. <u>East Asian Executive Reports</u>, July 1985, p. 8, 21.

Japanese firms would also like to be allowed to copy the structure of programs that are the property of specific firms but which have become de facto standards. <u>Japan Times</u>, May 23, 1988 and June 14, 1988. This was the heart of the dispute between IBM and Fujitsu.

11

Intellectual Property, Technology, Assets and Strategic Choices in the United States

Atul Wad

INTRODUCTION

In policy discussions about intellectual property rights (IPR) the emphasis tends to be on defining and recommending the "proper" mechanisms and environments to ensure adequate protection of IPR and on the need for such protection. The assumption is that if this proper environment were to exist, U.S. firms would be able to operate far more effectively in foreign markets.

However, an equally important perspective with regard to IPR is that of the individual firm, especially the small and mid-sized firms that do business overseas. Such firms, U.S. or other national origins, rarely have the luxury of being able to wait for the "proper" policy climate in a country before commencing business there. Rather, the policy environment, and the general business climate, have to be taken for what they are, and the problem or challenge faced by these individual firms is how to succeed under such circumstances.

The purpose of this chapter is to explore the issue of IPR from the perspective of the individual firm (particularly the small or medium-sized firm). It is a preliminary analysis based upon interviews with several U.S. firms from the midwest and is intended primarily to elaborate on the issues and to contribute to a conceptual framework of IPR.

This chapter is an attempt to examine some of the issues by drawing upon the viewpoints and experiences of individuals who are involved in this technology marketplace -- either as direct participants (i.e. private firms) or as intermediaries to these transactions(e.g. consultants). An attempt has been made to cover a range of sectors and consultant specialties. The sectors covered included chemicals, telecommunications, process engineering, software, food and food processing, pharmaceuticals and health care. The main objective of the interviews was to obtain some qualitative data on the manner in which intellectual property and technological assets are interpreted within the firm and also to identify and understand some of the specific strategic concerns that relate to these issues. This report is still a preliminary step in what is intended to be a more detailed study, covering more firms and sectors and attempting to identify and develop more systematic propositions and relationships and establish more useful analytical categories.

The firms interviewed for this chapter included the following:

1. a large food production company with sales of $7.5 billion;
2. a mid-sized company that specializes in computer controlled production and process R&D systems in the chemical, petrochemical and petroleum industries;
3. a medium-sized telecommunications company which manufacturers digital cross connect systems and echo cancelers;
4. a consulting company that specializes in analysis and assistance to manufacturing firms in licensing, joint-venture negotiations, and intellectual property issues;
5. a computer software company that recently received an infusion of venture capital and whose main product is an object oriented programming language;
6. a start-up health services company that is a spin-off of a larger health service corporation and is in the prototype development stage for a computerized home nursing unit;
7. a large chemicals company, one of the largest in the country.

The interviews with these companies, as well as with some experts in technology licensing and intellectual property matters, focused on how issues concerning IPR and technology were approached within the company, how they were reflected in the company's operations and strategy, and what types of problems were faced in this regard.

What emerged from these interviews was the importance of the concept of technological assets as an overall framework for the analysis of IPR as well as other strategic concerns to a firm doing business in today's global environment.

The specific arguments are firstly that IPR cannot be treated in isolation from other aspects of a firm's environment. Secondly, the specific manner in which a firm deals with the IPR question is a function of its more general strategic orientation and priorities (to the extent that they exist). Finally, the specific strategies and choices that are best suited are themselves determined by the characteristics of the firm and its environment. The conclusions discuss three areas -- technology intelligence, technology valuation and international business support services -- which were identified as potentially valuable to firms in making strategic decisions with regard to their international operations.

TECHNOLOGICAL ASSETS

There is a growing pressure on the individual firm, whether large or small, to explicitly and consciously undertake systematic measures to optimize its returns on its technological resources, know-how, and associated capabilities -- its technological assets.

The concept of technological assets as used here describes the resources and capabilities of a firm to develop, commercialize, modify, and use technology and know-how in its business. It therefore includes direct assets such as R&D capabilities, patents, trade secrets etc., as well as "complementary assets" such as marketing, manufacturing, and distribution.1/

Admittedly, it is a broad concept that requires further refinement and specificity. However, it is useful in encapsulating the domain of attributes of a firm that influences its ability to perform effectively in a technological sense. In this sense, it is a multidimensional concept that includes both "hard" and "soft" characteristics of a firm, and resources that are either directly or indirectly related to the firm's ability to gain returns from its technological strengths.

Technological assets does have a positive connotation, but in principle it should also include the technological weaknesses or liabilities of the firm. It is the balanced composite of strengths and weaknesses that constitutes the overall assets of the firm. As such, technological assets does have an accounting flavor and raises interesting questions about the possibilities of technology "audits," technology "balance sheets," and "technology flows" in the firm.

A second feature of this concept is that it allows firms to be positioned according to their specific role in the technology marketplace, whether it is a net producer or user of technology. Thus, for a firm that operates in a technology-intensive environment and is primarily a technology developer, it's technological assets could be determined by its R&D strengths, its know-how, its ability to commercialize technology, and other such factors that influence the degree of innovativeness of the firm.

However, a firm with virtually no technology of its own, but which specializes, say, in technology brokering, the buying and selling of technology, would have strong assets if it were well-networked with and knowledgeable about the technology producers and users in that industry. Another example could be a firm in a developing country which again has little or no technology of its own. However, if it has a good name recognition locally, is competent in doing business in that environment, has the capacity to acquire or adopt external technology effectively, and has a good knowledge of the options and sources for the technology it needs on a global level, it can be said to have strong technological assets, although in a way that a firm in an advanced country with considerable technology generation and innovative capacities does not.

Thus, technological assets may be seen as the attribute of a firm that is the main determinant of its success in a global technology marketplace. Such assets themselves are of little value unless they yield returns to the firm that contribute to its profitability and competitiveness. These returns may be in the form of direct increases in profits, market share, and growth, or they may be more intangible returns that will in turn promote profitability and growth. For example, returns could be realized:

1. through increases in market share and sales, or consolidation of market dominance.
2. through establishment of credibility and legitimacy, particularly in those sectors where these are important. In industries where standards and quality are of crucial importance, the reputation of a firm and the credibility of its product are important influences on the prospective buyer.
3. through the generation of fees and royalties or technologies developed by the firm. Particularly in large firms, technologies are often developed that the firm has no use for, but which can have value to other firms. In the past many large firms would pass these technologies on to their suppliers or to noncompeting firms, but recently the trend is toward trying to license or sell these technologies in order to recover the costs of their development and hence optimize the returns from the firms' technology assets.
4. through spin-off benefits, for instance by the creation of demand for other company products and services.
5. through defensive results, for example, a patent can be taken simply to keep out the competition. In highly competitive industries where the technical barriers to imitation are low, such defensive patenting can be essential to the firm's survival.
6. by attracting financing needed by the firm. This is particularly true for start-up firms seeking risk or venture capital. Having no track record, and often no hard assets, a solid record of innovation, represented perhaps by a number of good patents, combined with a well-thought-out business plan and a confident, inspiring management team is needed to convince potential investors of the prospective work of the company.
7. by attracting top quality people to the firm. An important incentive to researchers and

engineers is the extent to which their job provides opportunities for recognition and status within their field and the direct personal benefits they can gain as a result of their work. Firms with a known reputation for high quality research and innovation and those that offer specific incentives and rewards for outstanding performance are therefore likely to attract better and more motivated people and to retain them longer, which in turn is of long-term value to the firm itself. Such an image is perhaps more important in industries where expertise is in short supply.

IPR has generally been treated as a specific and separate issue that firms must deal with in terms of, to a large extent, methods for patent protection overseas. However, if one views the question of IPR from a broader perspective, optimization of technological assets, it is more pervasive in various aspects of corporate functioning and structure. Specifically, the question is one of protection of technology, but also one of determining strategies and options to optimize the returns to the firm from its technological assets within an international climate. Each climate, however, has varying levels of protection, competition, and opportunity. This suggests that a firm view a number of its strategic concerns in light of it own technological assets. This would include the more obvious issues such as a firm's policy toward patents and IPR, as well as other concerns: (1)criteria and philosophy for entering strategic alliances and partnerships, (2)investment in R&D and the relative emphasis given to external sourcing, (3)relationships with external sources of research such as universities and research institutes, (4)strategies for entering into new business areas, (5)overall competitive strategy, (6)criteria for working with subcontractors, (7)personnel policies.

Such an analytical approach is particularly useful in the case of small and mid-sized firms which generally treat IPR as a somewhat nebulous concept that has little direct relevance to them. Of course, in many instances, such firms also lack any overall strategic orientation as well. Couching the problem in terms that are meaningful to the firm (in its own vocabulary) could serve a dual purpose articulating IPR to the firm and expressing the importance of strategy in general.

The case studies were valuable in identifying some of the more important issues facing firms in this regard. They also revealed that different issues affect firms in different ways depending upon the particular characteristics and situation. In particular, the following factors appear to have an influence on the relationship between IPR and technological assets on the one hand, and strategic choices on the other: (1)the international technology environment; (2)the structure of the industry; (3)the regime of protection; (4)corporate structure and characteristics (5)the volume of transactions. These "parameters" help to define how different issues are articulated to different types of firms and, taken together, how these issues and parameters provide the first step towards a categorization of firms with respect to their technological assets and options for optimization.

The International Technology Environment

The U.S. position of unquestioned technological dominance is gradually eroding as other countries become more prominent in the advancement of technology and in its commercialization. This not only refers to the obvious countries such as Japan, West Germany, and France but also to some of the Eastern European nations and a few of the Newly Industrialized Countries (NICs).

There are an increasing number of different sources of technology around the world, both in conventional technological areas as well as in newly emerging fields. These are not for the most part "breakthrough" technologies, but incremental improvements in products or processes which can be of significant importance to the competitive position of a firm. This technological multipolarity has a positive and a negative side. More sources of technology means more options for a firm seeking technology. On the other hand, more sources of technology implies the potential for new competitors and new threats to a firm's established business. In this situation, technology and competitive intelligence become all the more important.

Accompanying this proliferation of technology

is a fiercer competitive environment where technological capabilities play an important role. This puts a greater pressure on the firm to maximize the returns from its technological assets.

Technological multipolarity also has implications for how a firm views its own internal R&D. The "make or buy" decision now has an expanded set of factors upon which to be based. The increasing availability of new product and process technologies in various countries makes it more difficult for a firm to decide whether to carry out its own R&D in-house or to simply look outside, perhaps overseas, for what it needs.

Furthermore, the threats of piracy and infringement of intellectual property rights have grown as more countries and firms participate in technological change. Often, the regimes for protecting intellectual property rights in different countries are not as powerful and well-enforced, or are dissimilar to that of the U.S. The optimization of technological assets then encompasses the need for more effective methods for the protection of IPR, and for alternatives to the traditional methods of protection. The costs associated with infringement, and patent violations are also rising and are often excessive for a small or mid-sized firm. The protection offered by legal channels and processes of litigation, even if affordable, is of limited value.

The rising costs of R&D and technology development also create a pressure to get the most out of a firm's investments in technology. This could be in the form of greater market shares, higher margins, licensing of technology etc. This applies not only to firms that develop their own technology but also to those that source most of their technology externally, since rising R&D costs are reflected in increased costs of technology transactions.

In addition, a number of other factors characterize today's technological and business environment:

1. The mobility of scientific and engineering personnel, particularly in some industries, causes real threats of information leakage.
2. The increasing internationalization of production and of technology-based transactions

(joint-ventures, acquisitions, licensing, mergers etc.), create more windows for information leakage and IPR violation.

3. The speed of communication and information transmittal has resulted from new information technologies thus changing the environment. News about new developments in one country is received elsewhere in a matter of days if not less often narrowing the time available for a firm with a new product or process to exploit its potential.
4. Finally, as technology transactions increase in frequency, and more firms participate in the process of global technological change, technology per se increasingly becomes a commodity to be bought and sold in the marketplace. This is reflected in the growing number of "technology brokers" and "technology fairs" around the world. To participate successfully in this marketplace, a firm must have a better sense of how technology is priced or valued (both, its own and that of others) and how to keep abreast of new developments around the world. It must also have a finer sense of where it fits in the spectrum of the marketplace -- is it primarily a buyer or seller and what does this imply. It is not necessary for a firm to have its own in-house technology development capabilities in order to participate in this new technology intensive environment. In fact, opportunities are continuously emerging for firms that are able to take advantage of this situation by positioning themselves appropriately -- as manufacturers that can make the best use of available technology, as service providers that specialize in technology related activities, and as intermediaries in the technology marketplace.

In other words, for the average technology-based (though not necessarily technology-intensive) firm, the global context of technological multipolarity and the accompanying complexity presents itself in the form of various issues:

1. How do I protect my technology from imitation, and where are the threats likely to come from?

2. What is the value in the market of my technology?
3. Who should be my partners if I am to make the most of my firm's technology?
4. Where is the competition likely to come from?
5. How can I improve my technology by importing or acquiring know-how from elsewhere, how can I find out where these sources of know-how are, and what are the associated costs?
6. Given this growing marketplace in technology with more and more firms becoming both buyers and sellers, where is my niche in this matrix of transactions? Am I a net provider/producer of technology, an imitator or an acquirer?
7. Where can I find support and assistance for my international business and technology activities?

Structure of Industry

The characteristics of the industry play a major role in determining how a firm in that industry approaches the issue of IPR and optimization of technological assets. The importance of technology to competitiveness varies across sectors. In the chemical industry, technology is generally viewed as a key factor in the competitiveness of a firm, and this is reflected in substantial emphasis on patenting, licensing in and out, and a corporate "culture" that emphasizes the importance of technology. It also reflects on where the R&D is done. In the software industry, most R&D is done in-house, again because of the importance of technology and also because of the threats of IPR infringement. In the chemical industry, especially among large firms, little R&D is subcontracted out, and even then only on very specific projects and with protective agreements negotiated beforehand (confidentiality, required one year lapse before publication of results, etc.).

Besides the importance of technology, the nature of the technology in a particular sector is also relevant. The more "intangible" the know-how, the lesser the tendency to patent or to reveal information. Computer software is a solid example. More "material" technologies, for example new materials such as nylon and teflon, are associated with greater patenting behavior. Of course, in any one sector, there are a multitude of relevant technologies, but often it is the character of the core technology that determines the overall approach to technology in general. The extent of imitability of technology, or of certain parts of it, is important. For instance, a chemical pilot plant firm interviewed estimated that about 75 percent of its systems involved technology that could be easily replicated and that about 25 percent was impossible to duplicate or very expensive to copy. These latter technologies apply mainly to the smaller items in the system, the circuitry, board design, wiring, software etc. As such, there was no perceived pressure to copyright or patent in order to protect technology. Similarly, since their systems are used for R&D, they tend to become obsolete fairly rapidly and the time available for possible infringement is short. The core know-how of the company rests in its knowledge of how to put these systems together efficiently, rapidly, and based on the latest technology available. The rate of technical change and new product development, when rapid, can also force a firm to devote more resources to new models or versions of existing products, as in the software industry. Rapid technological change also emphasizes the need for good techno-business intelligence.

Relevant as well is what specific aspect of technology needs to be protected. Generally, there are various elements to a particular technology, some of which are already in the public domain or are easily imitable. Often the technology (if it is the product) is well-known and the competitive advantage lies elsewhere (e.g. manufacturing process). The key question is where does the proprietary knowledge exist? The better the understanding within the firm of the specific elements of the technology that are the basis of its overall assets, the more effectively it can protect and optimize returns on these assets. The analysis of this core technology asset is therefore very important.

In a large food company that was interviewed, the primary function of in-house R&D is to extend product lines (e.g. new flavors for a line of yogurt, new packaging etc.) and to ensure compliance with quality and regulatory standards. There is a fair amount of patenting of such research and this is undertaken explicitly to protect the technology. However, much of what the company seeks to protect relates not to the technology per se but to the manufacturing processes. This protection is achieved through trade secrets. The use of secrecy agreements in joint ventures and in research that is subcontracted out is quite common.

The degree and nature of competition also influence firms in their technology dealings. In highly competitive environments, greater emphasis is placed on secrecy and defensive behavior. For example, in the health area, it is common for firms to patent new products and processes simply to keep out potential competition even if the firm has no intention of commercializing that product. In some industries, foreign competition is more serious and recognition of this is reflected in stronger lobbying efforts and pressures on governments to increase IPR protection.

In the food industry, alliances between companies are rare, with most firms being fairly independent and placing more emphasis on vertical integration with marketing, distribution, suppliers etc.

The degree of government regulation is sometimes important. In the food industry, a substantial portion of in-house R&D is devoted to ensuring compatibility with government standards. Alliances with other firms, generally uncommon in this sector, are nevertheless found in areas relating to quality and health standards.

Of particular importance is the relative position of the firm within the industry. In food, for example, some of the larger firms devote considerable resources to in-house R&D, whereas others tend to rely more on external sourcing. The R&D carried out by government-supported laboratories (USDA and FDA) is a major source of technology for these firms. Relative to other industries such as chemicals, technology in the case of the interviewed food company generally plays a less important part in determining the competitiveness of the company, though other firms tend to place a greater emphasis on R&D. The company is to some extent a technology follower, and depends substantially on the external sourcing and acquisition of technology, either through its suppliers or from government labs.

The company has established a specific strategic technology group with the express mission of external technology sourcing and intelligence and its integration with the company's strategic plans and goals (and very recently, its corporate R&D). This also reflects a growing awareness within the company of the increasing importance of technology to its competitive position.

This is partly in reaction to what is happening in the industry as a whole -- certain areas such as packaging and microwave products are rapidly changing and require greater attention to technology. However, it also reflects a realization on the company's part that it tends to underfund and underemphasize technology relative to some of its competitors. Thus the company's increasing emphasis on R&D is occurring at a time when the R&D/sales ratios of some of its competitors, which were higher in the past, are remaining at constant or declining levels. However, in the long run, the company will continue to be driven by its marketing strengths.

One of the firms studied specializes in a niche market in the chemical, petroleum and process engineering fields. It designs and builds pilot plants for research purposes. In this instance, the company has virtually no in-house R&D but is driven by the research needs of the industry it serves. There is little concern with IPR protection since most of their business is of a one-of-a-kind nature and becomes obsolete rapidly. However, the scanning and monitoring of technology globally is important to the firm.

There is little competition for the company, except to the extent that its clients opt to undertake the pilot plant development in-house. However, in most cases, these customers prefer to subcontract the pilot plant work for two reasons: it is more cost effective, and because of such factors as the "not invented here" syndrome, it tends to be more technologically effective as well. Also, the company now has a track record in this type of work. On the other hand, the company faces considerable "NIH" based opposition from the R&D groups but has over the years learned to deal with this.

A medium-sized telecommunications firm that

was also interviewed produces digital cross connect systems, echo cancelers, and multiplexers. The technology in this firm's area of business is generally relatively well-known and easy to copy. The advantage is derived from the manufacturing process. There is sizable competition for the company's products, but its leadership depends firmly on its manufacturing process advantages, which are kept secret. In addition, the firm also has strengths in terms of the quality of its product, responsiveness to customer needs and after sales service. The market for its products has the characteristics of a wholesale market and as such after sales service makes for a difference in competitiveness.

Similarly, marketing is extremely important. The industry is such that legitimacy and reputation are essential to success and the company has excellent market relations, is well-known and trusted. This goodwill factor counts a great deal towards its success.

The telecom industry is driven by standards set by the large corporations and governments. The company's products and its R&D is directed towards meeting these standards and ensuring compatibility. Most R&D is done in-house, sales are carried out by its own sales force. Components are purchased from general suppliers, since they are fairly standard products themselves and there is very little subcontracting for specific components.

Regime of Protection

This again varies widely not only across countries but across fields and sectors. The most notable is the software industry which is characterized by major controversy over the methods of protection of software, the effectiveness of copyrights and patents, and the protectability of software. Often what is of value in this particular industry is the "look and feel" aspect of the product. On the other hand, in the telecommunications industry, the firm interviewed utilized technology that was widely known. What was proprietary was the manufacturing process and substantial security measures were taken to protect this -- confidentiality agreements, a very careful hiring and firing process, classification of documents, etc.

The levels of protection overseas affect different sectors differently. In the case of the software firm, the real threat was from domestic competitors. Foreign competition and threat of piracy, though taken seriously, was not considered the most significant danger. On the other hand, in the pharmaceutical and chemical industries, foreign markets that do not offer strong protection are generally avoided. For the software firm, the key to protection overseas was to have a strong and visible presence in that market, either directly or through an authorized dealer or distributor. The tendency for software copyright infringement was seen as encouraged by the lack of such a presence.

Most protection in this industry is achieved through copyrighting of the software, manuals and documentation. However, there is also some limited patenting, in those cases where the product is totally new and serves a new market. However, this is only possible in special cases.

One of the ways software companies protect their technology is in effect by continuing to innovate and be "ahead of the game." However, the techniques of copy-protecting disks is phasing out because of too many problems involved.

An issue that emerged anecdotally but has serious implications is the tendency of some countries to tacitly endorse IPR violation. An example was given of a foreign government actively seeking a licensee for a new biotechnology drug that had already been patented. The search was for other firms that had developed the same drug but had lost the patent race. The plan was to license the technology (presumably at much lower cost than from the patent holder) and be prepared to negotiate a court settlement should a lawsuit be filed. Apparently, the costs associated with such an approach were viewed as lower than a standard license arrangement. What this implies is that patent holders need to be constantly vigilant of other firms that were also developing the same products or processes. On the other hand, there is little that can done if such strategies are endorsed by national governments, except in a punitive sense.

The notion of tacit protection was brought up in several instances. For example, the standard of living in a particular country and the purchasing power can be such that there is no real market for computers except among large businesses and government agencies. Therefore, to the extent that these users demonstrate responsibility for IPR rights, there is a tacit type of protection in effect in that country. Similarly, if a country does not possess adequate capabilities in the relevant areas of R&D, it would be difficult for a firm or individual to try to replicate a technology-intensive product. Not only would the development be difficult, but the lack of the proper technical support would limit the market potential.

Corporate Structure and Characteristics

Apart from the sector in which a company operates, certain characteristics of the corporation are also important. Size is one. Large corporations with a range of products and product areas and geographical spread tend to have more structured approaches to such activities as technology sourcing, licensing, intelligence, and acquisitions. Often this is in the form of a Corporate Technology Office. The degree of awareness of technology as part of the corporate culture is also important. Some large corporations in technology-intensive areas have in-house training programs, seminars, and other events to emphasize the importance of technology to the company. Such awareness is seen as part of corporate loyalty. In smaller firms, the attention is more focused and technology related activities are often the responsibility of a small informal group within the firm. Small firms also tend to look to alliances and joint-ventures as useful mechanisms to enter new markets or to bring in new products.

Other corporate characteristics of importance are its ownership, particularly when there is significant foreign ownership (and foreign firms have been known to "buy into" high-tech firms for the "window" it provides to the technology); the rate of growth of the firm, which if high and based on technological superiority can encourage searches for acquisitions to enter new markets, expand manufacturing capacity etc. as well as increase subcontracting; and the relative role of the firm in the R&D spectrum of that industry. In any industry, some firms are more likely to be technology leaders, whereas others follow the industry technological trends. For follower firms, keeping abreast of new developments is essential in identifying new product opportunities; for the leaders, it is important for competitive reasons.

Volume of Transactions

The volume of transactions that characterize the business of a firm, whether they are technology or product transactions, affect several aspects of how a firm approaches technology assets. For example, if the firm has large product sales volumes and has strong brand recognition and visibility, the potential of IPR infringement is greater. Good examples are the consumer products made by such names as Cartier, Benetton, Rolex, Louis Vuitton, etc. On the other hand, even relatively high-technology items which have a strong visibility attract "cloning" behavior (e.g. the IBM PC).

Where there is a large volume of technology transactions, there is a greater need for proper pricing and valuation of technology. There is a growing number of firms that specialize in the "valuation of technology," which can be used for negotiation purposes in licensing and joint-ventures and acquisitions, for litigational purposes in cases of infringement, and internal evaluation purposes (e.g. the value of in-house R&D). The valuation of technology is also important when a firm is considering alliances (what is brought to the table) and for "make or buy" decisions. Some of the considerations in this valuation process include: the level of protection of the technology, the nature of the technology (breakthrough or incremental), the level of competition, length of time to get the product to market, the availability of alternative technologies (uniqueness), number of patents involved, extent to which other sales may result for the firm, and the structure of the market and the specific niche to be addressed (and the size of the niche).

The volume of patenting is itself important. The telecommunications firm interviewed undertook patenting because one of its largest customers was

AT&T, and a large number of patents increased its reputation and legitimacy with respect to AT&T. A start-up firm in Australia was mentioned as having sixty-three patents and no product, and the patent record had been influential in its raising venture capital. Significant patent behavior can therefore serve marketing and financing goals. A strong reputation in good quality research as reflected in a record of strong patents can also attract better researchers to the firm. In some firms, internal incentive systems are also used to attract such people, particularly where there is a shortage of qualified personnel.

CONCLUSIONS

This chapter has attempted to illustrate, based on case study material, some of the issues that confront firms in terms of making the most of their technological assets. Certain "parametric" factors seem to influence how these issues are articulated to different firms in different industries. In particular, the importance of technology intelligence is evident for a number of reasons -- competitive strategy, new product development, leveraging of internal R&D and marketing strategy.

Technology sourcing and intelligence (TSI) is emerging rapidly as a new consulting specialty and corporate function. Several large U.S. corporations have a TSI type office or function at the corporate level that is charged with seeking out and monitoring relevant new technological developments. Often, this function is integrated with the technology strategy function of the corporation.

For the small and mid-sized firm, however, it is more difficult to build an in-house TSI capacity. Yet, such firms can benefit greatly by being properly informed about new product and process developments around the world. While the private consulting sector appears to be responding to this need, small firms tend to find these services expensive and there may be a role for the government to play in this regard. Perhaps the support of TSI activities at universities or research institutes would be useful, if firms were to have access to these services at affordable costs.

Also increasingly important is the need to

more systematically value technology -- in terms of a variety of technical, market, cost/financial and spin-off benefit considerations. Technology valuation is needed by firms that license technology in or out, and by those that are concerned with the real market value of their technology, either when entering negotiations, making investment decisions, or when dealing with IPR infringements.

Technology valuation services are particularly important to small and mid-sized firms, since they are unlikely to have the in-house capacities for such analyses. A few firms are emerging that specialize in this form of assistance.

Finally, what emerged from the companies interviewed for this chapter was the overall need for business support and advisory services for small firms involved in international business. This need extends beyond IPR protection to include all aspects of international business-market studies, partner identification, government clearances and approvals, tax and customs assistance, product sourcing, etc. Such services are essential if the full potential of the U.S. small and king-sized companies is to be achieved in international business. Most firms acknowledge the need for such assistance, but there are few providers of these types of services except for scattered assistance available from some government agencies. Whether the demand for such services is strong enough to sustain a totally private enterprise is as yet an unanswered question. However, as small firms become more international in their operations, and as competition from other countries increases, the need for such support services will become essential. The critical question is whether these services should be subsidized by the government or left to the dynamics of the market. It should be noted, however, that most other countries have some form of official government support for their firms in their international operations.

From a research viewpoint, the important role of firm level research in gaining a more detailed and operational understanding of the issues and problems confronting firms needs to be recognized. While macro level policy analyses are useful and informative, they tend not to be able to capture the rich vertical detail that is offered through firm level case studies and research. While this has been a preliminary investigation into the concept of technological assets and IPR from the firm perspective, there is need for much more research at this level so as to develop more rigorous analytical categories and relationships that in turn can enlighten and refine the formulation of policies to support industry and to improve our understanding of technological processes within the firm.

NOTES

1. David Teece, "Profiting from Technological Innovation: Implications for Integration, Collaboration, Licensing and Public Policy," Research Policy, vol. 15, no. 6, December 1986.

12

Macroeconomic Perspectives on the Use of Intellectual Property Rights in Japan's Economic Performance

Michael Borrus

INTRODUCTION: INNOVATION AND IMITATION IN JAPAN'S INDUSTRIAL DEVELOPMENT

Japan's system of intellectual property protection is typically treated as a trade barrier in recent official U.S. evaluations, on the ground that large Japanese firms successfully orchestrate the system to extract proprietary technology from U.S. competitors.1/ Indeed, Japan's giant companies are extremely skilled at using their country's system of intellectual property protection as a competitive weapon. However, in this they are probably no more skilled than America's great corporations have been, at least since the early twentieth century, at building patent monopolies to safeguard their own dominant market positions. What was said at AT&T in the 1920s can as easily be said today at Hitachi, Mitsubishi, and their comrades:

> It seems obvious that the best defense (of market and technology position) is to... maintain such a strong engineering, patent, and commercial situation...as to always have something to trade against the accomplishment of other parties.... Ability to stop the owner of a fundamental and controlling patent from realizing the full fruits of his patent by the ownership of necessary secondary patents may easily put one in position to trade where money alone may be of little value.2/

The largest players with the greatest resources

will always be able to effectively manipulate an expensive-to-operate system to their own advantage.

Nonetheless, Japan's system of intellectual property protection for technology is significantly different from other industrialized countries. The differences can be traced at least in part to Japan's interpretation of the contribution of social value accorded imitation versus innovation. Until recently, intellectual property has been considered more as a common good to be shared and used than as a right of exclusive possession accorded to the creator.3/ Thus, for example, trade secret protection is weak, trademark protection is slow with no interim penalties for infringement, and copyright law has stringently high notions of creativity and severe limitations on what can be protected.4/ Similarly, Japanese patent law can operate effectively to force licensing for widespread use, to encourage cosmetic differentiation as a way around blocking patents, and to discourage enforcement of existing rights by failing to force disclosure of prior art or to punish infringement.

In short, particularly with respect to technology, the system as a whole seems to draw a different balance than in other industrialized countries. At least since the Second World War, during Japan's rapid postwar reconstruction, the balance appears to have been drawn in ways that favor technological diffusion over innovation. Rather than favoring and rewarding creativity in development, Japan's system of intellectual property protection encourages and rewards creativity in use. The user who improves (in terms of functionality, cost, or quality), adapts, or otherwise takes creative advantage of a less restricted flow of technological ideas is seen as creating as much as or more social value than the originators of technology. This was one reason that when Hitachi was caught illegally obtaining IBM technology in the famous 1982 sting, the Japanese company was felt in Japan to be the aggrieved party. Its appropriation of IBM technology was essential to its socially valuable activity of creating superior IBM-compatible products; while FBI involvement was seen as proof that the U.S. government was intent on frustrating the success of Japanese industry.5/

This characterization of postwar Japanese practice underlies this chapter's simple thesis:

Japan's system of intellectual property protection for technology has been discretionarily administered as one component of Japan's developmental industrial policy. Policy favored the import and forced licensing of foreign technology, its rapid imitation, adoption, use, and improvement by domestic companies, as a means of driving rapid economic growth without incurring the costs of autonomous, domestic technology development. The policy worked brilliantly, helping Japan to near technological parity with the United States in a few short decades.

As parity was reached over the past fifteen years and Japan exhausted the limits of this strategy, Japanese companies have increasingly become themselves innovators, autonomous new sources of technology development. As one indication, between 1975 and 1985 the Japanese share of U.S.-granted patents more than doubled, rising from 9 to 19 percent, and these were among the most highly cited patents which indicates that they are fundamental technology contributions.6/ As the change from imitator to innovator occurs, a corollary to our thesis seems reasonable: Japan can be expected to be increasingly more protective of innovation than during its developmental phase. Even as greater protection occurs, however, the system is likely to favor for some time domestic over foreign innovators. The discretionary institutions that favored imitation in the past are not easily dismantled, particularly when they can continue to advantage the domestic economy in acquiring the benefits of the technologies of the future.

The overall argument presented in this chapter is organized as follows. The first section characterizes Japan's developmental system, showing how it treated foreign technology, favoring diffusion over development, and use over creation. Section two then locates Japan's intellectual property system within the context of the developmental model described in section one, emphasizing with examples how it operated to advantage domestic producers. Japan's patent system is used as a reasonable proxy for the overall system of intellectual property protection, since it is a piece of the system that dealt most directly with the relevant (largely hardware) technologies of the past few decades. The concluding section briefly examines the directions of systemic change.

JAPAN'S DEVELOPMENTAL SYSTEM AND TECHNOLOGY

Japan has had extraordinary success at achieving technological parity with the United States in a remarkably short time. Its performance rests in a model of economic development that has several key attributes: (1)an emphasis on rapid economic growth through managed industrial restructuring, (2)the aggressive use of protection, (3)the import of foreign technologies, conjoined with the promotion of domestic market competition in technology development, application, and production innovation, and (4)a systemic commitment to education and increased skill levels throughout the work force.7/

Japan is a developmental economy, a state systematically committed in its business-government interactions to rapid economic growth.8/ Indeed, rapid economic growth has been the central political goal to which all other Japanese policies have been subordinated.9/ During its period of explosive development after World War II until roughly the mid-1970s, policy self-consciously helped to create comparative advantage and nurture economic growth as the production profile of the domestic economy shifted out of primary sectors and light industry into progressively higher value-added industries.10/

In a few short decades, Japan managed to move domestic production from a concentration on light industry like textiles, into industries requiring large-scale capital investment like ship building and steel, then into complex manufactures like autos, machine tools, and consumer electronics, and finally into the knowledge and technology-intensive industries like computers and telecommunications. At each step of industrial restructuring, the government played a crucial role in manipulating the access of foreign competitors to the domestic Japanese market, in restructuring the key domestic industries to promote their export competitiveness, and in helping to secure financial and technical critical mass. In essence, the government acted as both protector and promoter of Japanese industry.

In the role of controlling access to the domestic market, the Japanese government (particularly MITI) was an "official doorman [between the domestic and international economies] determining what and under what conditions, capital, technology, and manufactured products enter and leave Japan."11/ For example, foreign investment laws required governmental review for approval of all applications for foreign direct investment in the domestic economy.

Wherever a foreign technology was needed for domestic development, the government prevented the foreign producers from establishing a foothold in the domestic Japanese market by consistently rejecting all applications for wholly owned subsidiaries and foreign majority-owned joint ventures.12/ Foreign purchases of equity in Japanese firms were similarly restricted. Foreign import penetration was limited through high tariffs, restrictive quotas, cumbersome registration and permission requirements, and exclusionary customs procedures.

The price to the more technologically advanced foreign firms for limited access to the Japanese market was their licensing of advanced technology. Indeed, from the 1950s to the 1980s, Japanese industry entered into thousands of licensing agreements, paying only several billions of dollars for technology and know-how that had taken several hundreds of billions of dollars to develop.13/ Since MITI controlled access to the Japanese market and its approval was required for the implementation of licensing deals, it could dictate the terms of exchange. Its efforts were simple and effective.

MITI required foreign firms to license all Japanese firms requesting access to a particular technology. It limited royalty payments to a single rate on each deal, thereby preempting the competitive bidding-up of royalties. Often, it linked the import of certain technologies to the acquirer's ability to develop export products using that technology. It conditioned approval on the willingness of the involved Japanese firms to diffuse their own related technical improvements through sublicensing agreements to other Japanese firms.

The result of all these policies was the cheap acquisition and controlled diffusion of advanced technology throughout the domestic economy.14/ Foreign technology advantages were never permitted to dominate the domestic market unless they were embedded in the products and processes of domestic firms. And it is this rather unique developmental context that Japan's postwar system of intellectual property, especially its treatment of patents, is best understood.

JAPAN'S PATENT SYSTEM AND THE DEVELOPMENTAL TEMPTATION

Like most of its governmental institutions, Japan's patent system is not rule-bound and does not operate with transparent processes accountable to clear legal norms. Rather, the system is effectively an agency of MITI and is shot through with the administrative discretion that made MITI famous. It is a creature of the "administrative guidance" which characterized Japan's postwar industrial policy.15/ But by itself, administrative guidance does not guarantee a system that fulfills developmental goals. Rather, the system's characteristic features must lend themselves to the "developmental temptation."

Japan's patent system is premised on first-to-file, and lays all patent applications open to inspection. By themselves these features are neither unique nor necessarily developmental. During the postwar period, however, the system limited patent applications to single, narrowly focused claims, and discretionarily construed the scope of claim interpretation very narrowly. This encouraged a characteristic feature of Japanese patent practice, the massive flood of early patent filings by major companies aimed at preemptively staking out ground around a fundamental innovation. Just as for AT&T in U.S. historical experience, preemptive filing essentially operates to ensure that technology will be traded and used rather than locked-up to the inventor's advantage.

Significant pre-grant opposition procedures permit imitators to tie-up innovators in proceedings for extensive time periods, occasionally over ten years for critical new technologies. Moreover, filers are essentially not required to disclose prior art; there is not much of a discovery mechanism to find evidence of infringement, and penalties for infringement are extremely limited and do not run during the opposition period. The result is an overly lengthy patent process, with most burdens of proof placed on the innovator and most systemic incentives aimed at encouraging cross-licensing and use. MITI can even force licensing where the system's unique characteristics fail.

When combined with administrative discretion at each step of the process, the system's unique characteristics permitted it to be used as a component of developmental technology policy. During Japan's period of spectacular postwar growth, MITI administered the patent system to several technologies that it considered essential to Japan's economic success in such a way as to block the establishment of a dominant foreign position in the domestic Japanese market, thus permitting Japanese producers to play technology catch-up. This was true, for example, of semiconductors in the 1960s and optical fiber in the 1970s. Detailed consideration of the system's characteristic features shows how the Japanese accomplished this objective.16/

Significant administrative discretion without juridical review is a function of the Japanese patent system's placement within the governmental bureaucracy. The Japan Patent Office (JPO) head comes from MITI, and the JPO reports to the MITI Minister. Indeed, the JPO's work is often directly coordinated with MITI's Administrative Vice Minister and with the Directors General for Machinery and Information Industries and International Trade Policy.17/ Needless to say, this tight bureaucratic binding alerts the JPO to technologies designated by MITI as strategic for economic development, and creates the opportunity for political discretion in actions involving these technologies.

The exercise of discretion is enabled mightily by a lack of transparency in decision-making. The JPO rarely documents its reasoning. This not only makes the establishment of a record for appeal very difficult, but also provides leverage to frustrate the initial examination itself. Indeed, effective patent examination requires a continuous information exchange between examiner and filer; therefore, when using the system to disadvantage foreign filings, JPO examiners have been known to fail to communicate in a penetrable way.18/ The resulting speculative interpretation of the examiner's intent leads to misinterpretation and instant justification for hindering or rejecting foreign filings.

These temptations are compounded by grossly

insufficient staffing, due in part to a Japanese Diet limitation imposed in 1976.19/ From 1977-1987 the number of patent applications more than doubled from 161,000 to 341,000, and examination requests and examiner workload almost doubled; however, the total number of JPO employees -- including examiners -- actually declined.20/ Severe staffing problems obviously hinder domestic and foreign filers equally, but in a discretionary system, such problems also create a convenient rationale for the exercise of arbitrary administrative power.

In a first to successfully file system, discretion and staff limitations can be decisive where domestic and foreign firms are racing toward similar innovations. For instance, when an application is filed, discretionary communication can permit domestic applicants to benefit when, as in Japan, patent applications are open for inspection. Of course, by themselves, these two characteristics are very similar to European patent systems and have equally reasonable justifications. For example, opening applications to inspection discourages others working on identical inventions from needless, duplicative effort, and permits holders of prior art to advise overworked, understaffed examiners.21/ In that sense, the system's faults and its features can be mutually reinforcing.

The system's discretionary effects were substantially enhanced by the limitation of patent applications to single, narrowly construed claims, with equally limited scope of claim interpretation by the JPO.22/ The narrow claim focus and often literal interpretation by JPO examiners, predictably shaped Japanese patent practice to encourage the characteristic massive flooding of early filings by major Japanese companies. Even today, Japan incurs five times the typical number of U.S. filings. There is, moreover, no requirement that the invention actually be reduced to practice at the time of filing, and unlimited changes can be made in applications during the first fifteen months after filing. These features provide substantial latitude for preemptive strategies -- that is, for major firms to file sufficiently numerous and initially ambiguous applications to force cross-licensing and widespread use of proprietary invention.

The system's discretionary administration and

narrow claim interpretation are nowhere better illustrated than with Corning Glass's two decade long attempt to protect its basic patents in fiber-optic technology.23/ Corning's generic patents for optical fiber was issued in the United States and in Europe by the mid-1970s. In Japan, by contrast, several of the fundamental patents were administratively delayed for over a decade. The act of filing, however, opened the patents to inspection thus disclosing relevant information to Japan's major cable companies and prompting several rounds of expensive challenges. Meanwhile, Nippon Telegraph and Telephone, the monopoly buyer of fiber at the time, refused to purchase from Corning or even to recognize the validity of its claims to control the technology.

While urging that Corning license or venture with Japanese companies, NT&T simultaneously entered into a crash technology development program with the cable companies to engineer a production method that, at least in Japan, would not infringe Corning's patents. Corning was often urged to disclose greater information in its application in order to hasten granting of patents. On several occasions, its more detailed specification only served to provide its Japanese competitors with the information they needed to make cosmetic changes in imitative filings and thereby to attain patent protection before Corning on the same basic innovation. In the end, even though Corning was able to sue successfully for patent infringement in the U.S. and in Canada, the discretionary Japanese system had bought enough time for major Japanese companies to become established players in the optical fiber market.

The discretionary characteristics of Japan's patent system illustrated in the Corning example are exacerbated by other features of the system. For example, significant pre-grant opposition leading to deferred examination (up to seven years) can similarly favor domestic imitation over foreign innovation. This is particularly the case when, as in Japan, the patent term runs during the opposition period even though the patent has not been issued, and when the initial challenge is conducted by discretionary administrators. Thus, pre-grant opposition has been used very skillfully by Japanese industry to delay the award of patents to foreign innovators and to force licensing of the disputed technology. Indeed, oppositions have appeared in the past to be collusive. The same imperfections, phraseology, and the like make it appear "that all of the opposers have met to collectively define the issues, distribute the support documents, develop the arguments, and divide those issues and arguments among themselves, all by way of mutual agreement."24/

Smaller foreign companies, with more limited (than Corning's in optical fiber) but still distinctive technology positions, often run afoul of these features of Japan' system. Measurex, a U.S. producer of computer-based process control systems had such a typical experience with an infrared sensor technology it first patented in the United States in 1974.25/ Patents followed in 1977 in West Germany and Sweden. Meanwhile, by 1976, a Japanese competitor had copied the technology and filed for a flood of improvement patents, all of which were issued in Japan four years before Measurex's own opposition process was exhausted and the Measurex patent was issued in 1985. Only at that point could Measurex file notices of infringement, with a modest licensing fee likely to be all that it recoups. Measurex had lost years of sales and the unique opportunity to establish a dominant position for itself in the Japanese market.

In a rule-bound system, the features of the Japanese patent system that lead to these anecdotal outcomes are perhaps manageable. In a discretionary system, they can be orchestrated to disadvantage outsiders, particularly when the burden of proof is thrust on the outsider. Indeed, since there are few penalties for failure to disclose prior art, innovators must conduct a painstaking review of all Japanese patents laid open for review to determine if they draw upon its prior art. Even when that burden can be managed, strict enforcement and compensation against infringement is still very hard. Royalties run only from the time that proof of infringing use is completely established. And a review of patent infringement law suits in Tokyo District Court from 1975-1985 showed that an order to prohibit infringing behavior was never issued until after all applicable proceedings were exhausted.26/ The predictable end result is that, wherever discretionary administration permits, users can more or less infringe with impunity.

The most widely publicized recent example involves Fusion Systems, a smaller U.S. manufacturer of industrial equipment.27/ Fusion holds several U.S. patents on high-intensity microwave-driven light sources. They brought the technology to Japan and filed for protection 1975. Two years later, Mitsubishi reverse engineered the Fusion product and filed over 200 patents surrounding the technology. Protracted negotiations to resolve conflicting claims have been going on since the mid-1980s and the outstanding issues still unresolved. In the end, Fusion may spend $10 million and twenty years all in an effort to recapture control over its own technology.

The characteristic features of Japan's patent system exemplified in Fusion's experience result in an overly long waiting period to obtain patent protection, even when all the steps are executed correctly. Even today the system averages five to seven years to process application versus two to three years in other industrialized countries. When substantial technology advantage is at stake, as in high technologies ranging from microelectronics to amorphous metals, fiber optics, and ceramics, a ten to fourteen year waiting period is not at all uncommon. The wait, discretion, and systemic features all have combined to create a regime that can effectively force licensing of foreign technologies. Indeed, when the system itself fails and an application has already been published, MITI can discretionarily grant a compulsory license for an improvement invention upon request. While this feature has not often been used, it creates an obvious incentive forcing negotiations for licensing.

The overall system was, perhaps, best orchestrated as a developmental effect to support Japan's effort to build a fledgling microelectronics industry in the 1960s.28/ The effort was stymied by Texas Instrument's refusal to license its critical integrated circuit patents to Japanese firms without gaining permission to establish a wholly-owned production subsidiary in Japan. MITI discretionarily stalled approval of TI's Japanese patent applications thereby enabling domestic Japanese competitors to play technology catch-up and forcing TI to negotiate. In the end, TI was forced to fully license its competitors and to settle for a production joint venture (with explicit limits on its realizable market share in Japan).

The TI case is perhaps the cleanest example of the Japanese patent system being used explicitly as an instrument of Japanese industrial policy. But the essentially forced licensing and technology diffusion which results from the system's normal operation has a powerful competitive effect even when explicit industrial policy goals are absent. The characteristic features examined above tend to shift the terms of technology competition from innovation to manufacturing competence, product quality, and low production costs. These are, of course, the precise terms on which Japanese business has built its international competitive success.

SYSTEM REFORM AND JAPAN'S FUTURE INTERESTS

The full-blown developmental model briefly sketched in the first section of this chapter has been substantially dismantled over the last decade. Its success in generating technological strength has made its application less necessary. Government powers to structure market access and controls over capital availability and allocation are much smaller now and occasionally nonexistent. Yet, the effects of past policies linger in the enduring structure of tightly linked Japanese buyers and sellers. As a consequence, the domestic market remains relatively closed, especially in those high technology industries seen to be critical to Japan's future. Moreover, the promotional policies aimed at fostering competitive position and comparative advantage in the technologies of the future remain in full force. In addition, substantial subsidies to technology development and the panoply of incentives to incorporate new technologies from Japanese suppliers are also still prevalent.

Similar changes are visible on the horizon of Japan's intellectual property landscape. As Japanese firms become innovators, the administrative instinct appears to be discretionarily shifting to favor increasing protection of the innovator. The developmental temptation notwithstanding, the Japanese patent system appears to adequately protect technological innovation by domestic sources. It also appears to generally work for those foreign firms with the resources to play the game and who manage to avoid being subject to discretionary abuse. Despite the very real, if anecdotal experiences described in the previous section of this chapter, in recent years foreign applications have fared no worse than domestic applications with roughly 60 percent of both awarded patents.29/ Of course, foreigners account for only about 4 percent of all applications, and even the most active foreigners like IBM and Phillips, are outfiled by their Japanese competitors on the order of twenty to thirty fold.30/

Moreover, in several areas, notably chip-mask protection and computer software, Japan has moved to protect innovation (albeit it often under diplomatic pressure from the United States). The continued discretionary nature of the system still permits the claims of domestic firms to be favored in technology areas considered essential for Japan's future prosperity. But the system's enhanced respect for the Japanese innovator conjoined with vigilant pressure from abroad ought, in principle and over time, to force a measure of conformity in the treatment of the claims for intellectual property protection of both domestic and foreign firms.

This seems inevitable as Japan shifts in international fora to protect its own innovations against newly industrializing countries that now claim the same right to reverse engineer, copying what Japan once perfected as part of its industrial development strategy. Contradictions between its international position and domestic practices will make resolution of its international claims very difficult indeed. But these pressures provide little guarantee that Japan will end up protecting intellectual property to the same extent as in other advanced countries. Given its experience, traditions, practices, and enduring institutions, Japan is likely to draw the line between innovation and imitation in unique ways. Even as the innovator is better protected, the social usefulness of the imitator is not likely to be wholly sacrificed.

NOTES

1. This is a consensus position of U.S. officials in "The Effect of the Japanese Patent System on American Business,"Hearing before the U.S. Congress, Senate, Subcommittee on Foreign Commerce and Tourism of the Committee on Commerce, Science, and Transportation, 100th Congress, June 24, 1988 (Washington D.C.: U.S. GPO, 1988). Hereafter this reference will be cited as "Patent Hearing." See also the official statement of the U.S. Trade Representative in, 1989 National Trade EStimate Report on Foreign Trade Barriers (Washington D.C.: Office of the USTR, 1989), pp. 140 ff.

2. AT&T's J.E. Otterson, memorandum of 1927, cited in David Noble, America by Design (Oxford: Oxford University Press, 1977), p. 97, footnote 39.

3. Peter D. MIller, "Cavalier View of Patents Erodes Incentive," Japan Economic Journal, October 22, 1988, p. 23.

4. See USTR, Foreign Trade Barriers; and Karjala and Sugiyama, "Fundamental Concepts in Japanese and American Copyright Law," American Journal Comp. Law, vol. 36, no. 613, 1988.

5. This interpretation of the Hitachi-IBM sting is drawn from Clyde Prestowitz Jr., Trading Places: How We Allowed Japan to Take the Lead (New York: Basic Books, 1988), ch. 3 ff.

6. See, National Science Foundation, The Science and Technology Resources of Japan: a Comparison with the United states, NSF 88-318 (Washington D.C., 1988), pp. 33 ff. and tables. The NSF states that Japanese patents account for 45 percent more of the top 1 percent most highly cited U.S. patents than expected based upon their total number of U.S.-granted patents. Ibid., p. 34.

7. This model is drawn from the author's own work on Japan. This section is drawn in particular from Michael Borrus and Denis F. Simon, High-Technology in the Pacific Basin: Analysis and Policy Implications, (unpublished manuscript, March 1, 1989) prepared for the Conference "Foreign Competition in Science and Technology: Implications for U.S. Interests," at the National Academy of Sciences, May 11, 1989. For a brief review of the literature on Japanese economic success, and an interpretation similar to that in this paper, see Chalmers Johnson, Laura Tyson, John Zysman, Poli-

tics and Productivity (Cambridge: Ballinger Publishing Company., 1989).

8. This is the notion best developed by Chalmers Johnson, MITI and the Japanese Miracle (Stanford: Stanford University Press, 1982).

9. T.J. Pempel, "Japanese Foreign Economic Policy," in Between Power and Plenty, ed. Peter J. Katzenstein (Madison: University of Wisconsin Press, 1978).

10. The data that follows is available from several sources that cite official Japanese government statistics. See James Abegglan and George Stalk, Kaisha, The Japanese Corporation, (New York: Basic Books, 1986), ch. 1.

11. Pempel, p. 139.

12. This and the following paragraphs are drawn from the discussion in Michael Borrus, Competing for Control: America's Stake in Microelectronics (Cambridge, Ma: Ballinger, 1988), ch. 5.

13. Regis McKenna, et.al., "Industrial Policy and International Competition in High Technology," California Management Review, vol. 26, no. 2 (Winter 1984).

14. While such gatekeeper policies helped to create the preconditions for Japanese firm success with imported technology, it was intense market competition, structured and promoted by government policy, which drove Japanese firms toward world-class competitiveness. Five sets of policies in particular permitted the government to conform its intervention to facilitating intense market competition among domestic producers. These were policies affecting capital allocation and availability, market demand stimulation, cooperative R&D, education, and risk-reduction mechanisms. Borrus and Simon, ibid.

15. On the notion of administrative guidance, see Johnson, MITI, ibid.

16. The detailed description of Japan's patent system and its contrast to other national systems is drawn from several standard texts and articles. See, in particular, John P. Sinnot, World Patent Law: Patent Statutes, Regulations, and Treaties (New York: Matthew Bender, 1974); T. Doi, The Intellectual Property Law of Japan (1980); Stephen Ladas, Patents, Trademarks, and Related Rights; National and International Protection

(Cambridge, Ma: Harvard University Press, 1974); and Nicholas Breyer, "Japan's Patent System," Journal of the ACCI, October 1988, pp. 16-25.

17. Breyer, p. 16.

18. Testimony of Alfred Michaelsen, Vice President and general patent counsel, Corning Glass Works, in "Patent Hearing," p. 48.

19. Though ostensibly imposed for budgetary reasons, the timing of this limitation, coincident with liberalization of Japan's domestic market for computers, microelectronics, and other high technologies, permits the speculation that the limitation may have been intended as a countermeasure to liberalization. While entirely consistent with other liberalization countermeasures adopted in 1976, I have seen no evidence that the JPO staffing limitation was actually intended as such. On liberalization countermeasures, see, Borrus, Competing for Control, p. 126.

20. Breyer, ibid., citing JPO statistics.

21. Ibid., p. 18.

22. Since January 1988, the scope of patent applications and interpretation has been formally broadened due to Diet-initiated changes.

23. This story is based on discussions, and on the account in Prestowitz, ch. 5.

24. Testimony of Larry W. Evans, Director, Patent and License Division, BP America, in "Patent Hearing," p. 60, who goes on to claim that collusive behavior has been "verified privately by many Japanese patent attorneys."

25. This account is based on a presentation of David Bosson, CEO of Measurex, at the Professional Committee Meeting of the Japan-Western U.S. Association in San Jose on July 22, 1989.

26. Evans testimony, "Patent Hearing," p. 61.

27. See testimony of Donald M. Spero, President, Fusion Systems Corp., in "Patent Hearing," p. 39 ff. See also Miller, ibid.

28. Borrus, ibid., p. 120 ff.; and John Tilton, International Diffusion of Technology: The Case of Semiconductors (Washington D.C.: Brookings, 1971).

29. Breyer, p. 18.

30. Breyer, p. 23.

13

Intellectual Property Rights in Japan and the Protection of Computer Software

Dennis S. Karjala

INTRODUCTION

Japan should be an instructive case study of the relationship between intellectual property rights and economic development. Its past is conveniently divided into fairly distinct pre and post World War II phases, while a third phase has begun only recently. In its prewar phase, Japan moved from a preindustrial society through basic industrial development, learning and adapting basic western industrial technology to do so. In its postwar phase, Japan evolved into a society able to compete at the leading edge of nearly all areas of technological development, importing large amounts of advanced technology in the process. Japan's ability to maintain its powerful economic competitiveness during the third phase, however, may depend on how well the Japanese system performs internally in generating creative new technological advances.

This breakdown of Japan's industrialization history into three phases seems critical in deciding the relevance of the Japanese experience to the issues under consideration in this book. Developing countries may wish to inquire into Japan's experience of a hundred, fifty, or twenty-five years ago, depending on their current stage of industrial development. The highly industrialized countries, however, may be more concerned with what Japan is doing today and can be expected to do in the future. The two inquiries may merge partially to the extent that the past, especially such a successful past, can be considered predictive of the future; but two important caveats must be raised.

First, it seems reasonable to assume as a working hypothesis that importers of technology would be less protective of intellectual property rights in technology and more protective of domestic rights to copy and use technology developed in other countries.1/ Creators of advanced technology, on the other hand, would be expected to be more protective of the products of intellectual creativity. This hypothesis requires investigation, but if it is correct it advises caution in extrapolating too far from Japan's past.

Second, and perhaps more importantly, we are undergoing a fundamental change in the relationship between schemes for the protection of intellectual property and technological progress. Until very recently, intellectual property rights in technology have always evoked notions of patent, trade secret, and unfair competition law, as well as more general schemes for the protection of know-how, all of which are often subsumed under the label "industrial property rights." The knowledge represented by such rights is typically implemented by human beings, and in fact the legal rights them-selves (such as a patent right) may often be less important than the general knowledge and skill levels necessary to implement the technology on a significant economic scale. The future of technological development, however, may lie largely in information that does not instruct, or merely instruct, how to make or use a product; rather, the information is itself the product. This is the case with computer programs, for example, and to an important extent, with semiconductor chip masks. It seems likely to be the case with many products based on recombinant DNA technology. At least in the former two cases, the worldwide trend is to protect these information-based products under copyright or copyright-like statutes. Past experience with industrial property rights to that extent becomes less sure as a guide to Japan's future regulatory attitudes.

This paper begins with a brief discussion of Japan's industrial property rights regime and its possible relationship to Japan's past industrial development, primarily with a view to pointing out the kinds of questions one would like to investigate in detail in drawing lessons from Japan's past. It then turns to a discussion of the Japanese copyright regime, in particular the application of that regime to computer programs, in an effort to evaluate where Japan is now and to guess where it may be going in the protection of the newly developing information-based products.

INDUSTRIAL PROPERTY RIGHTS AND JAPAN'S PAST

A cursory analysis of Japan's historical treatment of industrial property rights is inconclusive on the hypothesis that Japan was less protective of such rights during its development stages than countries that were relatively more advanced technologically. Statutory and judicial protection of trade secrets and against unfair competition has been historically, and remains today, quite weak in Japan in comparison with that afforded in the United States. This fact may supply marginal support for the hypothesis. There is in Japan no general statutory protection for trade secrets (although such a statute is reputedly under serious consideration). Moreover, unfair competition law is primarily aimed at false indications of source or quality and trade disparagement, and there is no general rule against "misappropriation." One can therefore speculate that, even with a strong and enforceable patent law, weakness in the law in these areas permitted at least some appropriation of nonpatentable know-how, learned in the course of implementing imported patented technology under licenses.

On the other hand, general trade secret protection is most valuable against disloyal employees, because any licensor can, at least in theory, protect himself by contract. The explanation for the absence of trade secret protection in Japan may lie therefore primarily in the traditional reluctance of Japanese employees to switch jobs rather than a conscious policy to make foreign technological information more freely available to Japanese industry. Moreover, even in the United States the law against unfair "misappropriation" has had a checkered history and cannot fairly be considered a crucial contribution of intellectual property law to economic development.

Perhaps even more importantly, Japan has had in place throughout this century patent statutes that make no formal discriminations between domestic and foreign inventions and has apparently afforded meaningful protection to patented foreign technology imported into Japan, particularly since World War II.2/ The word "apparently" is used because so much of patent law, especially in Japan, is administrative that information about the actual operation of the system is anecdotal. It is possible that the Japanese Patent Office has systematically protected Japanese inventors more strongly than foreign inventors, but isolated examples of weak protection for foreign patents does not in itself make the case that discrimination was or is being practiced. One cannot seriously claim that Western countries in general or the United States in particular have clearly found the optimum point for drawing the balance between an incentive for invention and the free flow of technological ideas; weaker protection in Japan may simply represent a view that the balance is properly drawn at a different point.

For example, a recent article in the Wall Street Journal describes a small United States company with a basic patent on a microwave lamp that is beleaguered by a much larger Japanese firm that has flooded the Patent Office with "improvement" patents incorporating only slight changes. Armed with these improvement patents, the Japanese firm then seeks royalty-free cross licensing with the American company. While this may seem "unfair" in some abstract sense, it may only show that the Japanese value product competition more highly than we do in relation to the incentive to create.3/

In any event, whatever the Japanese actually did during Japan's period of industrial development seemed to work; Japanese industry was able, during its formative and developing years, to import, learn, and use nearly every aspect of Western technology that was important to it. Intellectual property law, particularly the patent law, undoubtedly played a role, in conjunction with other legal and social norms and administrative practices. Separating the relevant factors and assigning accurate weights to them is an interesting problem that remains to be carefully addressed.

INFORMATION-BASED PRODUCTS AND JAPAN'S FUTURE

Computer programs and mask works for manufacturing semiconductor chips represent a new breed of intellectual property -- products of human intellectual creativity that neither express thoughts, ideas, or feelings to other human beings nor by themselves serve any useful purpose; rather, they serve as coordinators of an appropriate physical environment to allow the performance of useful work or the creation of useful objects. To reverse a trite phrase, with these products the message is also the medium. The process of creating such products resembles the creation of traditional copyrightable works in the engineering design process, such as circuit diagrams or building plans, but in their use they act simply as parts of a machine or other system which are traditionally patentable subject matter. The worldwide trend is to protect computer programs under copyright law, and semiconductor mask works are now protected in the United States, Japan, and a number of other countries under a sui generis but copyright-like statute. While the debate continues over whether copyrights are capable of achieving the proper social balance in application to technological works like computer programs, few who have studied the problem believe that the traditional patent law can do the job either. Consequently, it seems likely that much of our past experience with patent law in relation to economic and technological development will be of questionable relevance in application to the emerging and future information technologies.

This means, in addition, that some understanding of the Japanese copyright system is an indispensable part of any assessment of the future role of intellectual property rights and economic progress in that country. The sections below take a brief look at Japanese copyright law and at some of the recent developments in the application of Japanese copyright law to computer programs.

Japanese Copyright Law

Japanese copyright tradition begins with Japan's first adoption of a copyright statute in

1899.4/ The Japanese Copyright Law (JCL) was amended from time to time and comprehensively revised in 1970; however, few of the statutory fundamentals were changed and even the older judicial decisions continue to influence modern interpretations. Moreover, because copyright enforcement in Japan, as in the United States, is essentially a matter for the courts rather than an administrative agency, traditional legal research methods reveal more about the actual operation of the system than in the case of patent law.

My coauthor and I have recently completed an exhaustive study of the judicial interpretations of Japanese copyright fundamentals in comparison with those of the United States.5/ Our initial hypothesis was that Japan was less protective of copyrighted works than the United States, primarily because the statute seems to set a higher standard of creativity and because it appears more limiting in the types of works protected. Somewhat to our surprise, a comprehensive analysis of all of the reported cases addressing such concepts as the nature of the works protected, the scope of protection, proof of infringement, and fair use defenses showed perhaps greater variety in Japan in verbal formulations of the standards but no consistent pattern that Japan has been or is either more or less protective of copyright than is the United States.

That Japan has consistently been willing to protect copyright rights does not in itself say very much about Japan's attitude toward the relationship of intellectual property rights to economic performance since in Japan, as elsewhere, copyright protection has never extended to technology. The "idea/expression" distinction of copyright law, which is firmly accepted in Japan, denies copyright protection to ideas, methods, and processes. Even a copyright in a book describing technological ideas, methods, or processes protects only against verbatim or near verbatim copying of the author's particular expression, not the idea, method, or process expressed.

Nevertheless, Japan's traditional willingness to protect copyright rights can be expected to have a spillover effect on protection in other areas of intellectual property law, including the radical decision (the Office of the United States Trade

Representative notwithstanding) to apply copyright law to technology in the form of computer programs. The close congruence between Japanese and United States copyright traditions should make us demand clear evidence before we accept claims that Japanese attitudes toward protection will be radically different from ours. An examination of the Japanese decision to protect computer technology under copyright and the initial Japanese judicial interpretations give some hints on the degree of copyright protection that Japan will afford to this new technology. Perhaps more importantly, it provides reasons for believing that Japan is searching not to limit protection for the purpose of permitting technological piracy but for a regime of legal protection that optimizes the degree of technological innovation in this important arena.

The Computer Program Protection Debate in Japan

In 1983, three years after the 1980 amendments of the United States Copyright Act expressly defined "computer programs" and included them within the ambit of copyright protection, the powerful Japanese Ministry of International Trade and Industry (MITI) proposed a sui generis Program Rights Law for the protection of programs in lieu of reliance on copyright. Soon thereafter, the normally less powerful Ministry of Education (MOE) made a counterproposal to treat computer programs as copyrightable works of authorship. Normally, MITI would have been expected to win the intramural battle; but in this case, the United States intervened heavily on the side of MOE. The crux of the U.S. objection was that MITI's Program Rights Law proposed protection for only fifteen years and provided for the possibility of compulsory licensing in instances necessary "in the public interest." The United States, which at least at the time had a significant lead over Japan in software technology, feared that Japan was adopting a scheme of lesser protection for the purpose of pirating our software, the last bastion of American technological supremacy. As a result, MITI capitulated and the Japanese amended their Copyright Law in 1985 to adopt MOE's proposal.

In analyzing this dispute even before it was

resolved, I argued that a permissive attitude toward program piracy made almost no sense from a Japanese point of view.6/ By 1983, both MITI and MOE viewed software as a vital long-term growth industry. Whatever else one may think of MITI, few would accuse it of choosing a regulatory course that focused only on short-term rather than long-term Japanese industrial interests. In fact, the debate in Japan was simply a bureaucratic turf battle over which agency was going to have regulatory authority over an important and growing new industry. Historically, industrial property rights (patent, trademark, unfair competition) have been within MITI's jurisdiction, but the Copyright Law, which theretofore covered primarily artistic and literary works rather than industrial or technological products, fell within the ambit of MOE. A simple amendment of the Copyright Law to include programs would have left MOE as the agency with administrative authority over copyright matters.

MITI's Program Rights Law was in fact very much like copyright in style; the major differences were the shorter term of protection and the compulsory licensing provisions. Significantly, these two provisions could not be effected by amendment of the Copyright Law because of international treaty obligations. Therefore, a new statute would be required, and the natural agency to administer such a statute would be MITI since the objects of protection are much closer in substance to works covered by traditional industrial property rights rather than works protected by copyright. Thus, the MITI proposal had a rational, nonconfiscatory basis that is readily understood in terms of an internal jurisdictional power struggle.

In this connection, it should be borne in mind that the application of copyright law to the protection of computer software is far from a natural or obvious choice.7/ In addition to the problem of protecting technology under copyright, a radical break from the tradition of applying patent and other industrial property laws to technology, copyright's long period of protection, the idea/expression distinction, the substantial similarity test for infringement, and prohibition of compulsory licensing are all problems that could potentially confound the dispute resolution mechanisms8/ and afford an undue monopoly to the first creator of a particularly popular program. In addition, the Berne Convention requires a minimum period of copyright protection of fifty years and prohibits compulsory licensing schemes, so the decision to protect programs under copyright may mean that no experimentation with shorter terms of protection or compulsory licensing systems aimed at more rapid dissemination of the technology will be possible.9/

Protection of Computer Programs in Japan

Although MITI lost the intramural battle, it appears that MITI was not without influence in the statutory changes that were made in the Copyright Act. The debate with MOE brought to the fore in Japan the nature of computer programs as industrial property rather than traditional literary works, and did so much more clearly than CONTU assumed when it recommended amendment of the United States Copyright Act to protect programs. Although it is not clear exactly who was responsible for the statutory language that was ultimately adopted in Japan and there is essentially no legislative history to explain exactly what was intended by the key provisions, the statute contains some express limitations on the protection of computer programs as copyrightable works that are amenable to an interpretation considerably less protective of these works than American courts have generally recognized in the United States.

This does not, however, mean that Japan is seeking a lower level of protection with a view to royalty-free importation of software technology. The appropriate level of protection for programs remains a matter of intense debate in both the United States and Japan (and elsewhere), and I for one have long been arguing that the Japanese limits on the scope of copyright protection of programs are much closer to the socially optimal balance between creation incentives and the free flow of technological ideas than the protective approach generally followed by courts in the United States.10/ There is no question that the Japanese are serious about protecting software. Their differing system of protection is simply a reflection of different estimates concerning where the protective line should be drawn to maximize overall social return.

Major disputes over operating software between Japanese computer manufacturers, such as Hitachi and Fujitsu, and IBM have been widely publicized and might be seen by some as indicative of a general Japanese desire for a lower level of protection. In these cases, the Japanese firms are trying to compete with IBM in the mainframe computer market in which IBM's worldwide position is dominant. IBM is so well-entrenched, in fact, that unless a competitor can offer a compatible system, competition is essentially impossible. The recent dispute between Japan's NEC and Intel similarly involved the effort of a Japanese competitor to offer a compatible part, in this case a key microprocessor for personal computers. Needless to say, the Japanese companies in these cases argued for a narrow view of copyright protection.

These same companies, however, are also beginning to find themselves on the other side of these disputes. NEC, for example, brought an action against Epson for infringing NEC's copyright on operating software contained in a personal computer marketed in Japan. This action placed NEC in the same position with respect to Epson as IBM is with respect to Hitachi and Fujitsu, and in the opposite position from that taken by NEC itself in the Intel litigation. It is simply implausible to assume that Japanese companies, as a group, are going to take a position that permits a confiscatory taking of their software products. Too many of them are major producers of software in their own right.

Moreover, there is no reason to think that the Japanese courts will be unwilling to respect copyright rights in software. Although there are as yet no judicial decisions interpreting the recent Copyright Law amendments, a spate of opinions have recognized and enforced copyright rights in various aspects of videogame programs (and their outputs) even under the preamendment law.

In addition, the one non-videogame program decision to date, also based on the preamendment law, involved a United States company as plaintiff, and the court came down with a highly protective decision.11/ In this case, the American company Microsoft had written a BASIC interpreter as part of the operating system for an NEC personal computer. The defendant decompiled the Microsoft program into source code, added explanatory comments, and published the result in a book, presumably for sale to owners of the program interested in making optimal use of it. The court found these actions by the defendant to be an infringement of Microsoft's copyright. The resulting decision received the support of Japan's leading academic opponent to the application of copyright law to computer programs. This author believes the decision to be overly protectionist,12/ but it should at least give comfort to those who fear that the Japanese will uniformly take a nonprotectionist attitude toward computer software.

CONCLUSIONS

Japan has a long history of intellectual property rights protection and there is no reason to believe that, in general, Japan will be less protective of intellectual property rights in the future. This does not mean that Japan will or should blindly follow United States demands for more or different levels of intellectual property protection, nor should we expect continued quiet Japanese acquiescence in specific approaches to intellectual property problems that have been adopted by the United States (notwithstanding the examples of computer programs and semiconductor chips). The relation between intellectual property rights, technological growth, and economic performance is complex, and ever "higher" levels of protection are not necessarily a social benefit. Higher levels of protection offer gains to society that come from a presumed increased incentive to produce valuable works. Higher levels of protection, however, also decrease the flow of technological ideas and information which can reduce the rate of technological advance and lower productivity of valuable works. These losses must be offset against the gains in determining the social utility of a proposed "higher" level of protection.

Ideally, we will set the level of protection exactly at the balancing point. In practice, of course, no one knows where that point lies, and the Japanese may be expected, and should be encouraged, to experiment. An analysis of current Japanese approaches suggests that Japan may experiment with levels of protection for some of the new information-based technologies that are lower than may be available in the United States, if the American computer software cases to date are any guide. Even if this is true, however, it is not because the Japanese are casual about "piracy." Every thoughtful commentator in Japan, for example, agrees that computer programs should be protected against verbatim copying. How much more protection, if any, should be given to achieve an appropriate balance between creation incentives and technological improvement is a question on which reasonable people differ, both in the United States and in Japan. We should welcome Japanese willingness to innovate in this important area and try to learn from their experience.

NOTES

1. For example, for the first 100 years of its existence, the United States was largely unprotective of foreign works of authorship. See R. Brown and R. Denicola, Copyright, 4th ed., 1985, pp. 636-42.

2. For a recent study of the patent law of Japan and its relation to imported technology, see Note, "The Role of the Patent System in Technology Transfer: The Japanese Experience," Columbia Journal of International Law, vol. 26, 1987, p. 131. For a general introduction to Japanese patent law, see, e.g., T. Doi, The Intellectual Property Law of Japan (1980), pp. 1-67.

3. Wall Street Journal, October 13, 1988, B4.

4. Japan adopted its Design Law and Trademark Law, as well as a major revision of its fourteen-year-old Patent Law in the same year.

5. Karjala and Sugiyama, "Fundamental Concepts in Japanese and American Copyright Law," American Journal of Comp. Law, vol. 36, 1988, p. 613.

6. Karjala, "Lessons from the Computer Software Protection Debate in Japan," Arizona State Law Journal, 1984, pp. 53, 79.

7. E.g., Samuelson, "CONTU Revisited: The Case Against Copyright Protection for Computer Programs in Machine-Readable Form," Duke Law Journal, 1984, p. 663; Samuelson, "Creating a New Kind

of Intellectual Property: Applying the Lessons of the Chip Law to Computer Programs," Minnesota Law Review, vol. 70, 1985, p. 471.

8. Fujitsu of Japan v. IBM is a good example. The arbitrators expressly eschewed comparing the programs involved for substantial similarity, the traditional copyright test for infringement. The arbitrators feared being overwhelmed with detail, which may well be another way of saying that copyright is simply not up to the job of drawing the social policy balances involved in protecting works of this type. The arbitrators resolved the dispute by ordering a complex system of compulsory licensing. No judge implementing the United States Copyright Act could have come to this noncopyright resolution.

9. Karjala, "United States Adherence to the Berne Convention and Copyright Protection of Information-Based Technologies," Jurimetrics, vol. 28, 1988, p. 147.

10. Karjala, "The Protection of Operating Software under Japanese Copyright Law," Jurimetrics Journal, vol. 29, no. 1, Fall 1988; Karjala, "Copyright, Computer Software and the New Protectionism," Jurimetrics, vol. 28, no. 33, Fall 1987; "The Limitations on Protection as Program Works under Japanese Copyright Law," Michigan Yearbook of International Legal Studies, vol. 8, no. 25, 1987; Karjala, "Protection of Computer Programs Under Japanese Copyright Law," European Intellectual Property Review, vol. 8, April 1986, pp. 105-111.

11. Microsoft Corporation v. Shuuwa System Trading KK, Tokyo Dist. Ct. decision of January 30, 1987, 1219 Hanrei Jihoo 48.

12. Karjala, "The First Case on Protection of Operating Systems and Reverse Engineering of Programs in Japan," European Intellectual Property Review, vol. 10, June 1988, p. 172.

14

Intellectual Property Protection in the European Community

Wolf Brueckmann

INTRODUCTION

International comparisons of the role which intellectual property plays in economic performance must take into account the increasingly important influence of the policies of the European Community. Intellectual property systems in the twelve Member States are becoming incorporated into a growing web of Community rules. This influence has been especially notable with respect to two aspects of intellectual property protection. Firstly, the Community is playing a major role in adapting traditional forms of intellectual property protection in Europe to the emerging technologies that are widely viewed as critical to future economic performance. Secondly, in the struggle to widen and strengthen intellectual property rights related to international trade, the Community has sought to forge a consensus policy among its Member States. This has taken the form of forging a common European position at the GATT Uruguay Round Talks and exercising influence in bilateral commercial relations with developing countries.

The first part of this chapter will evaluate actions taken in the European Community to protect emerging technologies within the EC market by focusing on two areas of intellectual property protection crucial to the development of emerging technologies: computer programs and databases. Is the Community taking the initiatives necessary to adequately protect these two areas and create a favorable intellectual property environment for Europe's economic performance in the high-technology sector?

The second part of the chapter will examine the policies the EC has adopted to encourage strengthened protection for intellectual property rights in the GATT. In addition, EC bilateral negotiations with several developing countries will be discussed. The effectiveness of these policies in creating favorable international intellectual property protection for EC high-technology industries will be assessed.

Europe's economic performance would be enhanced by intellectual property protection policies that could accomplish the following:1/

1. Increase EC global competitiveness. This depends upon the competitiveness of the EC sectors like the information industry which promise the greatest future growth. Intellectual property protection is an essential element to the development of these dynamic sectors. An environment must be established in which "European creators and firms can rely on legal protection for their products and activities at least as favorable to their development as that enjoyed by their principal competitors in their home markets."2/
2. Establish greater uniformity of protection. Creating a single internal EC market would eliminate differences in the copyright protection available within the Member States. Differences in national laws and procedures for the protection of intellectual property rights can obstruct or distort cross-frontier trade.
3. Reduce foreign misappropriation. Intellectual property rights developed within the EC must be protected against being "misappropriated by others outside its external frontiers." The EC Commission states that: "holders of intellectual property rights should enjoy a 'fair return' when those rights are exploited in nonmember States."3/

PART ONE: ADAPTING INTELLECTUAL PROPERTY PROTECTION TO EMERGING TECHNOLOGIES: TWO CASE STUDIES

Protection of Computer Programs

The Proposed Directive on Legal Protection of

Computer Programs issued on February 10, 1989 is based upon a careful analysis by the Commission of what system of protection would best serve the interests of Europe's software industry. The Commission concludes that protection by copyright is the most appropriate form of protection and will most effectively promote the growth of Europe's software industry. In its explanatory memorandum, the Commission observes that the "overwhelming weight of evidence" received during the comment process supported this decision.4/

Several considerations prompted the Commission to make this decision. Only protection by copyright can minimize the unauthorized reproduction that will permit EC research and investment in computer technology to continue at a sufficient level to keep pace with other industrialized countries. The Commission concludes that strong and uniform protection is as much in the interests of specialized small and medium-sized software firms as it is for existing major producers. The small firm is particularly vulnerable to being undercut by unauthorized reproduction.

Copyrights create an environment favorable to investment and innovation by European firms. In contrast to various sui generis forms of protection, copyrights provide an established framework of laws and principles as a basis for distinguishing what is or is not protected in a program. Modern technology makes the copying of computer programs extremely easy. Copyright protection is the best assurance to program authors that they can expect a full and fair return on their investment. Furthermore, the dynamic growth of the European software industry depends upon a flexible form of protection that will not lock the industry into a rigid framework. Copyright protection has demonstrated over the years a capacity for adaptation to technological change.

The Commission proposal for copyright protection is also motivated by a concern that European industry obtain protection as favorable as that available to competing firms in their home markets. Japan and the U.S., the two largest trade competitors of the EC, have recognized the protection of computer programs by copyright. The emerging international consensus is clearly moving in this direction. At a meeting of experts in March 1989, under the auspices of WIPO, only three country delegates expressed doubts on copyrights as an appropriate solution: Algeria, Brazil, and Czechoslovakia. This marked the failure of a ten year effort in WIPO to establish a regime of sui generis protection for computer programs.5/

It is also clear that a decision to abandon traditional copyright protection would deprive creators of programs within the EC of the significant advantages of protection under the Berne Convention and Universal Copyright Convention. Reference to these international conventions provide an essential underpinning for EC policies aimed at multilateral and bilateral cooperation to combat international piracy of software, as will be discussed further in the next section of this chapter.

To fully realize the stimulative effect of copyright protection for European economic performance, free circulation of computer software without any restrictions due to diverging intellectual property rules among the Member States must be assured. The Commission proposal therefore seeks to establish legal protection in these Member States where it does not exist and ensure that protection in all Member States is based on common principles. At present, four Member States have adopted protection by copyright: France, West Germany, Spain, and the United Kingdom. In addition, Denmark, Italy, and the Netherlands have legislation pending.6/

The Commission has identified several major areas of difference that must be addressed by harmonization measures:

1. Terms of protection provided by Member States range from twenty-five years from creation to seventy years after the death of the author. The Commission proposes fifty years from the date of creation.
2. The range of programs protected varies due to diverging interpretations of the "originality" criterion. The Commission uses "originality" as the sole criterion to determine the eligibility of protection, meaning, in short, that the work has not been copied. No higher or different standard of originality is established (greater than average skill or exclu-

sion of "commonplace" program).

3. Scope of protection afforded by copyright needs to be broadened. The Commission affirms that the exclusive rights should be accorded to computer programs as literary works, not "as if" they were literary works to which specified limitations might be applied. This is essential to prevent major divergences in the scope of protection afforded under individual Member State laws.

The Commission reaches a strong judgment as to the effects of uneven protection of software among the Member States. Countries with "clear and established protection" are seen as "currently in a more favorable position than countries where protection is uncertain. Such differences in legal protection distort the conditions of establishment and of competition in Member States for firms which engage in activities concerned with computer programs." The Commission sees a direct impact on the technological performance of the Community resulting from a uniform level of protection. The Commission states that "by harmonizing the conditions under which the results of research and development in the computer program field are legally protected on a uniform basis in the Member States, innovation and technical progress throughout the Community will be encouraged."7/ The same logic presumably would apply to affording uniform protection for the global economy.

Another major way in which copyright protection promotes a dynamic European software industry is the balance it strikes between too much and too little protection. The Commission proposal concludes that copyright "provides sufficient flexibility to permit a fair compromise between the divergent interests of producers or suppliers on the one side and users of computer programs on the other."8/ The problem is to find a means of ensuring that the fruits of skill and creativity are protected without creating exclusive rights to mathematical or scientific ideas and thereby stultifying the development of software-related industries. Copyright protection should not inhibit competition in the data processing industry and prevent the spread of computer technology.

A key decision is whether to exclude access

protocols and interfaces from protection. The Commission Proposal acknowledges the principle that to the extent that they constitute expression rather than simply ideas, access protocols and interfaces should be protectable. Article 1(3) states that: "Protection in accordance with this Directive shall apply to the expression in any form of a computer program but shall not extend to the ideas, principles, logic, algorithms or programming languages underlying the program. Where the specification of interfaces constitutes ideas and principles which underlie the program, those ideas and principles are not copyrightable subject matter."

Therefore, the Commission has decided against any sweeping exclusion of access protocols and interfaces. On the other hand, the provisions of the Proposed Directive do not attempt to establish a dividing line between expression and idea. The Commission concludes that this is a dynamic issue that depends upon the evolution of the computer industry as well as upon the success of the courts in drawing the line in concrete cases. Court decisions must attempt to "achieve a reasonable balance between the interests of right-holders in existing programs and of persons who can show that they have independently developed programs to achieve similar results to existing ones."9/

The decision of the Commission to take this approach in the Proposed Directive is crucial since the future development of a dynamic European software industry would be seriously undermined by any shift towards the exclusion of access protocols and interfaces from protection. Such an exclusion would weaken European protection for European computer programs. It would also serve the interests of those software suppliers, most of whom are outside the Community, who place programs on the market, developed in whole or in part, by copying the expression from access protocols and interfaces. These losses would compromise the main competitive advantages of a European program. Such a rule would give European programs less protection in the Community than their competitors enjoy in their home countries.10/

It should be noted that there is consensus among European, Japanese and U.S. industries that "computer programs expressed in any language shall enjoy copyright protection" but that "an idea...

underlying any computer program... shall not be protected subject matter."11/ However, the difficulty and complexity of defining what is meant by access protocols and interfaces make it virtually impossible to achieve a general, uniform definition upon which to draw a line between "idea" and "expression." Action by the courts on a case-by-case basis within the framework of established principles of copyright law would appear to be the best solution.

The danger that strong copyright protection for access protocols and interfaces will stifle competition (often cited by observers in developing countries with a growing domestic software industry) can be easily exaggerated. Commercial considerations place considerable pressure on software developers to make substantial information on interfaces available. Customers require interface information to utilize the programs developers offer. They also desire connectivity to other programs and systems. Software developers need to have third parties write to their interfaces to achieve that connectivity. For those reasons there are market pressures on software developers to make information on interfaces available, both independently and through participation in the implementation of international standards.12/

Protection of Databases

The creation of a common information market has become an important goal of EC policy. In 1987 an action plan to achieve this goal was adopted.13/ The handling and storage of information is increasingly important to all forms of economic activity. One European association notes the following trend: "A reduction in tangible assets and an increase in intangible assets, information, and its use is an accelerating process as the industrial base of society moves towards a service orientated structure.... It is information, analyzed and presented by the computer system, that... provides its owner with commercial advantage."14/

In the Green Paper on Copyright the Commission explores copyright protection problems raised by databases. It defines a "database" as "a collection of information stored and accessed by electronic means."15/ The Commission does not attempt to reach a conclusion on the necessity for Community action on database protection. However, disparities among the Member States in protection afforded to databases could have numerous economic repercussions. It could result in distortions in the concentration of database creation geographically, the distribution of investment in creating databases, and the availability of databases within the Community.

The Commission identifies three issues that the use of computerized information systems creates from a copyright point of view. The first issue is the incorporation into a database of literary works already protected under copyright. In this area solutions are attainable within the framework of existing copyright principles, and therefore the Commission concludes action to create additional legal protection would be "at best premature."

The second issue is the retrieval of works stored in computerized databases. Retrieval of data through printouts is generally accepted as an art restricted through copyright. However, display of information from machine-readable databases raises novel considerations. In some cases a user can misappropriate the entire value of a database through unauthorized downloading without ever "reproducing" a copy. The Commission is seeking further views about the necessity of introducing protection on this issue.

The most serious and controversial issue concerns the question as to whether the mode of compilation within the database should be protected. The Commission notes that questions can arise as to whether or not a given compilation of information is subject to copyright, depending on the level of originality and creativity which the compilation represents. The buying and selling of databases containing factual information is a rapidly growing business. Therefore the Commission has requested comments on whether a sui generis regime of protection should be considered.16/

Indications are that reaction from the business community to adapting sui generis protection is likely to be strongly negative. It would subject authors and users to a variety of uncertain, ad hoc levels of protection. Furthermore, it would deprive authors of the benefits of the Berne Convention and UCC, thereby giving databases produced in the EC inadequate protection in the rest of the world. It would also make it more difficult for potential users or subscribers in the EC to obtain databases produced outside the EC.17/

PART TWO: EUROPEAN COMMUNITY POLICIES ON TRADE-RELATED INTELLECTUAL PROPERTY RIGHTS

Creating strengthened protection for intellectual property rights within the global trading system is important for Europe's economic performance in two respects. Firstly, the EC is suffering major trade losses due to piracy and counterfeiting overseas. Although there is no comprehensive data comparable to that gathered in the U.S. by the International Trade Commission, the available evidence gives a rough indication that they have a major impact relative to total EC trade activities.18/

In addition, high technology industry exports whose competitive advantage depends heavily on non-material attributes (design, image, information content, etc.) are especially vulnerable to copying for commercial purposes at a fraction of the cost of developing the original product. The dynamic European high technology sectors are especially hard-hit by international piracy, thereby magnifying the impact on Europe's economic performance.

The Commission has become increasingly active in developing a consensual EC policy on trade-related aspects of intellectual property rights within the context of its responsibility for the common commercial policy. To a significant extent, Commission policy has responded to growing pressures from the European business community to strengthen intellectual property protection in foreign markets. A milestone in this evolution was intervention in 1982 by the European business community to reverse Commission policy at a decisive moment in international negotiations to revise the Paris Convention for Patents and Trademarks. Since the start in 1986 of GATT multilateral negotiations on trade-related aspects of intellectual property, European industry has made additional efforts to exert influence on the direction of EC policy. This has been done primarily through the

Union of Industrial and Employers' Confederation of Europe (UNICE) and through trilateral initiatives in cooperation with the U.S. and Japanese communities.

The evolution of a common EC position in the GATT Uruguay Round negotiating group on intellectual property will be explored in the next section of this chapter. The EC is now forced to make decisions about a crucial issue: What division of labor between GATT and other international fora where intellectual property protection is discussed (primarily WIPO) would best serve EC trade interests?

This chapter will examine recent EC submissions to the GATT on several key points relating to a future agreement on intellectual property in the Uruguay Round. Parallel to these developments at the multilateral level, the Community has also been involved in bilateral activities relating to intellectual property protection. The relationship between multilateral and bilateral policies is a basic question of strategy efforts to secure improved protection for intellectual property rights in the global trading system.

EC Policy in the GATT Uruguay Round Negotiations

To what extent is EC policy at the multilateral level helping to achieve the strengthened protection and enforcement of intellectual property rights so vital to European industries in general, and to Europe's information industry sector in particular? An assessment of the Community position as it stands at the midpoint (April 1989) of the GATT Uruguay Round negotiations will be made by examining three key issues: (1)the relationship between GATT and WIPO activities, (2)the part played by substantive standards in a proposed GATT intellectual property agreement, and (3)attracting the participation of developing countries in a future GATT agreement.

The EC submission to the GATT negotiating group in November 1987 marks a major shift from the position taken at the beginning of the Uruguay Round on the relationship between GATT and WIPO. Initially the EC was noncommittal towards U.S. proposals for a strong GATT role that would include three essential elements: (1)adequate standards of protection for trade-related intellectual property rights, (2)effective means to enforce those standards, and (3)effective dispute settlement procedures. The early EC position displayed strong sympathy for the view of many developing countries that WIPO should be the forum for discussions on intellectual property protection issues. During the early stage of the Uruguay Round the EC appeared to favor confining GATT to completing the work begun in the Tokyo Round of multilateral trade negotiations, which was limited to adopting an anti-counterfeiting code. The Community did, however, support expanding the coverage of the proposed code beyond trademarks to other intellectual property rights.19/

The November 1987 EC submission radically departs from that approach and endorses a broader role for the GATT: "The problems created by inadequate or sometimes excessive substantive standards are very serious and require multilateral solutions; ... a transposition within the GATT legal system of the rules that enjoy wide international recognition would strengthen the effective protection of the trade interests stemming from intellectual property rights."20/

This new EC approach was in large part a response to criticism from European industry. A UNICE position paper submitted to the Commission prior to the shift in EC policy observes that "basically, the Commission has elected to limit its priorities to the implementation of mechanisms aimed at enforcing certain widely recognized rights. UNICE stated that this was deemed too narrow by European industry."21/ This recommendation reflected growing recognition by European industry that the international intellectual property regimes currently administered by WIPO -- the Berne Convention and International Copyright Convention for copyright and the Paris Convention for Patents and Trademarks -- would be unable to protect them from extensive losses to foreign piracy.

Several factors are viewed by industry as contributing to the inadequacy of the current multilateral agreements. While some of the international intellectual property conventions require adherents to provide high standards for foreign right holders, others do not. Signatories to these conventions are merely bound to provide national treatment. In many countries, foreign right holders are only promised the same inadequate protection that domestic law provides to domestic right holders. The conventions were never intended to be used as enforcement mechanisms for intellectual property rights. While they ostensibly require governments to implement their provisions, they do not provide either bilateral or multilateral dispute settlement provisions to ensure compliance.22/

A second major development in EC policy toward the GATT Uruguay Round negotiations is the decision to support the negotiation of substantive intellectual property standards. The EC submission of July 1988 refers to "the necessity of developing a comprehensive GATT approach to substantive standards." It further states that "if achieved, the result will strengthen both the GATT and other multilateral fora, including the World Intellectual Property Organization."23/

The Commission proposes that substantive standards should cover the trade-related aspects of patents, trademarks, copyrights, computer programs, neighboring rights, models and designs, semiconductor chip layouts, appellations, and arts contrary to commercial practices. Guidelines with respect to each are proposed in the submission. From the perspective of the software industry, this enumeration of issues is seriously flawed. Acceptance of a sui generis approach to computer program protection is suggested by the treatment of computer programs as a separate category from copyrights. It would appear to be inconsistent with the Proposed Directive on Legal Protection of Computer Programs discussed earlier in this chapter. It also appears at odds with the EC commitment to "transposing" international rules "that enjoy wide international recognition," as expressed in the EC submission.24/ Currently most developed countries recognize copyright protection as provided by the Berne Copyright Convention should be granted to computer programs.

A more general defect of the EC position on substantive standards is the failure to make clear an intention to negotiate binding substantive standards within the GATT. If the signatories to a future GATT agreement are not bound to incorporate the standards into their national laws and to enforce them, then European industry would not realize the major benefit of bringing standards into the GATT. If the binding nature of the substantive standards is not established, the effectiveness of adopting dispute settlement provisions allowing for appropriate sanctions would be called into question.

A third major issue for the intellectual property negotiations in GATT is attracting the participation of developing countries in a future agreement. There is considerable concern in the business community that the EC might seek to encourage participation by lowering the effective level of protection of intellectual property rights. Minimum standards of protection cannot become subject to "split the difference" bargaining that may be appropriate in some types of trade negotiations. Those standards must not be allowed to drop below a consensus existing among those countries engaged in the bulk of the trade in goods or services which embody intellectual property and whose existing national intellectual property systems are supporting growth in trade and investment flows. Faced with the prospect of diminishing the level of protection in order to attract participation, many in the business community would prefer to begin with fewer signatories.

The question of how to create incentives for developing countries which have expressed opposition to a GATT agreement on intellectual property remains a difficult one. Efforts to create various exceptions to the obligations imposed by the agreement to accommodate the public policy objectives of these countries including "developmental and technical objectives" (a phrase used in the GATT Mid-Term Agreement of April 8, 1989), would undermine the basic purpose of an agreement. The basic incentive for participation is that the benefits and rights of the intellectual property agreement would be enjoyed only by the parties thereto. Special incentives of modest scope might be extended to developing countries, such as providing technical assistance for developing adequate national laws and for training government officials (examiners, customs officials, etc.) in the administration of the intellectual property protection regimes.

In the final analysis, the decisive incentive

must be a perception by decision-makers in developing countries that positive benefits in trade, investment, and technology transfer would accrue to their economies under improved protection for intellectual property rights. The EC stresses the self-interest argument in its most recent GATT submission of July, 1988:

> The Community is convinced that adequate protection of intellectual property not only helps prevent distortions and impediments to international trade but that it contributes to economic growth and development, for example through increased transfers of technology and of direct international investment. The available evidence is beyond dispute: in the absence of adequate protection of basic intellectual property rights, voluntary international transfers of technology and capital are generally reduced. In the absence of adequate protection, investment in research and development will also suffer.25/

Bilateral Relations

In its submission to the GATT of July 1988, the EC "remains firmly attached to the objective of furthering multilateral solutions" while acknowledging that "the alternative to effective multilateral action will undoubtedly be increased recourse to bilateral or unilateral measures of a character which cannot but undermine the multilateral system, be it in the field of trade or in that of intellectual property and to the detriment of most trading partners." Consistent with this position the EC has been critical of U.S. bilateral trade actions designed to obtain adequate and effective intellectual property protection.26/ It has supported the formation of a GATT Panel to review the U.S. decision to retaliate against Brazil on the issue of inadequate pharmaceutical patent protection.

In a number of specific instances, however, the EC has pursued trade-related intellectual property objectives through bilateral means under Article 113, responsibility to establish a common commercial policy. Illustrations are provided by several activities undertaken in recent years in response to specific copyright issues:

1. In response to the requirements imposed by U.S. legislation, a Council Directive was issued in 1984 to secure protection on an interim basis for European semiconductor producers in the U.S. market pending adoption of Community legislation, which was adopted in December 1986.
2. Representations were made to Japanese authorities in 1984 expressing concern about the possibility that Japan would adopt a sui generis form of protection for software. Subsequently the Japanese Government chose to provide protection under copyright law.
3. In summer 1986, the Community made representations to Nigeria on a variety of intellectual property concerns, including inadequate legal provisions against piracy of copyrighted material.
4. Since early 1987, the Commission has consulted with Malaysia on a bill for copyright protection that would adversely affect Community right holders and is continuing to monitor the situation.
5. The Community took bilateral action on a failure by Korea to grant certain intellectual property rights to EC nationals and enterprises that had previously been granted to U.S. nationals under the terms of a Section 301 agreement. After the failure of talks with Korean officials, the Community decided in December 1987 to suspend generalized tariff preferences against products originating in the Republic of Korea.
6. Improved cooperation on intellectual property protection is being raised by the Community in the context of a variety of bilateral trade discussions, such as those under the Multifiber Agreement and the Lome Convention.27/

The bilateral activity with Korea represents an important departure for EC policy because it went beyond consultations and resulted in a trade action, specifically the suspension of GSP. In contrast to the U.S., the EC does not make adequacy of intellectual property protection a criterion in granting GSP benefits. The Commission decision to establish such a linkage in response to Korean intransigence was therefore a significant departure.

Possible future linkages between intellectual property protection and trade action could result from EC adoption of new trade policy instrument in September 1984. It is designed to enable the Community to respond more effectively to the illicit commercial practices of third world countries, which are defined as practices either incompatible with international law or with "generally accepted rules" in the international trading community.

Complaints can be brought to the Commission by private individuals, associations or Member States. If the Commission concludes after internal consultations that action is warranted, it may take a variety of commercial policy measures (including raising duties or imposing quantitative restrictions) providing they are consistent with all EC international obligations.28/

The first application of the new commercial policy instrument to an intellectual property issue took place in response to a complaint against Indonesia by the International Federation of Phonogram and Videogram Producers in March 1987. The complaint alleged serious injury to EC industries due to the lack of protection in Indonesia against unauthorized reproduction of sound carriers. Consultations were held with Indonesian authorities. Although a commitment to take corrective action was given, no bilateral agreement has yet been negotiated that would consolidate this outcome.29/ While no trade actions were taken in the course of this first application of the commercial policy instrument, the availability of a new bilateral option was clearly established.

In the Green Paper on Copyright the Commission states that "in the field of intellectual property, and copyright in particular, the new instrument could conceivably play a significant role in the future." However, one essential prerequisite is to establish that infringements of intellectual property rights as recognized by multilateral conventions are taking place and causing injury to European industry. The Green Paper concludes that since the rules of the Berne, Universal Copyright, and Paris Conventions are "generally accepted" among countries accounting for most of world trade, violations of these rules would constitute "illicit commercial practices" within the meaning of the new commercial instrument. An additional prerequisite is that the intellectual property infringements can be shown to be attributable to a particular country because it has failed to enact adequate laws or undertake effective enforcement action.30/

The Green Paper also concludes, however, that the practical usefulness of the new commercial policy instrument will be dependent on the active cooperation of European industry. "The industries concerned will not only have to be prepared to use it, but also to prepare possible complaints carefully and communicate relevant information to the Commission."31/ Government officials must rely heavily on the private sector because insufficient manpower and expertise exists within government to deal with extremely complex intellectual property issues.

CONCLUSIONS

Europe's future economic performance is linked to assuring protection for intellectual property rights that its most dynamic industries must have in order to flourish. This chapter has focused on two specific challenges that must be met. The first is to adapt existing intellectual property regimes in the twelve Member States to the needs of emerging technologies. The second is the need to strengthen international protection of intellectual property. Our examination has shown that policies at the European Community level are playing a significant part in efforts to meet those two challenges.

Computer software and database protection were selected as two critical factors in creating a favorable environment for Europe's high technology growth industries. The Community is making a significant contribution by working towards adequate copyright protection for software throughout the twelve Member States. It has stressed the need to provide protection comparable to that in principal competitor states, thereby promoting the growth of a globally competitive uniformity of protection among the Member States. The future

Directive on Software will provide the European software industry a single internal market in which to grow.

The Green Paper analysis of database protection indicates that the Commission is attempting to identify and anticipate the issues in this important emerging area. The rapidly growing economic importance of databases is evident, and it will play a vital part in the creation of a European information services market.

In Part Two, the evaluation of EC policies to strengthen international practices of intellectual property rights was examined. At the multilateral level EC policy has moved toward strong support for a GATT agreement that provides not only improved enforcement, but also adequate substantive standards and effective dispute settlement procedures. EC officials have become increasingly sensitive to the damage which foreign misappropriation of intellectual property rights is doing to European industries. Our discussion also suggested that the EC is prepared to utilize bilateral means to achieve improved intellectual property protection. The new commercial policy instrument opens up an additional avenue of bilateral action. Exactly what mix of bilateral and multilateral efforts the EC will settle on remains to be seen.

NOTES

1. Commission of the European Communities, Green Paper on Copyright and the Challenge of Technology - Copyright Issues Requiring Immediate Action, COM(88) 172 final, June 7, 1988. Chapter One contains a useful analysis of how copyright protection impacts upon the creation of a single European market.
2. Ibid.
3. Ibid.
4. "Proposal for a Council Directive on the Legal Protection of Computer Programs," COM(88) 816 final -- SYN 183 (January 5, 1989), para. 3.6.
5. International Chamber of Commerce, "Summary of WIPO: Meeting of Committee of Experts on Model Provisions for Legislation in the Field of Copyright" (February 20 to March 3, 1989), p. 1.
6. Ibid., Explanatory Memo, para. 2.9.

7. Ibid., para. 5.4.

8. Ibid., para. 3.7.

9. Ibid., para. 3.7.

10. IBM Europe, Comments on the Green Paper on Copyright and the Challenge of Technology (September 1988), pp. 10-11.

11. "Statement of Views of the European, Japanese and United States Business Communities," Basic Framework of GATT Provisions on Intellectual Property (June 1988), p. 67.

12. IBM Europe, pp. 11-12.

13. The establishment at Community level of a policy and a plan of priority actions for the development of an information services market, COM(87) 360 final.

14. "Business Equipment and Information Technology Association," Draft Response to Law Commission Paper 110 (February 23, 1989), Appendix.

15. Green Paper on Copyright, p. 205.

16. Ibid., pp. 208-216.

17. United States Council for International Business, "Comments on Chapter 6: Databases," Green Paper on Copyright (June 7, 1988).

18. United States International Trade Commission, Foreign Protection of Intellectual Property Rights and the Effect on U.S. Industry and Trade (February 1988). No comparable study has been done for the EC market. See Green Paper, ch. 2.

19. European Community, "Statement by the Representative of the European Communities to the GATT Negotiating Group on Intellectual Property in Geneva," March 25, 1987.

20. European Community, Guidelines on Trade-Related Aspects of Intellectual Property Rights, (MTN.GNG/NG/11/W/16) (November 1987).

21. Union of Industrial and Employers' Confederation of Europe, Position Paper on GATT and Intellectual Property (April 29, 1987).

22. "Statement of Views of the European, Japanese and United States Business Communities," ibid., p. 15.

23. European Community, Guidelines and Objectives Proposed by the European Community for the Negotiations on Trade-Related Aspects of Substantive Standards of Intellectual Property Rights (MTN.GNG/NG11/W/26) (July 1988), p. 1.

24. European Community, March 25, 1987.

25. European Community, July 1988, p. 2.

26. Auke Haagsma, "A View from the European Community," in Intellectual Property Rights and Capital Formation in the Next Decade, eds. Charles E. Walker and Mark A. Bloomfield (Lanham: University Press of America, 1988).

27. Green Paper, pp. 226-29.

28. Ibid., pp. 232-35.

29. Ibid., p. 235.

30. Ibid., p. 234.

31. Ibid., p. 235.

PART FIVE

Conclusion

15

Developing a Framework for Intellectual Property Protection to Advance Innovation

Alden F. Abbott

INTRODUCTION

In recent years public policymakers have shown an increased awareness of the link between the legal protection of intellectual property rights and innovation. At the urging of the United States, intellectual property protection was included in the agenda of the ongoing Uruguay Round of GATT trade negotiations. Intellectual property protection has also increasingly been featured in legislative proposals designed to enhance the "competitiveness" of American industry. For example, the Semiconductor Chip Protection Act of 1984 gave the creators of semiconductor chip designs exclusive rights for ten years over the reproduction, distribution, and importation of a semiconductor mask work. Most recently, the Omnibus Trade and Competitiveness Act of 1988 closed a loophole in U.S. patent law by providing that importation or sale in the United States of a product produced abroad in violation of a U.S. process patent would infringe that patent. The 1988 Act also eliminated the requirement that an intellectual property holder alleging infringement show injury as a prerequisite to obtaining import relief under section 337 of the Tariff Act. There is every indication that intellectual property protection will remain prominent in the public policy debate over American competitiveness for the foreseeable future.

I will argue herein that public policymakers' newfound concern for the protection of intellectual property is well warranted. Indeed, intellectual property protection plays an essential role in inducing the R&D that is a cornerstone of competitive success in emerging technology-intensive industries. After summarizing the constitutional underpinnings of intellectual property protection and the principal forms such protection has taken in the United States, I will turn to the public policy debate over whether strong intellectual property protection is warranted. After concluding that robust protection is called for, I will then briefly discuss a few possible government initiatives aimed at enhancing intellectual property rights.

CONSTITUTIONAL UNDERPINNINGS OF INTELLECTUAL PROPERTY PROTECTION

Intellectual property rights are the legally protected property interests individuals possess in the fruits of their intellectual endeavors. The framers of the Constitution granted Congress the power to enact laws protecting intellectual property in Article I, section 8, clause 8, of the Constitution, which states:

> The Congress shall have power . . . To promote the Progress of Science and useful Arts, by securing for limited Times to Authors and Inventors the exclusive Right to their respective Writings and Discoveries.

In referring to promoting "the Progress of Science and Useful Arts," the Constitution clearly evinces an understanding that intellectual property protection spurs people to engage in the innovative activity that leads to scientific and technological improvements. The framers clearly believed that the protection of intellectual property would redound to the benefit of society as a whole. Madison's statement in The Federalist in support of the constitutional authorization for intellectual property legislation could not be more unequivocal: "The utility of this power will scarcely be questioned.... The public good fully coincides...with the claims of the individuals."1/

FORMS OF INTELLECTUAL PROPERTY PROTECTION

Congress has exercised its constitutional authority over the years to provide statutory protection for four principal forms of intellectual property: patents, copyrights, trademarks, and semiconductor mask works.2/ Trade secrets, which do not fall into any one of these three categories, are protected under state law. Intellectual property rights, like property rights in general, give the owner the legally enforceable right to exclude others from making, using, or selling his property, without having to contract with them.

Patents

Patent protection extends to the application of an idea. Patent protection may benefit society by encouraging inventors to make significant innovative techniques publicly known, rather than keep them secret. A patent allows an inventor of any "novel, useful, and nonobvious" product, process, or design to exclude others from making, using, or selling his invention in the United States for seventeen years. When the patent expires, the invention becomes freely available to the public without restriction. To qualify for patent protection, an inventor must apply for a patent and secure a finding that his invention is indeed patentable.

The grant of a patent empowers an owner to sue anyone he believes has been using, making, or selling the invention as claimed in the patent without authorization. Even if a patent is granted, it may be challenged in court for failure to meet required standards of patentability (for example, a patented item may be deemed "obvious"), for fraud in the patent application process, or for "patent misuse" (inequitable conduct by the patent holder). Furthermore, under existing legal precedents, the scope of a patentee's property right is limited; for example, a patentee's restrictive licensing practices may expose him to charges of antitrust violations.

Copyrights

Copyright law protects the original expression of an idea, whether literary, artistic, commercial, or other. An author or copyright holder (an author may assign his right to someone else) need not apply for a copyright; protection attaches as soon as a work is fixed in a tangible medium. Thus a wide variety of forms of property that may be fixed in a tangible medium -- such as written works, sound recordings, and computer programs -- are protected by copyright. Under current United States law, copyright protection generally extends until fifty years after the death of the author. Unlike a patented work, a copyrighted work need not be novel; the test is that the work originated with an author and was not copied from some other source. The work's general ideas and themes may have appeared in earlier works.

The copyright owner has the exclusive right to copy or distribute a copyrighted work and to perform publicly or display derivative works. Anyone who engages in these activities without authorization may be sued for damages, injunctive relief (a prohibition on further copying), and attorneys' fees. The copyright owner may also sue for damages and injunctive relief against anyone who is producing anything substantially similar to a "derivative" of a copyrighted work, such as a play or motion picture. In addition, the copyright owner has exclusive rights, with respect to most works, to display and perform the work. Copyright law confers less than a complete right to prevent copying. Under the "fair use" doctrine, limited copying may be allowed on the basis of such factors as the purpose of the use (copying for scholarly purposes enjoys greater approval than copying for commercial purposes), the nature of the copyrighted work, the proportion of the work that is taken, the economic impact of the taking, the motives of the defendant, and the First Amendment interest in limiting the scope of the copyright. Applying the "fair use" doctrine, the Supreme Court has held that private videotaping, off air, for home viewing at a different time than the broadcast of copyrighted programming constitutes a fair use and thus does not violate copyright law.3/

Trademarks

A trademark is any distinctive device (such as a word or symbol) that is appropriated and used in trade or commerce to indicate the origin or sponsorship of goods or services. A trademark remains protected as long as it is in use. Under federal law, trademarks may be registered and a trademark owner may sue those who use a trademark without his permission. Infringement occurs if there is a "likelihood of confusion" resulting from the unauthorized use of the same or confusingly similar mark on the same or similar goods or services. This principle reflects the fact that one of the primary benefits of trademarks is to reduce consumers' search costs by precisely identifying goods that have particular, well-defined attributes.

A mark that has come to represent a generic name of the goods (such as the term "thermos"), rather than the source or sponsorship of the goods, no longer enjoys trademark protection. Moreover, a limited "fair use" exception exists; under this exemption, for example, a retailer can use a mark to advertise that he has goods bearing that mark for sale. In addition, the Supreme Court has ruled that a U.S. trademark holder cannot prevent importation through unauthorized distribution channels of validly trademarked goods produced abroad, when the U.S. trademark holder and the foreign manufacturer of the trademarked good are under common corporate control (as in a parent-subsidiary relationship).4/

Semiconductor Mask Works

The Semiconductor Chip Protection Act of 1984 established intellectual property protection for the mask works that embody the design for a particular semiconductor chip. Under the Act, a semiconductor mask work's creator is given the exclusive right to reproduce, import, distribute, and sell the mask work for a period of ten years. A mask work must be original (it need not meet the criteria of "novelty" and "nonobviousness" which applies to patents) and must be registered within two years of its first commercial exploitation to qualify for protection under the Act. Only civil remedies are available for violation of the Act. Section 1343 of the Omnibus Trade and Competitiveness Act of 1988 provided a basis for excluding from the United States semiconductor chips that infringe a registered mask work, by providing that the importation of such infringing chips would violate section 337 of the Tariff Act of 1930 (which deals with "unfair methods of competition" and "unfair acts and practices" in import trade).

Trade Secrets

Trade secrets or "know-how" are protected by state, rather than federal, law. According to section 757, comment b, of the Restatement of Torts (1939), which many states have relied upon in fashioning their trade secret laws:

> a trade secret may consist of any formula, pattern, device or compilation of information which is used in one's business, and which gives him an opportunity to obtain an advantage over competitors who do not know or use it. It may be a formula for a chemical compound, a process of manufacturing, treating, or preserving materials, a pattern for a machine or other device, or a list of customers.

Although the subject of a trade secret must not be of public or general knowledge in a business, the necessary element of secrecy is not lost if the trade secret holder reveals the trade secret to someone in confidence and under an implied obligation not to use or disclose it. For example, the employee or licensee of a trade secret holder may be duty-bound to keep the secret in confidence. A trade secret holder may be able to sue for damages and obtain an injunction in the case of unauthorized disclosure by someone who had a duty not to divulge a secret or by someone who obtained a secret by improper means, such as theft or wiretapping. Trade secret laws, however, do not protect against discovery by "fair and honest means," such as reverse engineering (starting with the known product and working backward to determine how it was made), independent invention, or accidental disclosure. Federal patent law does not preempt state trade secret laws.5/ Furthermore, state-recognized trade secret property rights are protected from governmental taking without just compensation by the takings clause of the Fifth Amendment to the Constitution.6/

ECONOMIC RATIONALE FOR INTELLECTUAL PROPERTY PROTECTION

Intellectual Property Protection and Innovation

The exclusive rights conferred by intellectual property law give inventors, authors, and manufacturers incentives to devote resources to the creation of new literary and artistic works, symbols, and inventions. These new forms of property spur innovation; that is, by encouraging research and development (R&D), they bring forth new goods and services and lower the cost of producing existing goods and services. Intellectual property is essentially information, which, if not protected, can be used by free-riding competitors (firms that have not shared in the expense of creating intellectual property) of the property's developer at zero cost to the competitors. (Information has attributes of a "public good," that is, it can be consumed by more than one user without being reduced in quantity, and third parties cannot easily be prevented from using it.) Because of free-riding, firms have weak incentives to absorb the costly expenditures needed to develop intellectual property. Thus the pace of innovation is slow and a less than socially optimal amount of intellectual property is produced in a world without intellectual property protection. In other words, because firms can extract only a small portion of the social benefits flowing from the intellectual property they have created, a lack of intellectual property protection causes social underinvestment in R&D.

Even with intellectual property protection, however, some leakage or spillover of technological knowledge is probably inevitable in light of the difficulty of fully preventing disclosure of something as intangible as information. Given the mobility of personnel among firms and the embodiment of knowledge in products, the holder of intellectual property rights will be hard-pressed to prevent unauthorized third parties from having any access to the information he has developed. Some commentators view such incidental leakage as beneficial insofar as it facilitates the efficient spread of newly created knowledge without unduly deterring innovative activity.

Concerns about Intellectual Property Protection

Some authors stress the supposed disadvantages of intellectual property protection.7/ It is said that the "monopoly" conferred upon the intellectual property owner misallocates resources by allowing the profit-seeking owner to price above marginal cost (the cost of producing an extra unit of output) and reduce the output of goods embodying intellectual property. Thus the dynamic gains in innovation stemming from intellectual property protection must be weighed against the social deadweight losses that intellectual property rights impose. According to basic economic theory, deadweight losses occur because the sale of a good at greater than its marginal cost inefficiently limits the resources devoted to producing that good. Some consumers who would have been willing to pay an amount equal to or greater than marginal cost -- but below the "monopolist's" sales price -- are prevented from buying the good. These social costs are not offset by dynamic gains, insofar as an innovation would have been brought forth anyway at the same time without intellectual property protection. Additional costs may include the wasteful expenditure of resources by those who seek to invent around a patent or by those who use up scarce resources in competing for, but failing to obtain, a patent.

Even without governmentally established monopoly rights, it is argued, innovators may be able to garner an adequate return to their efforts through pricing strategies, such as selling the first items embodying an innovation at a price high enough that they can more than recoup their R&D expenditures. Alternatively, innovators may protect their intellectual property through such devices as "technological fences" which prevent unauthorized use (for example, the scrambling of television signals by program owners or the insertion of bugs to forestall copying of computer programs). Other forms of innovator protection include the joint provision of information-laden innovative goods and revenue-raising goods (for example, the joint dissemination of television programs and advertising), and the use of contractual arrangements in conjunction with trade secrecy law (for example, the lease of an innovative good to a user, with contractual penalties specified if the user disseminates information concerning the innovation to a third party).8/ The crux of these arguments is that purely private remedies may provide ample incentives for the creation of intellectual property.

The arguments against governmentally created intellectual property rights are unconvincing for several reasons. First, the exclusive legal rights conferred on an intellectual property owner do not necessarily give that owner an economic monopoly. Patented, trademarked, and copyrighted items typically compete with a vast array of substitute products and processes. To the extent that such competition exists, an intellectual property holder's ability to price the goods embodying his innovation at far above cost is constrained.9/ Moreover, intellectual property law creates less than complete property rights. A patent is of limited scope and temporary duration. In addition, since only significant innovations are patentable, routine technological improvements are not granted legal monopoly status. Copyrighted works can in part be disseminated without the owner's permission under the "fair use" doctrine. Moreover, trademark protection is lost when a term comes to signify the generic name of a class of goods. Trade secret law does not protect against inadvertent disclosure or independent development of a commercial secret. Furthermore, because of difficulties in monitoring the use of information, some unauthorized spillover of innovative ideas may be expected. For all these reasons, the exclusive legal rights created by intellectual property protection are sharply circumscribed, and hence the degree of deadweight loss due to that protection is limited.

Second, there is good reason to believe that the dynamic gains due to intellectual property protection vastly outweigh any deadweight losses. When an innovation brings forth a new good or service, the gross welfare gain to society is measured by the difference between the total value consumers assign to that good or service (in graphical terms, the area under the demand curve) and its total cost of production. Because deadweight loss (which represents that triangle under the demand curve composed of consumers who value the innovative product at greater than marginal cost but are unwilling to pay the price charged by the producer) accounts for only a small proportion of that gross welfare gain, intellectual property protection that is responsible for the development of an innovation confers substantial net welfare gains on society. The gains in one industry are often magnified by the propensity of innovators to confer collateral benefits on other markets as well. For example, the invention of the transistor not only benefited purchasers of radios but revolutionized a host of other industries. Admittedly, intellectual property protection may also waste some resources by spurring unsuccessful competitors' efforts to obtain patents and by causing some firms to try to invent around patents. Such activities may also, however, prove cost-beneficial, by engendering product and process improvements or additional innovative goods and services.

Third, although an invention might have come about anyway, even in the absence of intellectual property protection, this cannot be proved with respect to any particular invention. More generally, while it is certainly true that ideas will flourish whether or not intellectual property protection exists, this does not guarantee that the ideas would result in socially beneficial products and processes. Whether a particular research project will bear fruit is difficult to tell ahead of time. Although a certain percentage of projects may be expected to bring forth innovations, it may not be possible to identify the researcher or research design that will do so. This follows from the imperfect nature of information about product and process improvements. If there were no uncertainty concerning the exact means of bringing about technological progress, innovation would be a trivial task. A large number of research efforts will inevitably end in failure and impose losses on firms. Accordingly, risk-averse firms will be reluctant to hire research staffs and establish research facilities if there is no assurance that profits can be earned on that small portion of innovative projects.10/ Intellectual property protection provides that necessary assurance. Without such protection firms would run the risk that, because of free-riding, their innovations would earn insufficient profits to offset the losses stemming from failed research efforts. For the same reason, capital markets would be far less willing to provide funds for independent research efforts in a world without intellectual property protection. In short, without intellectual property protection, talented scientists and engineers would find it much harder to obtain the backing needed to explore new avenues of research, and innovation would proceed at a far slower pace to the detriment of society.

Fourth, purely private means -- such as pricing strategies, technological fencing, the joint provision of information goods and revenue-creating goods, and contractual arrangements -- are less than ideal. They do not avoid the creation of deadweight loss, since they are designed to allow the innovator to reduce output and to price above marginal cost. Indeed, they may lead innovators to devise distribution schemes that are more restrictive, and thus more socially costly, than those used when intellectual property protection exists, because innovators denied such protection face greater losses from free-riding than innovators who can rely on infringement suits.

Charging high prices to the first users may not be practical if there is initial uncertainty about the value of the information being provided. Moreover, a high pricing strategy may slow the socially desirable diffusion of knowledge by initially excluding many potential purchasers. Technological fencing may not prove feasible in all cases; for example, scarce resources may be wastefully devoted to developing countermeasures aimed at overcoming a bug that prevents unauthorized copying of computer programs. There may be antitrust law obstacles to the joint provision of goods which in certain cases may be deemed to constitute prohibited tying of a second good to a good that possesses market power.

Contractual arrangements designed to prevent the unauthorized disclosure of information may founder because of high transactions costs and difficulties in monitoring the behavior of the "borrowers" of information. Transactions costs combined with opportunistic behavior are highly important. Under a regime of no protection, if there are large numbers of potential information borrowers, each borrower may hold out in the hope that at least one of the contracting users will prove lax in protecting information or will accept a side payment to divulge it. This would be a logical strategy, since unauthorized use of information that leaks out is not illegal. Given the possibilities of leakage, however, contracts for the lending of information may not be entered into at all. This conclusion is particularly compelling if the developer of information cannot readily tell ahead of time which prospective borrowers will be lax and cannot easily monitor the behavior of borrowers after contracts have entered into force.

The key principle that emerges from this discussion is that it is much more difficult to arrange privately for the protection of intangible knowledge goods than for that of tangible goods. While purely private methods of protecting intellectual property should be allowed, innovators should also have an opportunity to avail themselves of guaranteed protection under intellectual property law -- a form of protection that may often prove more conducive to desirable innovation than strictly private approaches that enjoy no legal protection.

In sum, the economic arguments raised against intellectual property protection do not withstand scrutiny. Intellectual property law enhances social welfare by encouraging the creation of innovations that yield new, highly desired products and processes. The social gains attributable to intellectual property rights substantially outweigh whatever deadweight loss stems from the exercise of those rights. Thus, deadweight loss should be viewed merely as the social opportunity cost -- the price society must pay -- for bringing forth substantial social gains. Whatever its defects, intellectual property protection appears to be the best means known for bringing about beneficial technological progress.11/

SHOULD INTELLECTUAL PROPERTY PROTECTION BE STRENGTHENED?

Posing the Question

If we accept the proposition that intellectual property protection is socially desirable, the question remains whether the degree of protection afforded by current law is appropriate. Social welfare is best served if the scarce resources devoted to innovative activities at the margin yield the same return to society as resources devoted to other activities. If the "social rate of return" to innovative activity outpaces the rate of return to other activities (such as the production of long-existing products), social welfare will rise if more resources are devoted to innovation, a result that can be achieved by strengthening intellectual property protection. Conversely, if social returns to noninnovative activities are greater than returns to innovation, fewer resources should flow to innovation, and intellectual property protection should be weakened. The limited evidence that is available suggests that, on balance, intellectual property protection should be strengthened.

Economic Evidence

Empirical work on the link between patents and R&D confirms an association between intellectual property protection and innovation. For example, Bronwyn Hall, Zvi Griliches, and Jerry Hausman's analysis of 1970s R&D data for 650 firms found simultaneous year-to-year movement of patents and R&D, leading them to conclude that successful research leads both to a patent application and to a commitment of funds for development.12/ Applying a somewhat different approach, Ariel Pakes analyzed the dynamic relationships among (1)the number of successful patent applications by a firm, (2)R&D expenditures as a measure of the firm's investment in innovation, and (3)the stock market value of the firm as an indicator of its inventive output.13/ Pakes found that unexpected changes in patents and in R&D are associated with large changes in market-value. This led him to suggest that an event that causes a measurable change in the market value of a firm's inventive activity starts a chain reaction leading to more R&D expenditures far into the future, as the firm patents around the links of the chain almost as soon as they are completed. Accordingly, Pakes's conclusion that current patent applications are highly correlated with current R&D demand implies that patent activity is a firm's response to market signals that R&D will be highly profitable. By allowing firms to capture future gains to R&D, patent applications may spur them to carry out socially beneficial R&D projects.

Research also confirms that, because of spillovers of information, patents allow inventors to appropriate only a portion of social returns to R&D. Studies summarized by Richard Levin reveal that patent effectiveness as a means of appropriation differs from industry to industry, with patents being most effective in chemical industries, moderately effective in industries producing relatively uncomplicated mechanical equipment, and less effective in most other industries.14/ Adam Jaffe found circumstantial evidence of R&D spillovers from the original inventor to competitors.15/ Spillovers effectively diminish the value of patent protection and confer cost savings on third parties. Edwin Mansfield, Mark Schwartz, and Samuel Wagner found that about 60 percent of successfully patented inventions in the chemical, drug, electronics, and machinery industries were imitated within four years.16/ They also found that the imitator's costs averaged only about 65 percent of the innovator's costs. Similarly, Levin, Alvin Klevorick, Richard Nelson, and Sidney Winter found that major patented inventions could be imitated within three years or less in well over half the 129 lines of business surveyed; imitation costs for a typical innovation were less than 75 percent of the original innovation costs in over 80 percent of the lines of business covered.17/

Not surprisingly, R&D spillover and imitation effects appear to affect the incentive to patent. Summarizing and building on prior research, Ignatius Horstmann, Glenn MacDonald, and Alan Slivinski examined patenting in industries where competitors could earn profits through an imitation of the patented good or process.18/ In such industries the authors found a propensity to patent of zero to 100 percent, reflecting a positive but imperfect correlation between R&D expenditures and applications for patents. Research by Cockburn and Griliches suggests that, in industries where patent protection is more likely to be effective, the stock market values R&D efforts more highly than in industries where patent protection is relatively ineffective.19/ Higher returns to R&D due to strong patent protection may, of course, strengthen firms' incentives to engage in R&D.

Because of spillovers, the return to society on R&D is frequently much higher than the return to the innovating firm. Summarizing a number of studies, Mansfield reported consistently very high social rates of return to investments in new industrial technology -- generally in the 30 to 50 percent range, or higher across a wide variety of industries.20/ In contrast, private rates of return to innovative technologies have been far lower, often 30 percentage points or more below the social rates of return.21/ In light of these results, Mansfield concluded that intellectual property rights are of "fundamental importance" -- a failure to protect these rights adequately could lead to a less than socially optimal amount of innovation and a retardation of economic growth.22/ A recent study by Jeffrey Bernstein and Ishaq Nadiri derived similarly dramatic results.23/ The authors calculated social rates of return to R&D in five high technology industries by adding the sum of interindustry spillover cost reductions to private rates of return. This method yielded social rates of return to R&D equal to 1.5 to 2 times the private rate of return in the chemical products industry, 2 to 3 times the private rate in the nonelectrical machinery industry, 10 times the private rate in the scientific instruments industry, and 1.1 to 1.2 times the private rate in the electrical products and transportation equipment industries. Gross private rates of return to R&D capital were 1.5 to 2 times as great as gross private rates of return to physical capital in four of the five industries though only marginally higher in the transportation equipment industry.

Implications for Public Policy Toward Intellectual Property

The great divergence between social and private rates of return to R&D in a host of industries strongly suggests that there is a relative social underinvestment in innovative activities. In other words, society would probably gain if resources were redirected toward R&D from other private productive activities. The returns to society from such a reallocation of private resources would apparently outweigh the forgone gains society would have received if those resources had been dedicated to their former uses. The relative underinvestment in R&D reflects, of course, private innovators' inability to capture the returns due to informational spillovers. It probably also reflects the fact that, since R&D investments tend to be riskier than investments in physical capital, firms demand a higher return of R&D investments than of other types of investments. The findings of high technology industries support this interpretation: there are higher returns relative to R&D capital than relative to physical capital.

Acceptance of the premise that society would benefit if relatively more resources were devoted to R&D lends strong support to the proposition of strengthening intellectual property rights. Heightened intellectual property protection would enable firms to obtain higher returns on their successful innovations and thereby increase their incentive to engage in socially beneficial R&D.24/

POSSIBLE MEANS OF STRENGTHENING INTELLECTUAL PROPERTY PROTECTION

Below I briefly set forth a few reforms aimed at strengthening intellectual property rights in a socially beneficial fashion. This discussion is intended merely to be suggestive. A comprehensive, detailed analysis of alternative strategies for expanding the scope of intellectual property protection is beyond the scope of this paper.

Relaxing Legal Disincentives to Intellectual Property Licensing

Licenses are contracts that transfer to the licensees the right to use intellectual property. Licensing benefits society by expanding the number of people who have access to a new technology and facilitating the marketing of innovative products. Through licensing, the creator of a new technology may select the manufacturers and distributors that are best able to commercialize his innovation. By granting exclusive uses or territories to designated licensees, an intellectual property holder may give his distributors sufficient incentives to invest in vigorous promotion. In addition, by tailoring the exclusive rights he grants to different licensees -- and perhaps by retaining some exclusive uses for himself -- an intellectual property holder may be able to assure himself of sufficient returns to justify socially beneficial licensing. Licensing restrictions that tie a product embodying intellectual property to another product may facilitate the sharing of risk between a licensor and his licensees.25/

Existing legal standards, however, impose substantial risks on those who seek to maximize returns to their intellectual property through restrictive licensing practices. The legal treatment of patent licensing is especially instructive. The judicially created doctrine of patent misuse has been applied to strike down without careful analysis a variety of restrictive licensing practices on the grounds that they offend public policy. A finding of patent misuse has been based on patent holders' efforts to control commerce outside the scope of the patent claim -- by requiring a licensee to purchase unpatented goods from a particular source (tying), to license a group of patents when he wants only one patent (compulsory package licensing), or to pay royalties on the patented product based on the sales of an unpatented good (total sales royalties). A finding of misuse has also been based on patent holders' decisions whether to license particular parties and, if so, at what royalty or royalties. Courts have also struck down these and sundry other licensing restrictions under the antitrust laws on the grounds that they constitute unreasonable restraints of trade.26/

Although the courts are increasingly receptive to arguments that licensing restrictions should not be condemned if they promote economic efficiency, owners of intellectual property still face substantial uncertainty about the treatment their licensing restraints will be accorded by the courts. Even if they believe their licensing schemes would ultimately be upheld, they may be reluctant to enter into socially desirable licensing contracts. The threat of lawsuits by competitors, with the legal costs, delays, and uncertainties those suits impose (the fate of a marketing program could be placed in limbo), may be sufficient to deter a licensing program that would have enhanced innovation by promoting the diffusion of new technologies. Even worse, legal concerns about their ability to extract reasonable returns to innovations through restrictive licensing may dissuade firms from making socially beneficial R&D investments. In short, the uncertain legal climate with respect to joint R&D licensing may retard the rate of innovation.

Various proposals have been introduced in Congress to modify the legal treatment of intellectual property licensing.27/ Under some proposals, restrictive licensing practices would be deemed to constitute patent misuse only if antitrust analysis showed them to be anticompetitive and thus violative of the antitrust laws. This approach was endorsed by the Reagan administration. Other proposals would specify one list of licensing practices that constituted patent misuse and a second list that did not. The first set of proposals, calling for a case-by-case analysis of competitive effects, is desirable and merits enactment. It would reduce the antitrust risks associated with licensing by ensuring that no restraints would be accorded blanket condemnation without analysis of their actual effects. The second set of proposals is less desirable than the first. The latter proposals would ensure case-by-case scrutiny only of practices listed as not constituting patent misuse; restraints on the patent misuse list would still be condemned without regard to their possible efficiencies in particular situations.

An additional legislative approach to restrictive licensing practices would be to rely on a more focused, structured antitrust rule of reason, which would never condemn a licensing restraint out of hand. A restraint would be condemned only if (1)it would restrict output in a market that did not embody the intellectual property being licensed, or if (2)it tended to restrict output "unreasonably," without a substantial efficiency justification, in a market that embodied the intellectual property being licensed. An efficiency justification would have to center on why the incidental output restriction was well-tailored to facilitate a reasonable return to the licensor's intellectual property and did not unnecessarily restrict output without regard to this justification.

Under this proposal the risk that courts might employ an unguided rule of reason analysis and wrongly condemn efficient licensing restraints would be minimized. Thus an individual intellectual property holder would be allowed to extract substantial returns to his innovations. At the same time this proposal would effectively preclude competitors from misusing cross-licensing schemes (in which firms license their intellectual property to each other) as a sham to "cartelize" a product market or markets in which they operate -- the prime threat to competition arising out of restrictive licensing.

In short, proposals, precluding a finding of patent misuse, absent antitrust law violations and also mandating adoption of an antitrust structured rule of reason, could establish a climate conducive to the promotion of innovation through licensing without unduly sacrificing competitive concerns. Accordingly, they merit being enacted.

Reformers should also not neglect an obstacle to patent licensing that arises out of patent law. In 1969 the U.S. Supreme Court ruled in Lear v. Adkins that a patent licensor cannot contractually compel his licensee not to challenge the patent's validity as a condition to entering into the license. This aspect of the holding may preclude patent holders from entering into optimal license agreements. A patent owner may fear that a licensee will seek to avail himself of the benefits of a new technology while depriving the owner of a reasonable return to his investment in R&D. This might happen if, shortly after entering into the license contract, the licensee sought to avoid recompensing the licensor by challenging the validity of the underlying patent. Thus the developer of a patent will be less willing to license his innovation than before Lear was handed down. This phenomenon may have contributed to a decline in licensing that lowers social welfare by slowing the diffusion of new technologies.

Furthermore, by reducing the expected value of returns to patent licensing, Lear may have diminished innovators' incentives to engage in welfare-enhancing R&D. Accordingly, society would benefit if inventors were contractually free to agree with licensees that the licensees would continue to pay royalties while any challenge to the patent was pending. Indeed, incentives to license could be further enhanced if there were no legal obstacles to contract provisions authorizing licensors to terminate licensees who challenged a patent's validity. The passage of federal legislation thus clarifying Lear v. Adkins -- legislation that would assure licensors of a return to their investments until their patents were held invalid -- deserves high priority.

Strengthening Incentives for Process Patenting

Until very recently American holders of process patents -- patents covering the process by which a product is made -- were barred from bringing patent infringement actions against importers of goods produced abroad in violation of those process patents. They had to rely on indirect, less effective actions under the trade laws if they wished to keep such infringing goods out of the country. As a result, American firms' incentives to devote resources to process patenting activities have probably been weaker than socially desirable.

The limited process patent protection afforded innovators may well have undermined American competitiveness. Recent research by Mansfield indicates that Japanese firms' ability to earn far higher returns to applied R&D than American firms stems at least in part from the Japanese firms' greater reliance on process technology.28/ Mansfield found that two-thirds of Japanese firms' R&D expenditures went to new processes and process changes and one-third to improved products and product changes. The proportions were reversed for American firms: two-thirds of R&D expenditures were devoted to improved product technology and only one-third to improved process technology. Because new process technology (a driving force behind the reduction of production costs) tends to have a grater effect on an industry's rate of productivity increase than new product technology, Mansfield's study suggests that American firms' allocation of R&D funds is less conducive than Japanese firms' to innovation and thus to future competitiveness. Mansfield concludes that American firms might respond to the Japanese technological challenge by putting relatively more resources into process R&D. Investments in process R&D may be encouraged by a new law authorizing patent infringement suits against importers of goods produced in violation of American process patents. This statutory change was included in the Omnibus Trade and Competitiveness Act of 1988, enacted by Congress and signed by the President in the summer of 1988. By enhancing process patent holders' remedies against infringement, the new law should increase the expected value of process patents and thereby encourage firms to direct a larger share of their R&D resources to process patenting. This result may quicken the pace of innovation by American industries and thereby bolster their international competitiveness.

Still more can be done, however, to create a legal climate conducive to process patent activity. Because the importation of goods produced by infringing processes may be particularly hard to detect and prove, it is less likely that process patent violations will be observed and challenged than that imports violating patents on manufactured goods will go unpunished. Thus there may be a stronger incentive to engage in process patent violations than in violations of product patents. This suggests that especially harsh penalties should apply to breaches of process patent law.

Legislative proposals aimed at toughening sanctions against infringers might impose mandatory treble damages on infringers and importers when a finding of process patent infringement is made (treble damages awards are authorized, but seldom assessed, under current law), establish a long-term ban (perhaps seventeen years, the length of a full patent term) on the infringer's exportation to the United States of goods produced according to the pirated process technology, and impose criminal penalties (including possible jail terms) on infringing producers and importers that have engaged in willful violations. These proposals are only suggestive; a wide variety of alternative means of strengthening the rights of process patent owners should be scrutinized.

Federal Protection for Trade Secrets

Trade secrets are protected under state but not federal law. Unfortunately, state trade secret laws differ widely in their coverage; many antiquated laws were fashioned to protect physical, not intellectual, property. Only a dozen states have enacted the Uniform Trade Secrets Act, which provides powerful civil enforcement weapons, and only about half the states have passed criminal sanctions against theft of trade secrets.29/ Given the nationwide mobility of technical staffs and the easy dissemination of information across state lines, firms may face great uncertainty about the legal standard that will be applied if they seek to move against theft of their trade secrets.

In light of this uncertainty, risk-averse businesses may be loath to invest considerable sums in developing technologically valuable proprietary information for fear they will earn an insufficient return on their investment. Thus, companies may underinvest in proprietary information that would enhance technological development from the standpoint of social welfare. In short, the states have provided less than socially optimal protection against theft of trade secrets. Competition among the states to attract businesses has proved ineffective in bringing forth stiff laws against misappropriation of trade secrets. Even if such competition intensifies over the next few years, leaving trade secret protection to the states may continue to subject businesses to substantial losses and undesirable uncertainty for a considerable period of time.

Federal trade secret legislation therefore deserves careful consideration. Given the growing difficulty of detecting trade secret theft, standard deterrence theory suggests that stiff federal penalties may be required to dissuade persons from engaging in such theft. Criminal penalties, including jail terms and large fines, in addition to damages recoverable by harmed firms, merit close attention. Federal law already imposes criminal penalties on federal employees who divulge trade secrets and trade secrets are exempt from disclosure under the Freedom of Information Act.

Improving Foreign Countries' Protection of American Intellectual Property

American firms whose goods and services are disseminated internationally are harmed by the failure of developing countries to protect the intellectual property those companies have developed. The misappropriation by foreigners of Americans' intellectual property imposes many billions of dollars in direct losses on American firms and also diminishes their future competitiveness by reducing their incentive to develop new technologies. Fortunately, the subject of intellectual property protection is the subject of ongoing Uruguay Round GATT trade negotiations. In order to entice developing countries into agreeing to a multilateral GATT-sponsored intellectual property agreement (which would specify enforceable standards of intellectual property protection for agreement signatories), developed country negotiators will have to convince these developing countries that it is not in their long-term interest to eschew protection and continue to free-ride on developed nations' intellectual property. In order to garner developing country support for a GATT agreement, developed country negotiators may wish to stress that enhanced protection of intellectual property may: (1)create jobs in primary and supporting industries, (2)enhance labor force quality through on-the-job training, (3)encourage multinational corporations to transfer up-to-date technologies to developing countries, (4)shift jobs to higher productivity areas, (5)increase a developing country's capital stock, (6)enhance the quality of capital through innovation, (7)improve the allocation of the capital stock, (8)expand activities subject to economies of scale, (9)improve local economic efficiency, (10)lower the cost of producing existing products, and (11)spur the production of new products. Developed country negotiators might seek to bolster these abstract arguments by pointing to concrete examples such as the spectacular growth of indigenous copyright-based industries following Hong Kong's enactment of a copyright law in 1978.

Enhancing Incentives for Joint R&D

Joint R&D by competitors may encourage innovation by allowing firms to combine knowledge, share risks, and prevent misappropriation of intellectual property. The National Cooperative Research Act of 1984 was designed to eliminate unjustified obstacles to joint R&D ventures (JRDV). Nevertheless, significant antitrust disincentives to such ventures may remain; the NCRA's "safe harbor" still exposes NCRA registrants to possible unjustified suits for actual damages. Possible new legislative reforms that merit scrutiny include (1)the establishment of a safe harbor for efficiency-seeking joint production ventures that rely on R&D as an input, (2)a sharp curtailment or total elimination of private parties' right to sue JRDVs, (3)a reduction in the potential liability of JRDV members for attorneys' fees, and (4)replacement of the vague existing antitrust standard for evaluating JRDV activity with a precise structured rule of reason that is more sympathetic to welfare-enhancing R&D efforts. (Given the efficiencies that may stem from joint R&D, the structured rule of reason might, for example, provide that the inclusiveness of a joint R&D venture -- the percentage of firms in an industry covered by the JRDV -- would in itself have no bearing on the JRDV's antitrust legality. A JRDV's inclusiveness would give rise to antitrust attack only if it tended to reduce product output "downstream" by facilitating collusion.) Adoption of the structured rule of reason would remove an artificial source of competitive disadvantage for American firms vis-a-vis Japanese firms, which, unlike their American rivals, face no antitrust risks due to the JRDVs they form.

Public Subsidies for Joint R&D

An alternative to strengthened protection of intellectual property rights is reliance on public subsidies for R&D. The government might encourage innovation through direct R&D subsidies or through tax preferences for R&D. Firms might be allowed to expense their R&D costs (fully write them off for tax purposes in the year they are incurred) or to receive tax credits for them. Tax policies might be targeted; for instance, tax credits might be greater for (or directed exclusively to) new process technology, as opposed to the socially less beneficial new product technology.

A public subsidies approach enjoys some academic support. Using a simulation model, Michael Spence concluded that such an approach would be an effective public policy.30/ An optimal R&D subsidy may raise social welfare by causing firms to take into account the external benefits their innovations confer on society.31/ Indirect evidence that subsidies may have a major impact on R&D may be gleaned from American firms' response to the 1981 federal tax credit. Although that credit provided only modest incentives, it appears to have engendered a steady increase in R&D investments in the following years, even though the severe 1982 recession created countervailing disincentives for R&D.32/ In short, the apparent extreme sensitivity of American firms to increases in the expected rate of return to R&D projects gives some indication that an R&D subsidy might provide a big bang for the buck. While subsidies merit further study, they present some obvious problems. To take advantage of subsidies, firms would have an incentive to characterize their expenditures as related to R&D whether they were or not. Direct R&D subsidies (as opposed to "indirect" tax credits) would undoubtedly lead to some wasteful allocation of public revenues to noninnovative private activities. They might also produce resource misallocations by firms toward relatively ineffective innovative efforts that would not have been deemed cost-effective but for the availability of a subsidy. Moreover, economic theory suggests that this approach would lead to deadweight social costs, that is, the inefficiencies inevitably associated with raising subsidies through the tax system. Of course, taxpayers would have to bear the burden of direct subsidies. Thus, although public subsidies might bring forth an additional stream of socially desirable innovations, it is far from clear under what conditions they would prove cost-beneficial. Accordingly, further analysis seems warranted of the costs and benefits of encouraging R&D through public subsidies and of the specific forms that subsidies, if attempted, should take. Attention might focus on the relative merits of R&D tax credits (especially in light of research on the effects of the 1981 tax credit) and direct federal handouts.33/

SUMMARY

Since this nation was founded, intellectual property protection has been recognized as a key to socially beneficial innovation. Patent, copyright, trademark, and trade secret laws spur the development of new technologies by assuring firms of a return to the valuable information they develop. Arguments against strong intellectual property protection, based on the notion that intellectual property laws create monopoly waste, are unconvincing. The incidental power to restrict output -- a power limited by the tendency of new information to leak out -- is outweighed by the dynamic gains in innovation society derives from intellectual property protection. Indeed, evidence suggests that, far from being too strong, the existing intellectual property protection may be weaker than socially desirable. Accordingly, legislative changes aimed at stimulating the production of intellectual property merit scrutiny. These include lowering antitrust and patent law disincentives to intellectual property licensing, strengthening process patent protection, passing a federal trade secrets law, encouraging foreign countries to increase their intellectual property protection,removing disincentives to joint R&D, and providing public subsidies for R&D.

NOTES

1. The Federalist Papers (New York: New American Library, 1961), no. 43, pp. 271-72.

2. The constitutional basis of trademark protection is the Commerce Clause, Article I, section 8, clause 3.

3. Sony Corp. of America v. Universal City Studios, Inc., 464 U.S. 417 (1984).

4. K Mart Corp. v. Cartier, Inc., 108 S.Ct. 1811 (1988).

5. Kewanee Oil Co. v. Bicron Corp., 416 U.S. 470 (1974).

6. Ruckelshaus v. Monsanto Co., 467 U.S. 986 (1984).

7. Frederick M. Scherer, Industrial Market Structure and Economic Performance, 2d ed. (Chicago: Rand McNally, 1980), pp. 450-54.

8. Tom G. Palmer, "The Case for Free Trade in Ideas: A Historical, Economic, and Philosophic Reexamination of Intellectual Property Rights" (Fairfax, Virginia: Institute for Humane Studies, George Mason University, 1988).

9. Edmund W. Kitch, "Patents: Monopolies or Property Rights?" Research in Law and Economics (1986), pp. 31-49.

10. Ben T. Yu, "A Contractual Remedy to Premature Innovation: The Vertical Integration of Brand-Name Specific Research," Economic Inquiry (October 1984), pp. 660-67.

11. Most of the leading scholars who are concerned about the costs of intellectual property protection acknowledge that it is better than alternative methods of encouraging innovation. Scherer, pp. 457-58.

12. Bronwyn H. Hall, Zvi Griliches, and Jerry A. Hausman, "Patents and R&D: Is There a Lag?" International Economic Review (June 1986), pp. 265-83.

13. Ariel Pakes, "On Patents, R&D, and the Stock Market Rate of Return," Journal of Political Economy (April 1985), pp. 390-409.

14. Richard C. Levin, "A New Look at the Patent System," American Economic Review (May 1986), pp. 199-202.

15. Adam B. Jaffe, "Technological Opportunity and Spillovers of R&D: Evidence from Firms' Patents, Profits, and Market Value," *American Economic Review* (December 1986), pp. 984-1001.

16. Edwin Mansfield, Mark Schwartz, and Samuel Wagner, "Imitation Costs and Patents: An Empirical Study," *Economic Journal* (December 1981), pp. 907-18.

17. Richard C. Levin, et al., "Survey Research on R&D Appropriability and Technological Opportunity, Part I: Appropriability" (New Haven, Conn.: Department of Economics, Yale University, 1986).

18. Ignatius Horstmann, Glenn M. MacDonald, and Alan Slivinski, "Patents as Information Transfer Mechanisms: To Patent or Not to Patent," *Journal of Political Economy* (October 1985), pp. 837-58.

19. Ian Cockburn and Zvi Griliches, "Industry Effects and Appropriability Measures in the Stock Market's Valuation of R&D and Patents," *American Economic Review* (May 1988), pp. 419-28.

20. Edwin Mansfield, "Intellectual Property Rights, Technological Change, and Economic Growth," in *Intellectual Property Rights and Capital Formation in the Next Decade*, eds., Charles E. Walker and Mark A. Bloomfield (Lanham, Md.: University Press of America, 1988), pp. 3-26.

21. Ibid., p. 23.

22. Ibid., p. 24.

23. Jeffrey I. Bernstein and M. Ishaq Nadiri, "Interindustry R&D Spillovers, Rates of Return, and Production in High-Tech Industries," *American Economic Review* (May 1988), pp. 429-34.

24. This is not to suggest that all spillovers of information should be eliminated or that intellectual property protection is the only factor spurring firms to innovate. Some spillover benefits society by facilitating the spread of technological improvements.

25. John P. Palmer, "Patents, Licensing, and Restrictions on Competition," *Economic Inquiry* (October 1984), pp. 676-83.

26. American Bar Association, *Antitrust Law Developments (Second)* (Chicago: ABA Press, 1984), pp. 487-526.

27. Charles F. Rule, "Statement before the Subcommittee on Courts, Civil Liberties, and the Administration of Justice," Committee on the Judiciary, House of Representatives, Concerning H. R. 4086 and S. 1200 (Title II), "Patent Misuse Legislation," May 11, 1988.

28. Edwin Mansfield, "Industrial R&D in Japan and the United States: A Comparative Study," *American Economic Review* (May 1988), pp. 223-28.

29. Gregory L. Miles, "Information Thieves Are Now Corporate Enemy No. 1," *Business Week*, May 5, 1986, pp. 120-25.

30. A. Michael Spence, "Cost Reduction, Competition, and Industry Performance," *Econometrica* (January 1984), pp. 101-21.

31. Leonard K. Cheng, "Optimal Trade And Technology Policies: Dynamic Linkages," *International Economic Review* (October 1987), pp. 757-76.

32. R. Michael Gadbaw and Timothy J. Richards, eds., *Intellectual Property Rights: Global Consensus, Global Conflict*? (Boulder, Colo.: Westview Press, 1988), pp. 101-02.

33. The research tax credit enacted in 1981 (section 41 of the Internal Revenue Code) was a 25 percent credit for any excess of "qualified research" expenses (technological research aimed at uncovering information useful in the development of new or improved business output) over base period expenses (covering the three prior taxable years). The credit was reduced to 20 percent in 1986, when a 20 percent credit for "basic" noncommercial scientific research was added. The credit for commercially useful nonbasic research is really quite small since only a small portion of the *increase* can be applied to reduce taxes.

Appendix A

Symposium Agenda

"INTELLECTUAL PROPERTY RIGHTS IN SCIENCE, TECHNOLOGY, AND ECONOMIC PERFORMANCE: INTERNATIONAL COMPARISONS"

May 8-9, 1989, Washington, D.C.

MONDAY, May 8

9:00 Welcome by Sponsors

Tony Motley, President, L.A. Motley & Company; Former U.S. Ambassador to Brazil

John Boright, Director, Division of International Programs, National Science Foundation

9:30 Introductory Remarks: International Issues in Intellectual Property Protection

Emery Simon, Director, Intellectual Property, Office of the U.S. Trade Representative

9:45-12:30 Session I: Intellectual Property Rights, Science, Technology, and Economic Incentives

1. Economic Incentives, Research and Development, and Economic Growth
   Edwin Mansfield, Professor of Economics, University of Pennsylvania

2. Appropriating the Returns from Science and Technology
   Richard Levin, Professor of Economics, Yale University

3. Emerging Technologies and Intellectual Property Rights: New Property Rights for Computer Technologies
   Anne Wells Branscomb, Program on Information Resources Policy, Harvard University

4. New Property Rights for Biotechnology
   Kevin O'Connor, Biological Applications Program, Office of Technology Assessment

Roundtable Discussion

12:30-1:30 Lunch

1:30-5:00 Session II: International Comparisons of Intellectual Property Rights

1. The International Environment for Intellectual Property Rights
   Ashoka Mody, Industrial Economist, The World Bank

2. Brazil

   Intellectual Property Rights, Science, Technology and Economic Growth: Brazil
   Claudio Frischtak, Industrial Economist, The World Bank

   Microeconomics: Case Studies
   Robert M. Sherwood, International Business Counselor

3. Japan

   Macroeconomic Perspectives on Intellectual Property Rights in Japan's Economic Performance and Case Studies of Japanese Computer Industry
   Dennis S. Karjala, Professor of Law, Arizona State University

4. India

Intellectual Property Rights and Managing R&D in India
Falguni Sen, Professor of Management, Graduate School of Business, Fordham University

Roundtable Discussion

TUESDAY, May 9, 1989

9:00-12:00 Session III: International Comparisons of Intellectual Property Rights (continued)

1. United States

Issues on Intellectual Property Protection in the United States
R. Michael Gadbaw, Attorney at Law, Dewey, Ballantine, Bushby, Palmer and Wood

Microeconomics: Case Studies
Atul Wad, Center for Social Studies of Science and Technology, Northwestern University

2. Intellectual Property Protection in Europe's Economic Performance
Wolf Brueckmann, Director, International Investment Policy, U.S. Chamber of Commerce

3. Pacific Rim

Economic Development and Intellectual Property Rights in Southeast-East Asia: A Comparative Analysis
Gunda Schumann, Associate Expert, United Nations Centre on Transnational Corporations

Roundtable Discussion

12:00-1:00 Lunch

1:00- 3:30 Session IV: Developing a Framework for Intellectual Property Protection to Advance Science, Technology, and Economic Performance

1. Protection of Intellectual Property Rights: Research and Development Decisions and Economic Growth: A Global Perspective
   Richard R. Rozek, National Economic Research Associates, Inc. (NERA)

2. Developing a Framework for Intellectual Property Protection
   Alden F. Abbott, Counselor to the General Counsel, U.S. Department of Commerce

   (NOTE: This paper is based on research conducted by the author at the American Enterprise Institute during the summer of 1988.)

Roundtable Discussion

3:30- 5:00 Session V: Summary of Discussions and Concluding Remarks

Rapporteur: Henry Hertzfeld, Legal and Economic Consultant

Concluding Remarks: Francis W. Rushing, Georgia State University and SRI International

Carole Ganz Brown, National Science Foundation

Appendix B
Symposium Attendees

May 8-9, 1989

Alden F. Abbott
U.S. Department of Commerce

Catherine P. Ailes
SRI International

Luiz Henrique O. do Amaral
Danneman, Siemsen, Bigler and Ipanema Moreira, Rio de Janeiro

Joao Eduardo Lopes Araujo
Brazilian Association of Informatics Services

Mary C. Barber
National Science Foundation

William Bernard
National Science Foundation

W. A. Blanpied
National Science Foundation

John Boright
National Science Foundation

Anne Wells Branscomb
Harvard University

Carole Ganz Brown
National Science Foundation

Wolf Brueckmann
U.S. Chamber of Commerce

Maria Busquets-Moura
Brazil-U.S. Business Council, U.S. Chamber of Commerce

Manfred Cziesla
National Science Foundation

Carl Dahlman
The World Bank

Royal Daniel
Bishop, Cook, Purcell & Reynolds

Peter deVos
U.S. Department of State

Roger Doyon
National Science Foundation

John Dugger
U.S. Department of Energy

Sheri Fox
U.S. Department of Commerce

Claudio Frischtak
The World Bank

R. Michael Gadbaw
Dewey, Ballantine, Bushby, Palmer and Wood

J. P. Gupta
Embassy of India

Robert B. Hardy
National Science Foundation

Henry Hertzfeld
Legal and Economic Consultant

John Holmfeld
U.S. House Committee on Science and Technology

Hiroshi Iwata
Takeda Chemical Industries

Dennis S. Karjala
Arizona State University

Cristina LaBarbera
U.S. Chamber of Commerce

Monica Lemos
Brazilian Film Company (EMBRAFILME)

Richard Levin
Yale University

Edwin Mansfield
University of Pennsylvania

Keith Miceli
Brazil-U.S. Business Council, U.S. Chamber of Commerce

Ashoka Mody
The World Bank

Mary Ellen Moges
Consultant

Tony Motley
L.A. Motley & Company

Kevin O'Connor
Office of Technology Assessment

Pierre Perrolle
National Science Foundation

Marilyn Pifer
U.S. Department of State

Jonathan Putnam
Yale University

Proctor Reid
National Academy of Engineering

Bud Rock
U.S. Department of State

Paulo Milliet Roque
Brazilian Association of Software Companies (ABES)

Richard R. Rozek
National Economic Research Associates (NERA)

Francis W. Rushing
Georgia State University
and SRI International

R. Lawrence Sahr
The Carborundum Co.

Falguni Sen
Fordham University

Robert M. Sherwood
International Business
Counselor

Allen M. Shinn
National Science
Foundation

Gunda Schumann
United Nations Centre
on Transnational
Corporations

Emery Simon
Office of U.S. Trade
Representative

H. Stolberg
National Science
Foundation

Yoshitaka Tani
Takeda USA, Inc.

David H. Troncoso
Texas Instruments, Inc.

Atul Wad
Northwestern University

Charles Wallace
National Science
Foundation

Robert Weissler
Office of Technology
Assessment

Bruce Wilson
Office of the U.S. Trade
Representative

Yoichiro Yamaguchi
Beveridge, DeGrandi &
Weilacher

About the Contributors

ALDEN F. ABBOTT is Senior Counselor, Office of Legal Counsel, Department of Justice, responsible for rendering opinions on constitutional and statutory issues, with an emphasis on international trade, economic policy and intellectual property. Mr. Abbot worked on the US-Canada Free Trade Agreement. Mr. Abbott received the J.D. from Harvard Law School and holds an M.A. in Economics. His forthcoming book is entitled Intellectual Property and Innovation (American Enterprise Institute and University Press).

MICHAEL BORRUS is Deputy Director, Berkeley Roundtable on the International Economy (BRIE), University of California, Berkeley, where he is also Adjunct Lecturer in the School of Business Administration. He holds the J.D. from Harvard University and an M.A. in Political Science. Mr. Borrus has given testimony or consulted for the National Advisory Committee on Semiconductors, Office of Technology Assistance, U.S. Trade Representative, and U.S.-Japan Trade Advisory Commission among others. His most recent publication is Competing for Control: America's Stake in Microelectronics (Cambridge, MA: Ballinger Publishing Co., 1988).

ANNE WELLS BRANSCOMB is a distinguished attorney and communications scholar, and has written widely about the legal implications of the new communications technology. She is currently with the Harvard University Information Resources Policy Center and is consultant to the U.S. Office of Technology Assessment and a member of the faculty at the

Western Behavioral Sciences Institute and the Polytechnic Institute of New York. She has been chairman of the board of Kalba-Bowen Associates of Cambridge, Massachusetts, and a visiting scholar at the Yale Law School. She is editor of Toward a Law of Global Communications Networks and the author of a forthcoming book, Teletribes and Telecommunications. She has written more than forty monographs, reports, and articles in law reviews and communications journals.

CAROLE GANZ BROWN is Senior Program Manager at the Division of International Programs, National Science Foundation, with responsibility for managing S&T cooperation with Australia and New Zealand. Other responsibilities include assessments of worldwide S&T capabilities, analyses of international policy issues, and comparisons between U.S. and foreign research systems. Recent publications include, Science and Technology to Advance National Goals: Science Policies in the United States and Japan (edited with Dale R. Corson and Sogo Okamura), Manufacturing Research Perspectives: U.S.A.-Japan (edited with Arthur Gerstenfeld and Toshio Sata), "Assessing the Scientific Strength of Chile" (co-authored with Robert C. Stowe), and National Policies for Developing High Technology Industries: International Comparisons (edited with Francis W. Rushing). She holds a Ph.D in Logic and the Philosophy of Science from Stanford University.

WOLF BRUECKMANN serves as Executive Director of the U.S. Chamber of Commerce Intellectual Property and Telecommunications Task Forces, responsible for developing U.S. Chamber policy in two vital areas of concern: (1)stronger protection against foreign violations of patent, trademark, copyright and other violations of intellectual property rights; and (2)securing greater access for U.S. firms in foreign markets for telecommunications products and services. He also helps develop overall U.S. Chamber policy on the Uruguay Round of the GATT. Dr. Brueckmann received a Ph.D. in international studies from American University in Washington D.C.

CLAUDIO R. FRISCHTAK is Senior Industrial Economist, Industrial Development Division at The World Bank where he is also Industrial Economist, Industrial Strategy and Policy Division. Dr. Frischtak is Adjunct Professor of Economics at Georgetown University. He holds a Ph.D. in Economics from Stanford University. His forthcoming publications include "Competition Policies for Industrializing Economies" (forthcoming: World Bank Policy and Research Series), Industrial Regulatory Policy and Investment Incentives in Brazil (World Bank Report).

FLAVIO GRYNSZPAN is President of Riotec, the management company of the technology park he organized in Rio de Janeiro in 1986. Dr. Grynszpan holds a Ph.D. in Biomedical Engineering from the University of Pennsylvania and has many years experience in the interface between the research and production sectors. He has taught in the Industrial Engineering Department of the Federal University of Rio de Janeiro in the areas of management of technology innovation, technology transfer, entrepreneurship, and university-industry relationships. He is consultant to many Brazilian governmental institutions and was recently invited by Unido to be an international consultant in technology parks. He is vice-president of the International Association of Science Parks responsible for Latin America. Dr. Grynszpan is currently associated with Motorola, Inc. in Sao Paulo, Brazil.

DENNIS S. KARJALA is Professor of Law at Arizona State University, and in addition to his law degree holds a Ph.D. in Electrical Engineering. Professor Karjala has been a Visiting Research Scholar and Japan Foundation Fellow at the Faculty of Law, University of Tokyo, conducting research on problems of computer software protection, especially under Japanese law. He offers a seminar in computers and the law and regularly teaches courses in intellectual property law at Arizona State University. His recent publications include "The Protection of Operating Software under Japanese Law," "The First Case on Protection of Operating Systems and Reverse Engineering of Programs in Japan," and "The Limitations on Protection as Program Works under Japanese Copyright Law."

EDWIN MANSFIELD is Professor of Economics and Director of the Center for Economics and Technology at the University of Pennsylvania. Professor Mansfield has been a member of the Advisory Committee on Policy Research of the National Science Foundation and the American Association for the Advancement of Science's Committee on Science, Engineering and Public Policy. He has served as U.S. chairman of the US-USSR Working Party on the Economics of Science and Technology and was the first U.S. economist to be invited to visit and lecture in the People's Republic of China under the 1979 Sino-American agreement. He is editor of a series of books on technological change published by the University of Wisconsin Press and received the 1985 Publication Award of the Patent Law Association.

ASHOKA MODY is an industrial economist at the World Bank and has been a consultant to the Korea Traders Association and the Korea Development Institute; the Economic Advisory Council to the Prime Minister, Government of India; the Economic and Social Commission for Asia and the Pacific; and the Danish International Development Agency. Dr. Mody holds a Ph.D. in Economics and a Bachelor of Technology in Electronics. His most recent publications include "Technology Evolution in the Semiconductor Industry," "Information Industries: the Changing Role of Newly Industrialized Countries," and "Korea's Computer Strategy."

RICHARD P. ROZEK is senior consultant at National Economic Research Associates, Inc. in Washington D.C., where he has worked on projects including international intellectual property rights protection. Dr. Rozek holds a Ph.D in Economics. He has also been a senior analyst for the Pharmaceutical Manufacturers Association where he analyzed issues affecting the research-based pharmaceutical industry including intellectual property rights protection. Dr. Rozek has spoken at the National Institute of Health STEP Seminar on Measurement of the Returns to R&D. His most recent publication is "Technology Transfer: Licensing's Crucial Role."

FRANCIS W. RUSHING is Professor of Economics at Georgia State University and Senior Economic Consultant Science Policy Program, International Policy Center, SRI International. Dr. Rushing has researched and published on technology transfer; training and utilization of scientific and technical manpower; international science policy, trade, and international competition focusing on U.S.S.R., People's Republic of China, and Brazil. His most recent books include The Science Race: Training and Utilization of Scientists and Engineers, U.S. and U.S.S.R. (with Catherine P. Ailes); Economics; and National Policies for Developing High Technology Industries: International Comparisons (edited with Carole Ganz Brown).

GUNDA SCHUMANN is Associate Expert at the United Nations Centre on Transnational Corporations. Ms. Schumann received the M.C.J. from New York University School of Law and holds and M.A. in Sociology from the Freie Universitaet, Berlin. One of her recent publications is "Copyrightability of Computer Programs and the Scope of their Protection under the ITC/Apple Case and the Whelan Case", in Computer Law and Practice, 1988.

FALGUNI SEN is Assistant Professor of Management at Fordham University's Graduate School of Business. He has his Ph.D. in Industrial Engineering and Management Science from Northwestern University and specializes in the management of technology and innovations. His current research is focused on various aspects of formulating and implementing technology strategies in technology-based industries. Dr. Sen was a member of the faculty at the Administrative Staff College of India at Hyderabad, India from 1973-1977 and 1983-1985. He has also researched and consulted with a number of laboratories in the Indian Council of Agriculture Research, the Council of Scientific and Industrial Research, and the Defense Research and Development Organization as well as firms in the U.S. and Republic of Ireland.

ROBERT M. SHERWOOD, an international business counselor, has practiced law on Wall Street and as a corporate attorney. He has spent fourteen weeks since 1987 in Brazil and Mexico researching the influence of intellectual property law and practice at the grass-roots level. He has published and lectured on Latin American debt, technology transfer, and intellectual property protection and taught at the graduate level. He holds degrees from Harvard College and Law School and from Columbia University.

ATUL WAD is Director of Technology Programs, International Business Development Program (IBD) at Northwestern University, a university-based unit providing advisory services in international trade and technology to firms in the United States and overseas. He has also been Scientific Affairs Officer, United Nations Center for Science and Technology for Development. Dr. Wad holds a Ph.D. in Organizational Behavior and a B.Tech in Mechanical Engineering. Among his recent publications are Science, Technology and Development (Westview Press: 1988) and "The Globalization of Japanese Manufacturing", a report to the National Academy of Science.

For Product Safety Concerns and Information please contact our EU representative GPSR@taylorandfrancis.com Taylor & Francis Verlag GmbH, Kaufingerstraße 24, 80331 München, Germany

Batch number: 10726009

Printed by Printforce, the Netherlands